Wiring the Writing Center

Wiring the Writing Center

ERIC H. HOBSON

editor

UTAH STATE UNIVERSITY PRESS
Logan, Utah
1998

Utah State University Press
Logan, Utah 84322-7800

Typography by WolfPack
Cover Design by Stephen Adams

02 01 00 99 98   5 4 3 2 1

Library of Congress Cataloging-in-Publication Data

Wiring the writing center / Eric H. Hobson, editor.
    p. cm.
Includes bibliographical references.

ISBN 0-87421-255-3 (pbk.)

    1. English language—Rhetoric—Study and teaching—Data processing. 2. Report writing—
Study and teaching—Data processing. 3. English language—Computer-assisted instruction.
4. Report writing—Computer-assisted instruction. 5. Writing centers—Automation. I. Hobson,
Eric.

PE1404 .W56 1998
808'.042'0285—ddc21   98—25384
                                                                          CIP

CONTENTS

ACKNOWLEDGMENTS   VII

INTRODUCTION   *Straddling the Virtual Fence*   ix
              Eric H. Hobson

PART I: Models and Strategies for Wired Writing Centers

ONE   *The Look and Feel of the OWL Conference*   3
          Barbara Monroe

TWO   *Email "Tutoring" as Collaborative Writing*   25
          David Coogan

THREE   *Reflection and Responsibility in (Cyber) Tutor Training:* 44
          Seeing Ourselves Clearly on and off the Screen
          Rebecca Rickly

FOUR   *WAC on the Web: Writing Center Outreach to Teachers*   62
          of Writing Intensive Courses
          Sara Kimball

FIVE   *Have You Visited Your Online Writing Center Today?:*   75
          Learning, Writing, and Teaching Online at a
          Community College
          Clinton Gardner

SIX   *The Other WWW: Using Intranets to Reconfigure the*   85
          Who, When and Where of Network Supported Writing
          Instruction
          Kurt P. Kearcher

SEVEN   *Wiring a Usable Center: Usability Research and Writing* 103
          Center Practice
          Stuart Blythe

PART II: Critical Assessments of Wired Writing Centers

EIGHT   *Drill Pads, Teaching Machines, and Programmed Texts:*   119
          Origins of Instructional Technology in Writing Centers
              Neal Lerner

NINE   *Virtual High School Writing Centers: A Spectrum of*   137
          Possibilities
              Pamela B. Childers, Jeannette Jordan,
              James K. Upton

TEN   *The Community College Mission and the Electronic*   151
          Writing Center
              Ellen Mohr

ELEVEN   *Random Memories of the Virtual Writing Center: The*   163
          Modes-to-Nodes Problem
              Ray Wallace

TWELVE   *Computers in the Writing Center: A Cautionary History*   171
              Peter Carino

PART III: Resources for Wired Writing Centers

THIRTEEN *UnfURLed: 20 Writing Center Sites to Visit on the*   197
          Information Highway
              Bruce Pegg

FOURTEEN *Computers and Writing Centers: An Annotated*   216
          Bibliography
              Steve Sherwood

          WORKS CITED   231

          CONTRIBUTORS   242

          INDEX   246

ACKNOWLEDGMENTS

*A*S EDITOR OF A COLLECTION SUCH AS THIS ONE, I GET TO SPEAK FOR THE entire group of collaborating authors and express our thanks to the many people who helped to make this book possible. Likewise, there are individuals I wish to thank personally for their help during the time this project took shape.

Completing this project encouraged all of the authors involved to try on for size many of the online services described in the following pages. This project was completed almost entirely via the internet: the project was conceived of and planned via email conversations; invitations were extended and replied to online; every chapter was composed using a computer; most manuscripts were submitted, responded to, and revised online; editor/author consultations frequently happened online—although, regrettably, we did not explore synchronous consultations. Doing so, we believe, added a textural-critical layer to the discussions that would not have been present otherwise.

A number of people must be recognized for the contributions they made to the project. Writing center colleagues from across the country helped in more ways than they could know. Michael Pemberton (University of Illinois) came through in his unerringly reliable way by providing back issues of needed journals, particularly issues of *Computers and Composition*. Christina Murphy (University of Memphis) and Joe Law (Wright State University) graciously encouraged Steve Sherwood as he extended the work begun in their standard-setting annotated bibliography *Writing Centers: An Annotated Bibliography* (Greenwood, 1996). Joan Mullin (University of Toledo) and Ray Wallace (Notherwestern State University of Louisiana) listened to the ideas behind the project and their insight and support have made the project all the better.

Michael Spooner, Director of Utah State University Press, has from the project's inception helped define and make it a reality. Utah State University Press deserves the writing center and composition studies communities' thanks for believing that writing center professionals are a viable market.

On a more personal level, Carla McDonough (Eastern Illinois University) willing juggled parenting duties so I could work with fewer interruptions from, Garrett, our toddler. Her readings of and responses to drafts helped me work with each author to better accommodate the needs of a wide audience of readers. Chuck Bonwell (St. Louis College of Pharmacy) continues to serve as my mentor, confidant, cheerleader; his support in this and other projects reminds me what it is I enjoy so much about collaborating with him. As with other projects, R. Baird Shuman deserves much of the credit, because he is the person who showed me that writing is not only a demanding professional activity but a joyous one.

Finally, thank you to each of my collaborators/colleagues/friends (new and old) who enthusiastically took up my recent challenge when I invited you to join me in this project. Your work has combined to make an attention-getting finished product, one that provides readers much to ponder, replicate, and modify for their teaching settings.

Eric H. Hobson
August 1998

Straddling the Virtual Fence [1]

Eric H. Hobson

THE MERGING OF COMPUTERS AND COMMUNICATION TECHNOLOGY HAS created a new educational frontier, albeit a virtual one. Faced with seemingly endless possibilities for incorporating computers and electronic communication technology into the classroom and other learning environments, many literacy educators are attempting to stake their claim to some of the territory up for grabs on the internet, World Wide Web (WWW), and other emerging and yet-to-be-realized electronic environments. In a scenario akin to the land rushes of the nineteenth century, educators have climbed on to whatever available mode of conveyance (PC, Mac, UNIX, etc.) and have attempted to keep up with the hoard of other users who, metaphorically, are heading west into this virtual landscape. Yet, like their historical predecessors, many educators moving online do so with little chance of achieving their idealized visions of success and limitless bounty for their students and themselves: they use obsolete or inadequate technology; have little-to-no guidance; aren't prepared to deal with hostile neighbors and other predators; haven't planned beyond the initial trip.

As with most new developments, approval for the universal use of computer technology in the teaching of writing has not been unanimous. Many educators, particularly those in the humanities, distrust claims made to support a mass adoption of computer assisted instruction. Most teachers of writing respond to the presence of technology and teaching in one of four ways: rail against its dehumanizing potential; ignore it and hope that it won't affect them too much; explore its uses and implications tentatively; a small percentage embrace it enthusiastically. Regardless of our individual reactions to the presence of computer and electronically mediated technology in the writing center, one must acknowledge, as does Diana George (1995, 333), that

> the technology is here. We cannot ignore it. Furthermore, we already know that computer technology—the communication revolution—is more powerful than skills-and-drills workbooks on a screen. What we don't quite yet know, I am convinced, is how this 'New World' really will reconfigure our teaching and our tutoring.

Among writing teachers, writing center personnel often have been at the vanguard of the move to online instructional applications, developing a range of variations on tutorial and consulting services that translate to the unique conditions of electronic/computer-mediated communication. As Murphy, Law, and Sherwood's *Writing Centers: An Annotated Bibliography* (1996), and Sherwood's update of that information for this project (chapter fourteen) demonstrates, discussions of educational technology's role, particularly of computers and computer mediated communications, in working with writers in the writing center setting has been an on-going and, at times, contentious topic in the composition studies and the writing center communities. The writing center community's discussion of this issue is recorded most consistently within the pages of *The Writing Lab Newsletter*, and more recently in the archives for the email discussion group, Wcenter. This process of program development and critical assessment has been highlighted most prominently in special issues of *The Writing Center Journal* 8.1 (1987) and *Computers and Composition* 12 (1995) which focused on the role(s) of computers within the writing center setting. Writing in the special issue of *Computers and Composition*, David Healy (1995 "From Place") raises the following questions about wired writing centers:

> What is the ontological status of a virtual writing center, and what kind of relationship will clients develop with it? How will it be perceived by the rest of the academy? What possibilities and what threats are opened up by going online. (191)

"These are the kinds of questions," Healy continues, "that writing centers must confront in the age of information technology . . . . Online writing centers represent a window of opportunity. Our challenge is to be reflective and self-critical while the opportunities before us are still flush." (191-92)

Taking its charge from Healy, this collection brings together seventeen writing center professionals from across American education—public and private; large and small; secondary, community college, four-year college, and university—to discuss the possibilities and limitations that online applications offer to writing centers. Specifically, these individuals present models and strategies for developing, modifying, and maintaining online services that meet two important criteria: they are pedagogically sound; they support the writing center's mission generally and within the context of specific/local educational environments. While advocating that writing center professionals make use of and take full advantage of the current and emerging potentials for online writing center applications, there is also the need for an equally critical and careful examination of what is to be gained and lost from moving in the direction of more wired writing center work. As all of the chapters make clear, the online activities that are currently underway in wired writing centers—Online Writing Centers (OWLs), WWW home pages, etc.—are essentially first-generation experiments, optimistic forays into the pedagogical unknown. Given the relative newness of these applications, however, we would be remiss to advocate that the community dive into this type of activity without an awareness of the dangers (real and imagined) and shortcomings that can and do exist. The constant note in these chapters is this: explore these and other online applications with enthusiasm; however, never forget that the technology does not provide a writing center with anything that can replace the people who work there, who train the staff, and whose experience, intuition, and common sense underlies a very powerful form of guiding insight. As Dickie Selfe admonished the writing center community in his engagingly titled *Computers and Composition* article, "Surfing the Tsunami: Electronic Environments in the Writing Center,"

> Voices of dissent from workers and students in writing centers are or should be an essential element of the planning process if computers and composition specialists and writing center workers want to mediate—at least locally—the massive and often blind "will to technologize" in this culture. (312)

And, as Bruce Pegg demonstrates in chapter thirteen, the increased numbers of writing centers that offer or are planning to offer online services suggests an abiding interest in the subject of computer mediated applications for the wired writing center. That interest often crashes against the harsh realities of these writing center professionals' lives—often tenuous professional status; heavy teaching and administrative loads; heavy service expectations; etc.—in such a way as to make the immediate implementation of many of the online services described in the following pages improbable or of secondary importance to more pressing or more pragmatic issues. One common issue that limits the use of online writing center services is that most of the people currently directing writing centers and training the tutors who work in these centers usually have neither the time nor the expertise to explore all the available options and to create online tutorial services. Beyond this limitation, they often lack convenient or adequate access to the required technology and the computer skills needed to undertake the construction and maintenance of these services. Additionally, there are few print resources available on the topic of computer-mediated writing center activity. Articles appear in *The Writing Center Journal* and *Writing Lab Newsletter* on this topic, but rarely in a coordinated, connected manner. Ironically, the best articles and guides appear in electronic forums, such as *Kairos*, a medium still unavailable or unknown to the many writing center directors. This lack of access is especially acute for writing center directors and staff in community colleges and secondary schools where computers are neither always widely accessible nor internet access a given. Regardless of the allure of electronic media, paper documents such as this book remain a primary source for disseminating information among members of this academic community.

The wide-ranging, thoughtful, and innovative discussions presented in this collection's chapters are richly detailed accounts of the contributing authors' activities, plans, reflections, and critique as they explore the implementation and implications of online writing centers. Taken both individually and as a whole, these chapters significantly expand the breadth and the depth of the community's conversations about technology's role(s) in the writing center. They offer models for others to modify to their local needs. These authors also step back to critique their endeavors in light of many issues: information about technology's impact on educational activity; the differing developmental needs of less and more mature writers; less-than-ideal realities about individual's and institution's access to technology; and established writing center theory and practice. As a set of foregrounding thoughts then, this chapter responds to and weaves in and out of the following chapters and the web of associations, assumptions, connotations, citations, implications, and innovations that each author brings to this project.

PAUSING TO ASK

It is not too far off the mark to say that an increasingly large percent of my professional time and self-definition is mediated and largely determined by the myriad available forms of electronic communication. I benefit directly as a writer, teacher, and member of the writing center community from my colleagues' (those whose work this book reflects directly and those it echoes) efforts to theorize, tinker with, implement, proselytize, and praise the potential applications emerging for electronically mediated forms of writing assistance and professional development based in the writing center. As these technologies expand, develop, and become easily accessible, I anticipate that this linking of personal/professional identity to technology will only continue. Yet, trained in the humanistic and post-enlightenment-bleeding-into-postmodern tradition of skepticism and critique, I tend to step back and ask probing questions—even about things and systems to which I am growing increasingly dependent and indebted.

I have little doubt that computers—and other electronic communication technologies presently available or currently in planning, testing, or initial distribution phases—will continue to play a pronounced role in the work that literacy educators undertake. Who determines what that role will be and the shape(s) it will take, however, is not a given. As Dickie Selfe states, the wave of change is coming—about that there is no doubt. Therefore, as teachers charged with helping students develop needed literacy abilities, we must start to determine how we will interact with this change. Between the alternative of standing defiantly in front of the tidal wave of technological change or of harnessing its momentum to the needs of writing centers and their clients, Selfe opts for the latter for himself and likewise recommends that choice to the writing center community. I concur. There is a real need for writing center personnel who theorize and implement online and other technological, writing center instructional services and learning environments to explore the implications of these actions, to stop and to check the community's sometimes unbridled enthusiasm.

Peter Carino's reference in chapter twelve to Neil Postman's critique of technology's shaping influence on culture is particularly apropos given this book's overall careful (re)assessment of computer-mediated communications technology in the writing center. In both Postman's work and in Carino's use of this material is the warning that technology does not "pause to ask" about its impact on culture. This guardedness, shared by all of this book's contributors, is an important critical stance—more so than a comfortable "proceed with caution" stance based on timidity—because it allows these authors the space they need to carefully, insightfully, and precisely assess the results of their actions to date. Keeping with this collection's overriding agenda—pausing to ask—in setting the stage for the material that follows, I want to make a number of observations about the (sometimes ironic; always revealing) way in which the writing center community has wired itself.

Specifically, a number of issues that my contributing colleagues raise and/or reveal about technologically-rich writing center programs warrant careful scrutiny. As we grow increasingly aware, there are implications (positive and negative) to each decision that writing center personnel make about the role(s) that technology will/should play in their particular context. As such, the writing center community's members must carefully (re)assess their desires to join the electronic/virtual wagon train, even as they continue their initial online forays. Critical reflection will help us all decide how and to what extent we will move the types of educational encounters and philosophies held dear by the writing center community at large into the admittedly unknown (a simultaneously terrifying and exciting situation) territory/ies inhabited and made possible by wired writing centers.

WHAT IS THE WRITING CENTER (COMMUNITY)
TO (BE)COME?

My understanding of writing processes and literacy/ies is shaped in ways I do/do not easily recognize by my increasing reliance on the personal computer as my primary writing tool and on such electronic communication systems as email and the World Wide Web as both conduits for professional communication and collaboration and as mediums for classroom instruction. At the same time, my fundamental self-definition(s) as a writer and a writing teacher is most definitely *not* yet wedded inextricably to technology in terms of my thinking about, creating, and maintaining the interpersonal relationships found in traditional writing center instructional dyads—teacher/student, tutor/client, mentor/mentee—or in small-group, collaborative settings. This apparently paradoxical personal/professional reality is one that I think I share with writing center colleagues of my generation—first and second generation writing center practitioners.

Cynthia Selfe (1995) acknowledges "the complex knot of issues generated by technology use in writing centers" (309). While she pays attention to a wide range of issues, she focuses particular attention on the give-and-take reality that accompanies any new literacy technology (pencil, printing press, computer, MUD/MOO, etc.), what she describes as

the potential for increased communication, community building, information access, and literacy education that technology offers students and teachers, but also of the many dangers that technology poses for the academic ecosystem of writing centers, humanities and English departments, and universities—the ways in which technology many affect coach-student relationships; the nature of the teaching and learning that goes on in these richly textured spaces; the goals and the missions of writing centers, and the status of these places within educational communities; the lives and outlooks of coaches, staff, and students who labor within writing centers. (309)

As Selfe tells us, in the midst of our enthusiasm for and implementation of the various ideas, applications, dreams, and desires that inhabit the concept of the wired writing center, there is a pressing need to stop and consider what are the results—immediate and potential—of our online forays. What are the potential reconfigurations of writing centers and of the writing center community that result from its rush to go online, to explore virtual configurations?

The collaborative dream realized?

Although it is too soon to gauge the longevity of these claims, there is no hiding from the fact that the literature about technology and writing—both for the discipline of composition studies and the writing center community—rests on the assumption that technology allows those teachers charged with improving students' writing abilities to do their jobs much more efficiently. Within the closer confines of the literature on online writing centers, including material presented here, there exists a palpable enthusiasm for online writing activity, an almost utopian vision of what the computer mediated writing environment can help us to achieve.

As it has to a large extent in composition circles, so too is it becoming commonplace to encounter many of the following types of claims about the benefits of computers in the writing center: computers in the tutorial setting allow for more equitable and convenient access to center resources and services (Gardner, chapter five; Kinkead 1988); computers and computer networks encourage collaboration among writers (Farrell 1987, 1989, Jordan-Henley and Maid 1995 "MOOving"); computers decenter authority and enhance tutor training (Chappell, Johanek and Rickly); virtual tutoring represents the future (Coogan 1995, Crump, Jordan-Henley and Maid 1995 "Tutoring", 1995 "MOOving", Kinkead 1988). The consensus of these proponents of a tight integration of computer mediated tutoring activities is that the computer and writing activities facilitated by computer networks realize the social constructivist ideology and pedagogy advocated by the writing center community within the past decade. Particularly, computers can help to establish community among tutors and encourage collaboration among writers in ways that help to create writing environments and collaborative relationships that are more natural than the artificial ones found in the typical classroom (Crump, Chappell, Jordan-Henley and Maid 1995 "MOOving").

A technology defined caste-based community?

In the midst of our enthusiasm for emerging technological applications, and in the midst of our eagerness to tell everyone else about the uses to which we put these applications, the writing center community must recognize the potential for it to unwittingly develop and enact a hierarchy—a class structure—based solely on the extent to which centers do/do not embrace or foreground technology in their day-to-day operations. Much of the community's strength and vitality results directly from its willing acceptance of its members' diverse missions and practices, a recognition of each writing center's situatedness as a primary agent in determining its priorities and procedures. To lose this tolerance to a yardstick based upon websites, online tutoring, and other technological applications would be devastating. Yet, despite our well-meaning assurances to the negative, the potential for doing so is real.

At each conference sponsored by the National Writing Centers Association, as well as at writing center sessions at NCTE and CCCC, the sessions about computer applications in the writing center fill to overflowing and generate tremendous amounts of highly animated and optimistic discussion. As much as I enjoy these sessions, I am bothered by the looks of consternation on many colleagues' faces, looks that suggest they feel somehow out of the loop, or less viable than their techophile colleagues. In our rush to show what we can do and have done with computers within the context of a particular writing center, it is easy to forget a number of very powerful realities:

- not every center has access to the many resources needed to replicate these efforts;
- not every center's clientele have access to the technology needed to make such projects expedient;
- not every center can determine its future and fate to the extent needed to follow suit;
- not every center's mission or philosophical foundation is commensurate with the assumptions contained in many online writing center projects.

To forget these fundamental differences while we celebrate the technologically innovative achievements of others, is to celebrate uncritically. The composite result of that type of spotlighting (and, simultaneously shunting aside) sends powerfully norming messages about what the community values, about what constitutes full community membership and recognition, and about what types of activity the community validates. This type of community definition, replete with ex/inclusions, is a reality to which we must pay careful attention as we explore technology's role in the writing center and as we continue to discuss the results and the implications of these activities.

A computer lab for writing?

As writing centers develop online resources that increasingly reflect, mimic, replicate, or provide prototypes for many of the online resources found in computer assisted composition classrooms (or, vice versa), and as writing centers encourage more writers to interact with other writers virtually rather than within the close confines of the face-to-face (f2f) tutorial, at what point is the allocation of the current monetary and physical resources no longer easily justified? "What is the value added by the physical writing center?" might become a question that we are forced to respond to should our OWLs and other electronic services attract the focused attention of budget conscious administrators. The answers we supply must be ones we have thought through with care because they will be directed most often to administrators who understand the powerful sway that technology linked educational programs hold over the public through a deeply rooted cultural assumption that technology holds the answers to problems, particularly such vexing problems as found in literacy education. To reiterate Wallace's point (chapter eleven), if the writing center begins to duplicate (even if only in appearance) the computerized composition classroom and its virtual resources for writers, including online materials and conferencing capabilities, what has the writing center become? What will be its fate? At what point in its expansion into online applications, asks Wallace, does a writing center cease to be a writing center and become a computerized writing classroom? While this is not a popular question, and certainly is not a question answered by this or by the following chapters, it is quite possibly the most important question facing the writing center community as it wrestles with the task of if and how it is possible to take the writing center online with its services and guiding philosophies and value systems intact.

An obsolete service?

I raise these questions neither to sound alarmist nor to draw a line in the sand and tell my colleagues that they cross it at their own peril. Issuing ultimatums and yelling "fire" are not effective rhetorical options because they ignore the many pressures that combine within the complicated calculus of most writing center practitioners' program development and maintenance process. I know how hard it is to make time to step back from the pressing needs of the program and assess its present status and needs. In my day-to-day, frenetic existence as a teacher and writing center educator, for instance, it is quite easy for me to react to other writing center's highly visible technology adaptations and to think, "I'd better get a webpage up and running that looks as good as Utopia U's," or, "I need to get online tutoring started." What is more difficult, however, is to find/make the time needed to think ahead, to play out the possible scripts that represent my and my program's potential futures as a result of these online enactments. When I make the time to do so, however, like Wallace, one possible future I see finds the writing center and my work within it rendered at worst obsolete and/or redundant, or fundamentally redefined. What I have yet to determine in these scenarios is whether that potential for obsolescence is due to evolution or replacement of the services and attitudes that have defined the writing center and its community. As Peter Carino remarked during the later stages of writing this book, "We could end up complicitous in our own obsolescence if we jump on the bandwagon without asking where it is headed."

DO WIRED WRITING CENTERS SUPPORT
TECHNO-CURRENT TRADITIONAL RHETORIC?

As a quick review of the writing center community's literature over the past decade reveals, the community has expended a great deal of energy in the attempt to distance its existence, mission, and pedagogical practices from the "undesirable" taint of serving the conservative ideology imbedded in postivist approaches to writing (Ede, Hobson 1992, Lunsford 1991, Murphy 1991). This desire occupies the philosophical (although, probably not the political) heart of the "writing lab vs. writing center" debate that both Wallace and Carino allude to in their chapters. Writing center proponents found their rallying cries of "individualized instruction," "process," "collaborative learning," "peer feedback," "audience and community accommodation," in a frequently idiosyncratic mix of expressivist and social constructivist thought and practice (Hobson 1992, 1994, Carino 1995 "Theorizing"). The upshot of this concerted and deeply-felt activity was to link the term "writing lab" with pedagogy derided as bereft of validity: worksheets dedicated to grammar and mechanics; repetitive drill exercises for developing and demonstrating mastery of the language; and formulaic writing task which reflect conservative culture's value of form and convention over developing writers' critical thinking and communicative flexibility. In opposition to the label "writing lab," "writing center" has come to represent innovative, process-based and contextually-located pedagogy focusing on the student and her need to negotiate her position within many discourse communities (Wallace 1991).

While this overstated history travels well-covered ground, I do so to highlight the following, a situation I find distressing and entertainingly ironic: in their first forays online, many writing centers are creating themselves in the form of their antithesis, that nemesis writing lab. Put bluntly, many OWL's consist primarily of the contents of old filing cabinets and handbooks—worksheets, drill activities, guides to form—pulled out of the mothballs, dusted off, and digitized (see Pegg's review of WWW sites in chapter thirteen). In addition to a reliance on these types of materials, by allowing—even encouraging—writers to make use of these online resources, many of these writers write in isolation, simultaneously reinscribing tenets found in current traditional rhetoric's insistence on originality of ideas (collaboration is a form of cheating) and expressivist rhetoric's Romantic portrayal of the individual as the locus of a personal truth (Berlin, Hobson 1992). While I do not ascribe pernicious motives to my colleagues who have developed these sites—I firmly believe in their good intentions, as I hope they concede my good will and humor as I critique these sites—the explosion of filing-cabinet-like online information available at an increasingly large number of writing center websites, programs that espouse a commitment to seeing writing as complex social phenomenon in their tutoring and tutor training, raises several other points worth reflecting on.

WHAT CAN('T) AN OWL DO
THAT A WRITING CENTER CAN('T)?

OWLs, as entities that exist within the physical and virtual space of a computer system offer writing centers highly efficient and expeditious means to store large amounts of information in incredibly small areas (a hard drive; a 3.5" disk). Stored in the semi-public domain of LANs, Gopher files, and webpages, this is information that writers can access on their own and at their convenience. With this bulk digitized and stored in personal computers and other computer configurations, physical space once devoted to filing cabinets full of print materials and other records can become available tutorial space; staff can also be relieved from the repetitious and tedious clerical task of digging out these materials.

The argument that an OWL offers increased access to many traditionally under served client populations is quite compelling. It makes sense that internet access, for instance, does make it possible for many of the less-frequently served client groups that Gardner mentions to use writing center materials and services at their convenience. Convenience is an important issue for students who commute, who juggle work/family/school obligations, whose access and mobility are hindered by physical disabilities, who are enrolled in distance education programs, who take courses at night or on weekend schedules, and, perhaps, who are exceedingly shy (Kinkead 1988). Does convenience, however, necessarily translate to a quality of service equal to that found in the physical writing center? The jury is still out on this issue. This question is both essential and complex.

Helping novice writers develop the ability and confidence needed to practice the demanding activities of critical thinking, audience analysis and accommodation, idea invention and development, implementation of conventions within specific discourse communities is a subtle task, a point that Childers, Jordan, and Upton foreground in their thoughts about secondary school writing centers (chapter nine). Michael Spooner (1994 "A Dialogue"), Jeffrey Baker (1994), and Katherine Grubbs (1994) each raise important questions about how effective online tutorials are for working with less-mature writers, particularly given the medium's lack of paralinguistic cues from which both the tutor and client glean continuous information about the conversation's movement and success. Can an OWL, in its most common current configuration as repository of forms and handouts, accomplish results that are in the writer's best interests and that are consistent with the philosophical and pedagogical principles the writing center community has fought dramatically to make the centerpiece of the community's practice and self-definition?

While I think it is possible to do so—Gardner's and Monroe's chapters present compelling examples to the positive—it isn't easy. And, ease is the overriding factor behind the fact that the majority of OWL resources look suspiciously like skill driven, current traditional "writing labs." Formatting static webpages isn't that demanding an activity, once one learns basic HTML commands; their upkeep, however, can be incredibly time consuming, a process that a colleague recently referred to as "a sinkhole into which I seem to have cast all of my and my tutors' spare time trying to develop, debug, and maintain." If getting an OWL to the stage where most currently are is a demanding process, creating OWLs that are consistent with the best of the writing center community's social constructivist-influenced theory and practice takes an incredible commitment of time, resources, energy, and continuing/continuous education on the part of everyone involved—planners, administrators, tutors, clients. Most writing center programs do not currently have the resources or the expertise to undertake this, more pedagogically defensible, version of the wired writing center. As Ellen Mohr demonstrates (chapter ten), time is a commodity in short supply, without the exponentially increasing demands created by the addition of sophisticated online services.

On a much more pragmatic level, I ask, why is it that we feel compelled to pull all this stuff out of the closet anyway? Didn't we work very hard to relegate positivist-based pedagogy to the very margins of writing center activity (Carino 1995 "Theorizing", Ede, Hobson 1992, 1994, Lunsford 1991, Murphy 1991)? If we think that writers can benefit from such electronic handouts and forms, why not let the textbook publishers take on the task—one it seems they already do well, based on the incessant flow of handbooks and workbooks on floppy disks and CD-ROMs flowing across my desk? Is the time it takes to develop (or to digitize) these materials worth the investment and the associated risk of appearing to condone their uncritical use. Frankly, we can tell writers, and other stakeholders who may have an investment (ideological, financial, dependency) in these types of materials, where they can be found—like the U. of Michigan OWL, we can always provide links to such websites—without having to create them ourselves, and in the process of doing so implicitly give our stamp of approval to them and to the pedagogy and ideology to which they adhere. Might we do so for reasons other than pedagogical, driven instead by politics, opportunities for expansion and self-aggrandizement?

WHERE SHOULD WE FOCUS OUR ENERGY?

As each chapter in this collection demonstrates, writing center professionals are being called upon to do more and more, often with the same or fewer resources and with increased expectations. In addition to their roles developing, implementing, and overseeing important support services for all writers within their community, they increasingly wear any number of hats: technology coordinator and chief computer fixer, email and web guru, faculty developer and curriculum coordinator. Nowhere is this situation made more clear than in Ellen Mohr's detailed history of all of the computer related courses she has taken in the past few years and extent to which the presence of computers in her writing center has reconfigured both her time and her role in the center. She has moved from being continually engaged in tutoring and tutor training to having less time to be part of these central writing center activities. Now she spends a majority of her time working with such computer related issues as learning and teaching software packages; ironically, however, her evaluation process still assumes that she is responsible for those tutorial related activities on which she once focused her activity.

In, "Computer Centers and Writing Centers: An Argument for Ballast," an article that responds to the types of situations Mohr describes, Nancy Grimm points to the costs of trying to accomplish everything and to be everything to everyone when she writes that "writing center professionals need time to focus on issues unique to their location" (324) Using her situation as writing center director at Michigan Technological University as an illustrative example upon which to investigate the costs associated with developing the knowledge and skills base needed to plan and oversee expansion of the writing center into virtual space(s), she writes,

> If I had to develop expertise in hardware and software, for example, I would not have been able to engage our staff in the program of critical reflection that is leading to some interesting literacy research; nor would I have had time to carry the idea of peer tutoring to other departments on our campus. (324)

As Ellen Mohr candidly states, "I quickly discovered that I had better things to do with my time." As more writing center directors and their staffs push beyond the first phase of using online resources to advertise general information about the writing center and to make handouts available, Mohr's sentiment may become quite common.

WHEN ARE SOME THINGS PATENTLY ABSURD?

I marvel at the ingenuity and commitment that writing center colleagues bring to their efforts to explore the potential uses to which they can put new technology to work in the writing center. Projects such as those described by Rickly (chapter three), Gardner (chapter five), Monroe (chapter one), and Kearcher (chapter six), for example, inevitably make me root for their success. At points, however, we need to acknowledge that, in spite of our best intentions, the results of some of our online efforts approach the sublimely ridiculous, particularly when students take the products of our idealized intentions and use them to achieve their decidedly idiosyncratic ends. My favorite example of this technologically-mediated irony comes from a colleague's writing center, and is, I think, a story that has the potential to become writing center legend:

> In the hour or so before a regularly scheduled writing center staff meeting, the writing center director observes staff as they worked with clients, particularly the one staff member engaged in a synchronous online tutorial—something that the director had wondered if clients would opt to use, given the need to learn to use the needed chat program. Looking over the tutor's shoulder, the director talked to the tutor about the tutorial, its process, ease and difficulties, as well as the tutor's sense

of how the client was responding to the advice given and to the online tutorial itself. The tutor mentioned that the process was slow and that she really wished she could talk (f2f) with the client in order to push the discussion to a needed level of depth about the project. Sensing the tutor's need to return to the tutorial, the director moved on.

Two students were using the center's computers in the adjacent room: one printing a paper; one "talking" online. Glancing at the screen, the director realized with a jolt that the student was talking to the tutor sitting fewer than twenty feet away, a situation the tutor was not aware of. The student had opted for the online tutorial because, "I wanted to be able to leave anytime without feeling guilty. And, I thought I could just get my questions answered and not have to talk about all that other stuff the tutors always want you to talk about, like who I'm writing to and why I need more info."

RESEARCHING AND ASSESSING
THE "WIRED" WRITING CENTER

As demonstrated throughout this collection, there exist any number of exciting next steps for members of this community to explore within the concept of the wired writing center—video conferencing, distance learning, virtual conferencing spaces, etc. One area that has not received the detailed discussion it should, however, is that of needed types of research related to the technological innovations that writing centers have or are considering implementing. A host of questions about online tutoring, for instance, need to be investigated: What types of writers benefit the most from online tutoring? Are gains in writing development consistent between (f2f) and virtual f2f conferences? What are the dynamics of online talk in comparison to (f2f) conversation? The lack of detailed discussion about how to begin to methodically research and assess our online activity has many sources, including the following:

- We are caught up in the rush to get our programs online.
- We are just beginning to zero in on the types of questions we can and should ask.
- We are not generally familiarity with or conversant about research methodologies that might apply to this area of writing center practice, and we are general suspicion about the results of such study.

Stuart Blythe (chapter seven) provides a primer for those members of the writing center community who wish to build into their forays into electronic communications, for example, the types of careful and audience aware planning steps and research necessary to more successful tailor online services to the needs of actual, not hypothetical, users—users who often come to our services with radically different agendas and needs than we might wish for them or even imagine. Usability research is essential, at some level, to help us create and to justify technology based writing center innovations. Additionally, while it is not always easy, a point

Stuart reiterates, the benefits of doing this type of work are many and can lead us to begin to carry out other types of needed investigation.

Raising the issue of needed research is almost routine call-to-action for the writing center community, one put before the community, it seems, every few years (Neuleib 1984, North 1984 "Writing Center", Severino). As such, I replicate and reiterate comments and charges others have made while raising research issues that I consider promising, enlightening, warranted—even, admittedly, fun—that present themselves as a direct result of the community's exploration of the uses to which it can put technology. Implicit in the following research agenda are the makings of any number of tutor research projects, master's theses, doctoral dissertations, and grant proposals.

1. Who uses our OWL? How?

Although I know that initial data keeping is underway in many places, there are currently no published analyses of the user/audience demographics of any OWL or of how these users interact with the site and the available information and services. While this may not be the easiest data to collect, it seems essential for a number of reasons: to inform specific, concerned stakeholders about the OWL's activity, either to justify maintenance or expansion of budgeted time and monies; to identify the writing support needs of this population of writers, particularly if these needs differ from those identified among users of the physical writing center; to analyze if the current configurations of the service encourage a critical use of the service(s) and increasingly mature approaches to the writing process and the issues that surround it.

Several relatively simple data collection strategies offer a start in this research project, particulary "hit counters" and questionnaires. Because most OWLs are web based, using HTML coding, it is easy to embed a "hit counter" to track the number of times the site is accessed. And, most websites do so. Yet, to get a more accurate picture of how the site is used, these tallying devices need to be part of every page in the site. Considered individually and together, the numbers provide a rough composite of the site's high and low demand areas, findings that may correlate to user's perceptions of most/least usefulness. A fascinating project would be to see the extent to which these perceptions do/do not coincide with the findings of composition research into composing processes of novice and experienced writers.

The down side of this strategy, however, is the realization that the data collected is highly unreliable, as these counters do not discern between new users and users who, in moving within a site, return to a specific page several times on the way to other pages. Yet, for an initial, low-risk research project, this activity could yield tentative information on which to begin to test the validity of many assumptions that undergird the site's mission and structure.

Questionnaires offer another line of research into OWL users, their experiences, and motivations. Because of the manner in which OWL users access these sites, it seems entirely possible—most likely with the assistance of outside technical expertise—to trace many users to their home email accounts where a questionnaire can be sent. Additionally, it is easy to build a questionnaire into the site itself. In both cases, response depends on the user—they become a self-selecting group, and, thus, their responses cannot be taken as normative—a problem encountered whenever one attempts to research a population using questionnaire instruments. Yet, for the purposes of developing research questions on which to build research projects designed to garner more reliable results, this approach is a good starting place. Additionally, the gathered responses are often illuminating.

As to the question of how do writers use online services, Barbara Monroe has provided a groudbreaking analysis of online tutorial interaction. Chapter one of this book should provide a model for many writing center scholars who have the requisite background in linguistics and discourse analysis to replicate her study both to corroborate the patterns she found and to expand on them. There is much to be learned about issues of access, power relations, gender differences and user profiles, online conversational patterns, tutorial dynamics in the absence of physical and contextual paralinguistic cues from this type of analysis of the online tutorial. And, by extension, there is much to be learned about the physical (f2f) tutorial interaction from these studies as well. By comparing what we know about (f2f) tutorials with what we can learn about virtual f2f tutorials, we may begin to find answers to a pressing pedagogical question, one with important implications for writing center administration and planning: What client groups benefit the most from online tutoring in terms of their growth as writers?

2. What defines a successful online tutorial? What does one look like?

David Coogan (chapter two) and Barbara Monroe provide a jump start to an fruitful and needed area of writing center research by recording and analyzing the online tutorial and by raising a number of important questions about its relation to the type of face-to-face (f2f) interaction found in the physical writing center tutorial. This inquiry must continue if we are to answer a number of critical questions about virtual tutoring, of which the following are representative examples:

- Does/can the online tutorial work effectively and efficiently with higher-order composing concerns?
- What does the lack of paralinguistic cues in the virtual tutorial do to the tutorial in terms of how the interlocutors interact and how they define their roles, the conversation strategies employed, the way(s) in which turntaking and collaboration is signaled, how emphasis and empathy is presented, read, and maintained?
- What are the cues tutors use to assess their client's level of engagement and commitment to the tutorial?

- Do pacing differences between synchronous and asynchronous online tutorials affect the type and quality of the tutorial interaction and the participants' attitudes?

3. What are the costs of going online?

A refrain common to conference sessions devoted to computer applications in the writing center addresses the unexpected costs of getting and maintaining both computers themselves and online services. Yet, the discussion rarely gets specific: how much did it cost to do X at Y? Admittedly, the dollar costs of computer equipment is hardly static; however, there is a need for members of the community to make a public accounting of the costs incurred in wiring their centers. Other programs need a conceptual ballpark in which to play as they plan and budget their technologically mediated writing center activities.

Beyond presenting in specific dollar amount the costs of creating and maintaining such services as those described in this book, we need people to undertake a more detailed, broader perspective cost analysis. There are costs incurred in attempting any innovation in the writing center and, most of these costs are not immediately translatable into specific dollar figures. For places to start this line of inquiry, consider the following questions: How much is the director's time worth to plan for and to oversee the implementation and upkeep of an OWL? How will this time be replaced in order to ensure continued coverage of the director's preexisting duties? How much is the tutorial staff's time worth while they are trained to tutor in a virtual writing center? What are the costs in terms of replacement time for staff and equipment designated to these new endeavors? What is the impact of such innovation on the center's materials, fixed costs, and services budget? What are the costs in terms of the center's productivity, mission, and staff morale?

4. How should we theorize and/or modify the writing center's mission to reflect technology's influence?

At the same time that writing center practitioners are faced with the question of what to do with the available technology at their disposal, a number of converging factors suggest the necessity to reexamine the writing center's traditional mission in order to determine if it should be modified. Linked to the technological explosion in education is the rapidly expanding and highly competitive distance education market. Most colleges, many private companies, and even some secondary institutions, are beginning to offer credit bearing coursework via the internet and the WWW. In the face of these developments, the writing center needs to think carefully about its mission and its duty to students and to its home institution (often competing duties). This (re)assessment will require us to review the theories and practices on which we define our current mission, and may require us to retheorize the center in terms of its mission and configuration; we should also entertain the possibility that the writing center as we have known it has served its purpose and is now facing its demise or absorption into other service providers.

In this line of thought, Selfe and Hilligoss (1994) provide a possible starting point for intrepid members of the writing center community in their attempts to theorize and critique the wired writing center and its role within literacy education. They write,

> As teachers and researchers, we need to study literacy, with computers as an important feature of the setting and the means, a feature that changes literate practices and our understanding of them but neither wholly sustains nor destroys any given literacy . . . . If we have wrongly identified text with literate knowledge, the next fallacy may be "computer knowledge," in which the computer—even a certain kind of computer—becomes the new picture of literate orientation. This is a real possibility." (339)

While these issues are broad and daunting, they are ones that the writing center community must address in order to assure its intellectual and ethical high standards. They may also help to ensure its continued existence in the current or revised form.

CONCLUSION

At the end of this introduction and the start of this book, it seems only fitting that I stop straddling the virtual fence and take a position on the issue of the wired writing center. Given the overall guardedness of my preceding remarks, it would be easy to mistakenly conclude that I am not a proponent of online writing center and other forms of computer mediated writing center activity. However, I am an irrepressible optimist, albeit fused to a deeply embedded strain of pragmatist and realist. As such, the optimist in me strongly supports the efforts that are underway in the writing center community to explore what opportunities that await them in the virtual frontier of online education. My pragmatic/realist side whispers into the virtual wind, "Be prepared before you go. Acknowledge the risks, even if/as you choose to venture forth."

This guarded optimism may explain the source of one of my still unreconciled fears about online writing centers, a potential result of a lack of foresight about these very diverse and exciting developments described in this book. While I am concerned by the rush to do everything imaginable with the available technology within the context of the writing center, it is not the experimentation that gives me pause. My abiding hope is that in the midst of our enthusiasm, we do not abandon the very powerful set of ideals and values that have been the writing center community's hallmark. It is possible that the idea of the writing center we value may become so diffuse, spread so thin, that our virtual enactments no longer resemble that powerful ideal. It seems possible to sacrifice more than we realize (or, rue in hindsight) to the gods of technology, progress, and public demand.

Throughout the process of bringing this book to fruition, I have been continually reminded of the writing center community's ability and willingness to face up to its need for careful assessment and critique of its actions. Each author has done so in a way that serves as a model to those who wish to follow the trails they are blazing across virtual territories that may become writing center domains. I find my colleagues' exploration of such technologically mediated activity as synchronous online tutorials using such virtual environments as MUDs and MOOs exciting, engaging, and stimulating. In fact, it is the sum of the positive reactions I have experienced during the past four-to-five years of unprecedented development of computer mediated writing center resources that makes my present critique possible. Following in the footsteps of my intrepid virtual pathfinders, including many represented in the following pages, reading the narratives of their activities to date, trying on their virtual sites and services for fit (size, aesthetic, ideological), has allowed me to gain my current, cautiously optimistic, perspective about the wired writing center and its future.

Thus, in keeping with the overall careful, yet optimistic tone of this book, I echo the entertaining, but very serious, admonition with which Peter Carino ends chapter twelve:

> If OWLs are going to carry us into flight rather than eat us like rodents, if MOOs are going to produce more milk than dung, if we are going to cruise the information superhighway without becoming roadkill, our vigilance will need to equal our enthusiasm. I think this history shows that generally it has, though not always in the best proportions, and will continue to do so. The question will be whether we can remain vigilant in the inertia of our enthusiasm.

If the contibutions of the authors presented here—and, by extension, the contributions made by the members of the writing center community to whom these writers refer to and build upon—are as representative of the best that this community has to offer as I believe they are, the future looks very good indeed for this community of educators to enact and maintain a richly textured, critically self-aware vigilance directed at the reasons we choose and the methods we embrace for wiring the writing center. No doubt the efforts to come will be as challenging, as productive, as exciting, as revealing, and, in all honesty, as much fun as the efforts that have brought the writing center community to its current space(s)-place(s).

NOTES

1.   I wish to thank Peter Carino, Ray Wallace, and Carla McDonough for reading and responding to drafts of this introduction. Their input proved essential.

PART I

Models and Strategies for Wired Writing Centers

CHAPTER ONE

The Look and Feel of the OWL Conference

Barbara Monroe

THE ONLINE WRITING AND LEARNING (OWL) AT THE UNIVERSITY OF MICHIGAN grew out of our face-to-face (f2f) peer tutoring program in many ways. Although our OWL website includes links to other OWLs that offer electronic handouts, our primary purpose is to respond to writers' needs, online, person-to-person. Like many OWLs, our online tutorial is technically conducted by means of asynchronous electronic mail, which clients can also access through the web. When we first decided to offer writing conferences online in 1994, we saw this move as simply an extension of our peer tutoring program. Not surprisingly, then, our online and f2f tutorials are close kin, borne of the same principles and practices. Our writing conference, both online and off, is based on a one-to-one, rather than one-to-many, instructional model and a collateral power relationship: peer-to-peer rather than a teacher-to-student. Consistent with that rationale, our OWL and f2f conference use the same activities, such as conducting diagnostic work and establishing conference priorities. Our tutors also worry about the same pedagogical issues, such as finding ways to engage clients as collaborative partners in the conference enterprise. And both OWL and f2f tutors work within the same constraints inherent to our walk-in program: our tutors can not count on seeing the same clients or the same paper assignment again, and so their conferences attempt to be comprehensive and specific at the same time.

But a key point of difference is that an OWL conference is a written artifact with its own look-and-feel, and as such, can be productively described and analyzed as a genre unto itself. Largely through trial and error, and verified by client feedback studies as part of our training seminar, our tutors have developed what we believe is an effective online pedagogy, specific to an asynchronous electronic environment. While the formal features of the OWL conference have stabilized over the past three years, each OWL conference reflects a tutor's own persona and conferencing style.[1] The centripetal trends of our OWL conference give it shape as a genre; individual tutors's variations on that form suggest the centrifugal pull on that genre, very much in a Bakhtinian sense. As a genre onto itself, the OWL conference can be productively described and analyzed. At first glance, the

OWL conference has a standard shape, but a closer look reveals a wide range of discursive practices at play within that formal framework.

THE LOOK OF AN OWL CONFERENCE

The actual procedure of our online tutorial is not unlike that of our f2f service. The OWL conference begins when a client first "comes in" (by way of our webbed OWL) and fills out a mailform (http://www.lsa.umich.edu/ecb/OWL/mailform.html). This form asks the client to identify what year student he is, what class the paper is for, and when it is due — information that gives the tutor a context for the conference. The mailform page also asks the client to explain the assignment and identify what kind of help he is seeking before asking him to copy, paste, and submit his paper. The tutor reads the paper through and thoroughly, usually more than once, before writing a response and sending the "conference" back to the client. Within 48 hours (as per our policy), usually much sooner, a client receives a "conference" from the tutor in the form of a personal email message, signed with a first name, a thoughtful, friendly, well-composed response from an experienced reader and accomplished writer in her own right. This is what a conference might look like to the client:[2]

Hi Curtis—

[1]   My name is Sean and I'm an ECB OWL tutor. I've read your paper, and I have some suggestions for you. I guess I'll give my general feedback and then my specifics. My specific stuff will be set off ***Like This***

Generally, I think you've got a nice, picturesque little tableau here: pretty well detailed, and certainly very pretty. If you're trying to think of avenues for expansion of the material, there are a couple of things I can suggest:

One thing to think about is a sort of narrative. I understand that this is not a specifically narrative essay, but there is an observer who is describing this scene. Why is this the scene that sticks with you particularly? Is this a general, timeless scene, or do you really want to foreground one particular time, and if you do, what is the narrator doing there, and why is it so important? I think there are shadows of these issues already sort of dancing at the edges of your essay, so if you bump them up you'll take up space and you can add more of a human dimension to this scene.

The other thing I'd encourage is just to really really really push at your description: make it as specific and sensory as possible. I'll show you what I mean in the specifics, so I guess we might as well just move right along to those:

On Tue, 18 Mar 1997, Curtis McDonald wrote:
>
> Name: Curtis McDonald
> Class the paper for: Eng125
> Assignment : Describe a landscape

> help looking for: how could I expand the paper? It is too short.
>
> The Harbor
> It was rare to have such a sunny day in this city.
[2] ***what city?***
> The sky was blue with no clouds; it merged with the tranquil ocean at the
> far end of the world. The wind blew gently and brushed away all the
> dampness. The afternoon sun shared its warmth with everybody, driving
> away the cold of the winter. I decided to go for a walk.
This is pretty much perfect, as far as description of the weather, I think. It's beautifully detailed. My one quibble is that all we see here is the sky: what about the city? What does the sidewalk look like in the sun after a long winter? How about the grass? The buildings? In other words, why not turn your attention to the rest of the city instead of just the sky overhead. Also, if you wanted to bump up the narrative aspect: what's happening inside the narrator? Why specifically does the narrator go for a walk? Just for the good weather, or something else?

> I arrived at the harbor sidewalk. The gorgeous view offered by the
> sidewalk attracted many citizens to spend their spare time here. I sat down
> on one of benches on the sidewalk and immersed myself into
I think you just want "in" here instead of "into."
> the beautiful sunset. I could see the high rise skyscrapers on the opposite
> side of the Victoria Harbor, forming a continuous wall of concrete.
> TheCentral Plaza, like the Empire State building in New York, stood up
> against the other structures.
Okay good, it stands out: How? What does it look like? I can't really see it (the Empire State has a very specific shape, is the Central Plaza similarly shaped, or does it just stand out the same way?)
> The sunlight shined on the reflective glass walls of the buildings, making
> them look like
You don't need the "like" here, I think.
> golden-plated. Above the harbor, the sea gulls circled to find their dinner,
> singing happily and enjoying this evening.
> This sidewalk is one of my favorite places, because I could see the
> ocean, and I used to go to here when I feel
I think you want past tense here: "felt."
>gloomy.
Is the narrator feeling gloomy now? If so, why? (These questions are just intended to open up avenues to expand the text, by the way, not just to be a jerk.)

> I like to hear the waves bouncing on the sidewalk, creating a harmonic
> symphony. I would gaze at the waves of the ocean, wondering how deep
> the ocean is. Being close to the sea gives me a calm and peaceful feeling.

Okay this paragraph is very good, except for the last four words. It's not that there's anything wrong with the words themselves, it's just that they're not as specific as they could be: what exactly do you feel? Heavy eyelids? Warm skin? Do your arms rest lightly on your legs? Do you feel like you're underwater? What, in short, is the physical manifestation of this feeling?

>   I also like to watch the people at the sidewalk. I saw quite a lot of
> people were relaxing under the warm sunshine. Two old men sat onthe
> edge of the fence fishing, lowering their tackles, and waiting patiently for
> the fish to eat their bait. A bunch of tourists walked along the sidewalk
> taking pictures. Two young executives dressed in suits leaned against the
> fence looking to the far side of the ocean. As if they were trying to escape
> from the high pressure in this fast-paced city.
>   A pair of lovers walked along the sidewalk hand in hand, smiling and
> whispering in each other's ears. Another couple sat on the bench hugging
> each other. Three teenagers roller bladed on the pathway, trying to do some
> difficult jumps.

The people watching here is good. More material here: linger a little longer on each. That is: let us watch the fishermen for a paragraph instead of a sentence. How do they tie on their bait? How do they cast? The same with all the rest. You don't have to spend an equal amount of time on all of them, but I think these people could be watched a little more, and that'll add to your description.

>   Above the ocean were numerous boats and ships. They left long white
> lines after they cut through the serene surface of the ocean. Ferries
> crisscrossed between huge cargo ships. Fishing boats came home after a day
> of hard work, I could almost see the smiling faces of the fishermen from a
> distance.

This is a nice image, but again, I can't "see" the different types of boats. Aside from numerous, what do they look like? Small fishing boats and freighters don't look alike, so you can spend some time here looking at each type of boat.

>   The orange street lights finally light up. The street lights line up in a
> row along the sidewalk. On the opposite side of the harbor, the skyscrapers
> gradually died down. Big neon advertising signs light up. I could see small
> lights comes out from each family kitchens, I could almost smell the dinner
> they were making.

Great! Getting smell into a description is always a good idea. I'd say that you really want to push this: what elements of food do you smell here? Meat? Fish? Or is it less identifiable? Even if it is, it should smell like something, which will remind the narrator of food.

>   Dong . . . dong . . . dong . . .
>   I looked at the clock tower from the pier, it was already seven o'clock.
> Though I did not want to leave, I have to say good bye. I knew I would
> come back again.
> Good bye Victoria Harbor.

***Now we're back to narrative here: why say goodbye? Is this an event, a leaving for a long time, if not for good? If it is, it weights things differently, and we should understand that throughout. In other words, you can play up the occasion for this telling, the narrative reason for this description.

[3] Anyway, I hope this has been helpful. Thanks for Flying OWL!

Sean

If an OWL conference is read straight through by the client, he might hear the tutor sequence his remarks much as he would in a f2f conference. The conference visibly has three parts that have become standard practice in our program: [1] *the front note*, opening overview comments that introduce the tutor and establish rapport, that acknowledge the client's stated concerns (e.g. development) and set (or re-direct, as the case may be) conference priorities (e.g. focus, counter-arguments, insufficient support); [2] *the intertextual commentary*, remarks within the text of the paper itself that locate specific instances of the conference priorities; and [3] *the end notes*, closing remarks that serve as a disclaimer, encourage revision, and/or remind the client of our f2f service.

While these three parts lend the OWL conference a generic framework, we see a wide range of rhetorical strategies at play within each of those parts. A descriptive analysis of each part—the front note, the intertextual commentary, and the end note—will identify what has become standard about those strategies.[3]

A CLOSER LOOK AT FRONT NOTES

Most of the work of the OWL conferences gets done in the front note. This work always includes these four main activities: 1) opening the conference by introducing the tutor by name and the conference procedures; 2) discussing the assignment parameters; 3) addressing the client's stated concerns; and 4) summarizing writing strengths and indicating revision priorities. The praise and criticism implicit in this last touchpoint of the front note are usually handled in tandem, but in a rich variety of ways.

Opening the conference

In the opening lines of the front note, the tutor greets the writer by name, introduces himself, and lays out how the conference will proceed. This procedural orientation includes telling the client that this front note is general commentary, with intertextual comments pointing to specific examples of the general critique layered within the writer's text that follows. Sometimes tutors thank clients for sending in their papers and encourage them to answer back if they have questions, but most save that for their closing remarks in the end note. In fact, a few prefer to save all the summary commentary for the end, a strategy they believe encourage clients to keep reading; those that follow this format always tell their clients where they can find the general commentary and immediately launch into their intertextually comment. Experienced tutors settle into their own self-devised template wording for this first line or so, some more expansive than others:

> Hi Sue,
>
> It's Sean again. I've read your paper and I have some comments for you, some sort of general stuff and some specifics. I guess I'll give you the general stuff first, and then move into the specifics intertextually. My intertextual comments will be set off ***Like This***
>
> ========
>
> Hi William! Thanks for sending a paper to our OWL — I hope I'll be able to be helpful to you.

With even a simple opener as the one immediately above, the tutor immediately begins the interpersonal work of the conference. Sometimes a tutor makes overt attempts at connecting, when appropriate, based on what the writer has shared about himself in his writing:

> I've really enjoyed reading your fascinating paper. I have a very close friend whose brother is autistic and I feel that I have a much broader understanding now of what's going on with both of them.

Discussing the Assignment

In the next portion of the front note, the tutor customizes the conference to the specific writer's needs and the requirements of the assignment based on what information the client has supplied in the web mailform. Because this information grounds the assumptions for the conference, the tutor takes care to "say-back" his understanding of the assignment. If the tutor is not sure that the client has met the required guidelines, he will explicate what he sees as possible points of difference, giving alternative explanations but leaving the final decision to the client:

> If you're trying to write the kind of review you'd see in a newspaper, I think you're on track (though you may go overboard sometimes). If, however, you're supposed to be constructing an argument based on the movie [Independence Day], I think you may want to seriously re-think the essay in terms of what we can learn from the movie in spite of the fact that it's terrible (what does it show that such a bad piece of cinema is one of the top grossing films of all time? Why did it hit so many of our buttons, so to speak?) Anyway, since your tone is so much closer to the former interpretation (like a newspaper), I'll assume that's what you're shooting for, and restrict my comments to how well that style is working.

Tutors often let clients know if they have had the same class and the same assignment, a gesture that promotes a peer relationship and establishes tutors' credentials at the same time. Sometimes the tutor explicitly evokes the instructor as the final word as a way of reassuring the client and, paradoxically, as a way of urging him to revise, as in the following two examples:

For example, you refer to the author's use of the term "the border," but don't explain what it is. Okay, I understand that your teacher will understand this reference and be familiar with the article, but often it's a good idea to show that you have a good understanding of the terms and issues as well (which I think you do, so it shouldn't be a problem).

========

That is, why not include a really detailed analysis of that, since it's important (also, teachers LOVE close readings where you pull apart a piece of text and squeeze every last thing out of it that you can get.)

Mentioning the instructor as evaluator can also serve as a kind of disclaimer, especially when the tutor really does think the paper is substantially complete:

It seems to me that it's exactly what your instructor's looking for: a personal anecdote that has a larger meaning. I think the structure of your essay is fine: a good, short intro, a tightly-drawn retelling of the fight and retaliation (with the exception of a few minor structural details that I'll talk about later), and an introspective conclusion. Very nice work.

A tutor might own up to her limitation, given an assignment in an unfamiliar discipline, but the covert strategy here is not really to disclaim responsibility. A tutor's apparent self-disparagement may aim to soften the blow of criticism–

Your audience, you say, is educated non-biologists (which fits me to a T), and for such people, I think you're going to need to really look at your material and think of the clearest, most concise way of saying what you want to say (because I was confused sometimes, and I've had to wade through more than my fair share of Darwinian theory). I guess I'll show you what I mean within the text. . .

—and at the same time to invite the client to make some choices—in other words, actively engage and collaborate:

I have to admit that I'm not that familiar with the workings of a psych research paper, so some things I'm gonna have to trust you on, or I'll register my concerns about argument or structure or whatever, and then you can consider whether those comments are appropriate for a study like this.

Addressing Client Concerns

Either while discussing the assignment or subsequent to it, the tutor directly acknowledges and responds to the writer's questions and concerns.

Beyond that, the tutor also gives the writer some indication of the relative importance of those concerns, both in terms of this paper specifically and the writing process generally. The ultimate goal of the one-to-one conference, online or off, is to produce better writers, not better papers, a mantra of our program. In that spirit, the tutor gives specific suggestions rather than recites generic rules. In the following example, the writer obviously knows the general rule that introductions need to launch the paper and engage the reader; what she does not know is how to apply the rule in this instance. Or she is simply blocked. The tutor's suggestions are specific enough to propel her toward revision but also general enough for her to have to make choices as well as do the actual writing herself:

> Alright you asked, and I'm answering: no, I don't think the introduction is as effective as you want it to be. I think a better way of approaching both the introduction and the paper in general might be to give us a specific organism or family of organisms and show how natural selection effects them (You know: the British Peppered moth example, a population separated by water which speciates, heck any one of a number of things. Something for the introduction could be the genesis of the term natural selection (as opposed to the kind of artificial selection which had been practised for years prior, breeding horses, dogs, pigeons and so on to get various traits.)**

The concern that clients most often say they want help with is "grammar." Admittedly, the OWL conference is not very conducive to sentence-level instruction. Indicating errors with the body of the paper, intertextually, impedes readability, especially when a paper has many surface errors. More important, we actively work against the image of the writing center as "fix-it shop," so just "correcting" papers without comment is not an option. Although the medium is not friendly to grammar/mechanics instruction, clients nonetheless need to be aware that surface error is distracting to the reader and/or disrupting meaning. And it is possible to have intelligent and useful discussions on grammatical and mechanical issues online, discussions that go beyond reciting the rules. In the following example, the tutor talks about local problems in terms of stylistic decisions:

> Overall, you've got a really nice story. There are some grammatical issues that come in to play, namely comma splices. There are a few examples of what could be considered run-on sentences, but I almost hesitate to comment on those. When you write a paper such as this and fall back into a past time, there are several liberties that can be taken. I'll try to elaborate on what I mean. I once wrote a paper about when I was twelve, and I did my best to make it sound as though I was twelve. By including run-on sentences and vocabulary that was particular to a twelve-year old, I hoped to make my readers believe that my narrator was, in fact, a twelve-year old. Your story jumps back to the second grade, and your "style" fits that time period. Your use of the word "Well" in transitional spots is one way to affect your voice. When I read, "Well, I went to . . . etc.", it reminds

me of the way a kid might tell a story. It's a smart usage on your part, but you may want to read through your paper once more to make certain you're using it strategically. Over-usage will rob the best literary devices of their effect. :)

Tutors always follow up within the text itself, in the intertextual part of the OWL conference, in order to establish the pattern of error, but only for a page or so, explicitly noting to clients that they need to follow through. For really difficult syntax work, clients are encouraged to come in for f2f conferences. Even for papers with less prevalent problems, like spelling, tutors still remind clients to polish and proofread their final drafts, with special attention paid to specified problems.

Handling Praise/Criticism

The information that the client supplied on the mail form has driven the conference thus far. At this point in the front note, acknowledging the writer's concerns, either justified or not, gives the tutor the opening for talking about a paper's strengths and weaknesses, or what tutors call "the good news and the bad news." This is the part of the conference that tutors worry the most about and spend the most time on. Ironically, the spontaneous effect that most tutors strive for in handling praise and criticism takes very deliberate effort.

Standardization of the praise/criticism portion of the front note has emerged both as matter of policy and as a matter of practice. Our policy directive is simply that tutors be honest in their appraisals. They should always be able to identify strengths important enough not to have to resort to damning with faint praise. Genuine praise can boost a writer's trust in a tutor's criticism, which he will more likely value and take as constructive. How to give praise without patronizing and criticism without alienating is a delicate balance. In practice, female tutors tend to be more indirect in their criticism than our male tutors. In any case, tutors use a range of rhetorical strategies that aim to strike a delicate but productive balance between praise and criticism.

In complimenting effective features of clients' writing, tutors often use generic, even cliché, words of praise, like "interesting" and "great," surprisingly without sounding routine or insincere. Most often, praise is followed by an elliptical allusion to something specific in the paper. Other lexical and syntactical features are striking in this portion of the front note: hedging language to buffer criticism (i.e. "little bit", "sorta" and "kinda"); conditional modals (as in "you may want to. . ."); and client-referential comparisons; "[Details] aren't as particular as you may want them to be").

Praise and criticism can be arranged within a paragraph in straightforward or complex ways, playing both to and against reader expectations. Expecting to find the criticism right after the praise (as is so often the case with teachers' end comments), the reader can simply look for the linquistic cue that marks the transition, such as "but" or "however" or some other contrastive phrase:

So far, I think you've done a decent job of comparing the two perspectives on glory here, and showing how they accord with one another. However, I think you may want to interrogate your argument a little bit more. That is, you show that there seems to be (I'll get to the seems in a minute) a connection here, but what does that do to our understanding of the works? Why should such a connection exist? What does it tell us about the societies that produced these works, or about the type of literature they are? One of my professors put it this way: so what? that is, you've noticed something in the text—there are these similarities—now so what?

But in the following example, the tutor places the contrastive phrase ("though") at the end of a sentence instead of at the beginning. Bluntness is further deflected by the use of "I-language" and a studied nonchalance:

I'm wondering about your plans for the future, though—and your instructor probably will, too. Are you going to college to somehow augment your present career? What are you getting a degree in? What are your big dreams? Do they dovetail with your current career goals? Just some questions that wandered through my head . . .

Another common strategy is to frustrate the reading expectation that praise and criticism will follow each other, like a one-two punch—perhaps by reversing that sequence or by not signaling the transition at all—

It is obvious that you have a very strong command of the language, and have put much effort into making this essay come across as knowledgable and intelligent. I am afraid that you may have gone beyond your goals here, and your paper comes off sounding stilted and over-written.

—or intricately intertwining praise and criticism in a rich discussion that throws into the mix assignment expectations and revision strategies as well—

It seems to me that you've satisfied the requirements of this assignment just fine—your instructor wanted you to list the details of a typical work day and that's what you've done. . . . I'm not sure how much latitude you have with this assignment (although I would imagine you have *some*), but it seems like there's a couple of ways to tackle it: a strict chronology (which you've done nicely), some particular aspect of management that hits upon everything you do in a day, but not in chronological order (like working with the sound engineers or something), or maybe you could even write about a day that's both typical and atypical, like the time you did back-up partying for Maria. You probably did all the stuff you usually do that day, but having the Maria anecdote as a focus would probably liven up the paper a whole lot. Or maybe, just to grab the reader's attention, start off with a cool anecdote, then just kinda slide into the day to day workings of a sound studio. I mean not all of us are lucky enough to have close encounters with rock stars as part of our working world—I'd go ahead and make a bigger deal of it (in a cool and nonchalant way, of course:-) The thing about chronology (first I do this, then I do this) is that it's not the most engaging way to present a day in your life. And you have an interesting life! Don't get me wrong, the way you've got the essay structured is fine, I was just tossing some ideas out that may not have occurred to you in case you want to play around with them a little.

—or showing how a writer's strength can be applied to a writer's weakness:

On the whole, it's apparent that you have very strong command of your words and an ability to express complex matters often quite concisely. However, this commanding tone takes a sharp turn in the paragraph beginning "Traditionally, medicine has taken . . . " What this might make the reader think is that you pulled out a thesaurus for the earlier paragraphs and then got too lazy. I don't think this is the case, but it is possible to see it this way. What you might want to do is keep your tone and language consistent throughout. I find that it makes the piece flow better and is easier to read when you use only one of the two styles you have employed. Overall, though, you have a real solid piece of work that just needs a few minor touch-ups.

In the above example, the tutor also used different points of reference for the standard against which the paper is measured. In one, the tutor abscribes the criticism to a generic audience, "the reader" ("What this might make the reader think is that you pulled out a thesaurus for the earlier paragraphs and then got too lazy") but distances himself from that assessment ("I don't think this is the case") only to re-instate that criticism, using a displaced subject ("but it is possible to see it this way"). The tutor uses "I-language" and direct-address "you," in the same sentence ("I find that it makes the piece flow better and is easier to read when you use only one of the two styles you have employed"). The issue of intentionality aside, the shifting pronouns have the sum effect of shifting agency and responsibility, thereby mitigating a direct hit to the client's ego.

In fact, the generic reader becomes the fall guy in many OWL conferences. Certainly the most fun criticism to read is that couched in humor, although the target of that humor should never be the client. In the three examples below the tutor gently deprecates his own advice; in the third, he also pokes fun at the vagaries of the ever-bothersome generic reader that the writer has to please:

I know it sounds goofy, but it works.

=====

I know that some of these comments seem sort of rambling and in truth, they are: I'm just trying to offer areas where you might continue your investigation of the parallels between these two texts, and possible things to think about in order to tighten up your argument.

=====

So what am I suggesting? okay, this may be pretty unreasonable, but I think you can flesh this story out more, take your time in uncovering the goings on, and make it into a novella or novel even. I think to have a conclusion where the whole species is wiped out, to achieve that sort of closure, you need a longer form, otherwise it feels too easy for the reader: you gotta make 'em suffer before you bring 'em relief, otherwise you mess with their catharsis and no one likes that.

Tutors who want to make sure that the comic intent is clear to the client use emoticons, such as :-) or ;-). The comic intent itself is a way of hedging—as if to say "just joking"—at the same, making a critical point.

Nonetheless, it is important that after the hedging, the shifting pronouns, the humor—after all these strategies for breaking the bad news gently—that the client be told the truth as the tutor honestly sees it, even if the bad news is the client needs, in effect, to start all over:

The problem then is mostly in terms of organization of the content. Your introduction, while giving a sort of nifty metaphor of natural selection as the quality control center of biology, for example doesn't really help us get to what natural selection really IS, how it functions, and so on. I'd also say that how you talk about nat. selec. sounds more like your drawing on a Lamarckian model of evolution (which technically speaking ISN'T nat. selec.), and not a Darwinian, natural selection based model. Your audience, you say, is educated non-biologists (which fits me to a T), and for such people, I think you're going to need to really look at your material and think of the clearest, most concise way of saying what you want to say (because I was confused sometimes, and I've had to wade through more than my fair share of Darwinian theory. I guess I'll show you what I mean specifically in the text:

"I guess I'll show you what I mean specifically in the text:" This last sentence is a typical transition from the front note to the intertextual commentary. Although the client surely could guess that the front note has concluded (even if the tutor had not already told him in the opening of the front note), just as surely he might think that the whole conference is over and not think to scroll down and look within the text for more. More importantly, the transition serves to re-create rhetorically a "live" conference, where tutor and client are actively looking at the text together in real, synchronous time, the tutor pointing to specific instances of the concerns he has mentioned in the front note—a dynamic and dramatic effect created by using present or future tense in the transition sentence that ends the front note and often heightened by ending that sentence with a colon or ellipsis, as in these transitions:

I'll show you what I mean in my intertextual comments, which I suppose I should just move on to now:

===

Alrightee—let's go ahead and get into your text to take a look at syntax and spelling . . .

===

Anyway, I think I'm being really vague, so I'll move on to the text, and maybe I'll start making more sense:

A CLOSER LOOK AT INTERTEXTUAL COMMENTARIES

This part of an OWL conference gives tutors a place to point out specific instances of concerns and strengths summarized in the front note. In other words, the intertextual commentary is the follow-through of the front note. Tutors typically compliment and criticize clients' rhetorical choices, but they also work more closely on sentence-level revision. They will critique sentence structure, suggest alternative word choices, even correct mechanic errors. In effect, the intertextual commentary is a kind of "red-lining," comparable to an editor's markings. In an OWL conference, these notations are set off ***like this***, usually with a line break before and after the comment. Because the tutor is working on so many levels—from global issues identified in the front note to local surface error—this portion of the OWL conference is both visually and rhetorically complex. While conference activities and rationale remain consistent with those of a f2f conference, one striking rhetorical feature of the intertextual commentary is that the criticism becomes markedly more blunt here than in the front note.

Local and Global Commentary

Interspersed comments—especially those where the tutor responds reactively to what he has apparently just read—visibly recreate the look of dialogue on a page and experientially capture dialogue's back-and-forth feel:

>Pullman plays the US president who seems to have no one working
>under him in this film. He drives to labs, he drives jeeps into the
> desert, he flies a fighter plane.
***I know! I know they're strapped for pilots, but give me a break! You don't get rid of the chain of command like that . . . ***

Not surprisingly, we see tutors using the same rhetorical strategies in this part of an OWL conference as they do in the front note, again consistent with their own tutoring style and online persona:

This may be overstating the case. Natural selection acts very very very very very very very very very very very very slowly, and it's hard to see its effects as far as change goes (although all the panoply of species out there are its progeny).

They continue the interpersonal work of the one-to-one conference as well, assuming the effort is a collaborative one and using the peer relationship as a leverage point, still invoking the higher power of the instructor at times:

I'm also dying of curiosity, and I bet your instructor will be, too: what sort of gear? Don't get too technical, but us lay people know nothing about the arcana of sound production, and I'd like to know more.

While the front note lends itself to global comments, intertextuality lends itself to close reading and suggestions for local revisions, in effect, giving tutors the opportunity to point out specific examples of their general remarks. This opportunity, though, becomes especially problematic when commenting on surface error. For some reason, this issue seems to trouble tutors the most, in both f2f and OWL conferencing, both as readers and as tutors. As readers, they tend to notice surface-error interference first and more than any other feature of clients' writing. As tutors, they are torn about how to work with clients at this level of need. On the one hand, they do not want to do all the work and nor are they an editing service; at the same time, they do not want the mistakes to go unremarked and perhaps give clients a false sense of security. Even when the tutor has advised the client in the front note that he is going to have to, in effect, start all over, thereby rendering comments on surface error seemingly irrelevant, instruction can be valuable for future drafts, whether the client revises or not. The most effective method seems to be not unlike that of the f2f conference: identify a pattern of error and then point out several instances of it, perhaps for the first screen or two. With each instance, the tutor perhaps gives less explanation, as if to assume that the client sees the pattern too. Just fixing all the mistakes is not only pedagogically unsound but also impedes readability. When a text is seriously error-ridden, tutors might decline commenting at all, instead insisting that the client come in for a f2f session.

In commenting on surface error, the tutor usually explains the rule in lay language (if he has not already done so in the front note). In the following example, the tutor not only suggests that sentence structure has discipline-specific parameters and stylistic implications, but also shows the client how to write a more active sentence:

***I may be off on this one, since I'm not sure how science people feel about passive voice these days (they used to love it). Anyway, this is a passive voice construction, which just means that you've made the subject into an indirect object (or something like that). In short, instead of saying "It was decided," if you wanna make this active, just say WHO decided it, ie "we decided . . . " ***

Often tutors refer to their own practice or development as writers when they make recommendations and share their own ways—some cognitive, some kinesthetic—of understanding style and sentence structure:

This is one of a few sentences that I found could have been broken into two. After you've made your next set of revisions, read your paper aloud and that will allow you to find many sentences like this one, that almost leave you gasping for air at the end of them. That's when you know you should break them up.

As in a f2f conference, tutors rarely strike a teacherly tone when talking about "rules"—quite the contrary: often they implicitly or explicitly indict the system for being so arbitrary:

Right now, you've got what's known as a comma splice here, which means that you've stuck two complete sentences together with a comma. I know, it sounds stupid, but I didn't make the rules. Anyway, you can fix it by either putting a period there, adding an "and", or changing the comma for a semi-colon (;) Personally, I like the last option best, but then, I use a lot of semi-colons.

A close reading involves much more than just grammar and mechanics, of course. Meaning can be obscured or obstructed by any number of problems, from choosing the wrong word to using faulty reasoning. What makes this intertextual part of the OWL conference more overwhelming than it is in a f2f conference is that the text becomes shot through with asterisks, which seriously impedes readability. The issue of readability may be more apparent than real—that is, reading interjected remarks is more difficult for non-participants in that conference than it is for either the tutor or the writer. A tutor has to assume that the writer will know his own text more intimately than either the tutor or an outside reader and will care enough to take the effort to decipher the text for the pearls of wisdom that are undoubtedly embedded there.

Compliment and Critique

The intertextual commentary also gives occasion for compliment, specifically, (seemingly) spontaneously, and so perhaps more powerfully than in the front note. Compliments can serve a number of functions, all of which can advance better writing. A tutor might compliment a particularly fine example of a general writing principle (in the case below, in a personal narrative), reinforcing that principle by overtly stating it:

Great! This sort of detail gets us into the moment in a visceral and moving way.

Ideally, the tutor may find an example from the client's own text of a revision that the tutor has recommended earlier or generally—

This is a cute bit: the child's eye view of Wisconsin. You may want to consider other moments where your child's perspective would be different from that of you as an adult looking back on the events. What are you wearing? What kind of things are you going to pack? What activities are you leaving behind?

Perhaps the most distinguishing rhetorical feature of the intertextual commentary is tutors' bluntness, often in the guise of humor and sarcasm. This trend in our OWL conferences occurs in all categories of suggestion, although tutors tend to be more tentative and kind when talking about grammar, and with all clients, except ESL clients, who are generally treated with more deference and less humor. This bluntness may be a function of the tediousness of actually doing an OWL conference: for most tutors, writing is simply more taxing physically and mentally than talking. Or tutors may feel that they need to disambiguate their words in the absence of paralinguistic cues, and they want to make sure clients get the message. But the bluntly critical posture of a tutor's intertextual commentary—in contradistinction to the delicate handling of criticism in the front note—suggests the dialogic character of this part of an OWL conference. Unlike the front note, which derives its genre characteristics and reading expectations from the teacher's end-note on paper texts, the intertextual commentary is not a direct descendent of the teacher's margin notes. In fact, this commentary is not marginal at all because it is not spacially limited by vertical space. Rather, the intertextual commentary is more like a conversation between peers. That the conversation is playful and sometimes contentious is significant, because both speech behaviors are predicated on an assumption of mutual status:

[from a conference on a science-fiction short story featuring killer beetles]

I'm not sure all of this is necessary. I like some of the detail, but it feels like overkill to me, especially since this guy's our first victim. Usually the first victim is akin to the character on Star Trek who I call "Ensign Deadguy." Ensign Deadguy is always the unnamed character who goes with the Away Team to go investigate something with all the main characters. Ensign Deadguy, as his name implies, dies, but not before he/she has a few lines which establish him/her as a human being, even if an uncompelling one. This way, the danger of the thing being investigated is established, but we don't kill a character that we have major emotional attachment to. In short, we end up too committed to this guy, and he's beetle fodder.

In the following two examples, taken from the same conference on a psychology paper on baseball cap wearers, the issue of word choice becomes a running joke:

[from client's paper]

>Perhaps they are wearing caps because they missed their showers.
***This just might be how I was raised, but I'm not sure if "missed" is the best verb to use with taking a shower. Perhaps, "slept late" or "didn't have enough time (combine it with the grooming part) would be a better choice. Maybe it's just my upbringing. Something to consider though. ***

[later in the same paper. . .]

>Early morning classes may have more cap wearers since the
>probability is higher that they got up late and missed their shower.
Again, my favorite verb, missed.

Online humor is always a tricky strategy, for it can so easily be misconstrued as sarcasm, which the tutor in the following examples may not have intended—or then again, she may have:

> logic dictates that,
**** Unless you are Spock or something, logic does not dictate anything. It may be a logical case that. . . . or it may be that "logic shows that . . . " but logic does not dictate anything per se. No one is obligated to be logical. . . .

But it is when tutors are taking issue with clients' arguments that they most often turn contentious, although a humorous posture may disguise aggressive intent. The following excerpt is taken from an OWL conference on a Stephen-King-like short story, and the tutor has taken issue with the client's imprecise use of language throughout the conference:

> "Well his skin is all cut off,"
Ah, but if the skin alone was cut up, it couldn't have been a lawnmower (actually it'd be more like the weed-whacker). A lawnmower would leave DEEP incisions in the flesh, into the muscle, and probably even the bone. This kind of flaying would go against their lawnmower hypothesis (and I think that Dan would know that, just by looking at the body on the scene.)

The pointed criticism in the following examples are not couched in humor, however. Clearly, tutors want to make sure that their clients get their point.

> In accordance with this rationale
All you are really saying is "therefore" so why use 5 long words when one will do the same thing?

Even tutors with less playful online personas level criticism more directly here than in the front note, although the comment may run several paragraphs, just as it might in a front note:

***My immediate reaction is that you have gone out of your way to overcompli-cate your writing. You clearly have a strong command of the language, but I think you overuse your vocabulary, and make things sound awfully complex when the complexity is not necessary. That's cool, but you will definitely muddy the waters for your argument when you do this.

Take this example from the above paragraph:

"It is the complex concerns associated with so called state and personal pater-nalism in medicine that this essay will audit." The term "this essay will audit" is kind of vague. In what way do you intend to "audit" the complex concerns? Are you going to simply enumerate and explain them, or is it your intention to attempt some kind of justification and understanding of the issues as well. Is your accounting going to trace the roots of this custom? Are you going to explore the multitude of anthropological concerns, that contribute to the culturally biased process by which we determine which individuals are or are not destined to be the subjects of paternalization?

You see . . . the more technical vocabulary you use, the more technical and thorough your argument needs to be. An audit of a subject is considerably more complex and far-reaching than a simple essay on a certain aspect of a single cultural custom. Unless you plan to write a book, I would avoid characterizing your work as an audit.****

Tutors level criticism this incisively in f2f conferences as well. The rhetorical questions in the example above suggest an oral style. When that style of questioning is tranferred to a written medium, the criticism seems more pointed than it does in a f2f conference—or so it would seem to non-participants. Since this strategy is the defining and distinguishable characteristic of intertextual commentary, we might ask how efficacious is this strategy specifically, and by implication, OWL conferencing generally?

Apparently, frank criticism works for some clients, based on the unsolicited thanks, the revised papers, and the repeat customers that our OWL receives. From this cumulative and experiential evidence, we do know that the OWL conference, even a highly critical one, can be effective. The following excerpts are taken from a conference between a female client and a male tutor, a non-traditional student and father of three school-age children:

> I watch my husband Brad interacting with our son Sean, and I can't
> imagine how their lives would be without one another. Since birth,
> Brad has participated a great deal in Sean's care. He feeds, bathes,
> changes his diapers (even the "messy" ones), and when necessary does
> an occasional load of laundry. I wouldn't say he goes out of his way
> to do household chores, but he helps.

It is wonderful to see that Brad "helps" with these chores, but who is he helping? Is it his wife? Does this indicate an assumption about Jesse's role, even by his wife? It wouldn't hurt your essay to recognize your own assumptions about fathers and their roles within the family. Division of labor is about the most gender-loaded issue I can imagine.

****When Brad's wife does the dishes, does she refer to herself as "helping" Brad? See what I mean about assumptions . . . you say it is equal, but he "helps" which implies that it is someone else's responsibility, and he is lending a hand . . . This kind of helping is NOT an equality based division of labor.***

> Now we're not without conflicts on whether or not the work is
> divided equally between us, that would be unrealistic. Here is an
> example: When I get home from a full day of school, (sometimes I go
> grocery shopping after) I pick Sean up from the babysitter, (which is

> another 14 miles roundtrip) get home, put away the groceries, fix
> Sean something to eat, bathe him, read him a story, and settle him in
> for the night. Brad on the other hand gets off work at 11:30 p.m.
> arrives home at 11:45 p.m. and doesn't have any household or child
> care chores to do.

Hmmm . . . I wonder. Does laundry and vacuuming and picking up toys and planning meals and doing dishes and feeding the cat and taking out the trash and sweeping the kitchen and mopping the bathroom and cleaning the toilet and . . . all have to happen between the time you get home from school and the time you go to bed at night? Would it be unreasonable to delegate some of these chores to the night shift? Say after 11:45 pm?*

> A study examining why more fathers do not use paternal leave,
> found that a substantial number of women did not encourage (and
> even discouraged) their husbands taking paternal leave . . .

**** because they did not want to risk the child's bonding with the father????? Balderdash!!!***

> As James Levine, director of the Fatherhood Project at the Families
> and Work Institute, has said: "Fatherhood is in the midst of an
> evolution, not a revolution. We shouldn't be discouraged by the
> accordingly glacial pace of change."

**** Nor should women be willing to accept the claim of equal involvement in the parenting role if the truth does not match the rhetoric. The point you are making seems to be defending the false belief that modern men are changing the face of fatherhood. I think this willingness to accept a glacial pace of change is another example of men using the family structure as a means of maintaining a positive position in the power relationship, and an easier job of it regarding division of domestic labor.

The tutor closes the conference with this end-note:

[I'm] a Father of three in a household where both Father and Mother are full-time students and part-time workers. The value of a full time domestic is fully understood by both of us, and we regularly regret that we cannot afford one!

I enjoyed your essay, and as I said, I expect you will receive a more conventional response from the "official" OWL tutors. I just wanted to point out to you how easily your essay has been allowed to slip into the social mold, and into rationalizations about why Brad's wife somehow ought to be expected to carry a heavier load than Brad. What do these assumptions teach Sean about the husband/wife father /mother relationships?

Thanks for using the OWL, I hope my remarks have been helpful, friendly, and inoffensive. These issues can be pretty highly charged with emotion at times, and it is good that you are able to take a more objective look at things. Also, it is good that you are writing about the one thing you know the most about . . . your self and your life.

Good luck, keep writing!
—Frank

The next day, the tutor received this response from the female client:

Hi Frank,
Thank you for such a quick response to my paper. I do like writing, but my first paper recieved a poor grade. It kinda took the "wind out of my sails," and I was afraid I couldn't write anything worthwhile. You have renewed my confidence in myself, and your comments are quite helpful. They help me see where some of my weak areas are. Again, thank you.

A CLOSER LOOK AT END NOTES

While it would seem that Frank's blunt criticism would destroy any writer's confidence, it had quite the opposite effect on this particular client. Perhaps cushioning the blow was Frank's end note, which reaffirmed their peer connections as non-traditional students and, in this case, as parents. Like the front note, the end note follows a fairly standard form, and often tutors template their own wording, modifying it very little for each client. Some simply sign off, without much more ado, especially if they've already given full-bodied responses before and within the client's text. The end note usually serves other rhetorical functions as well. Tutors frequently include some kind of disclaimer, in part to delimit their authority, should their advice prove different from that of the evaluating TA or professor, but also in larger part, to re-assert clients' agency in taking or leaving tutors' advice. A tutor may even overtly apologize for possibly overwhelming the client with too many suggestions. Or the tutor might nutshell the conference to one or two major points, to make sure an overwhelmed client fails to see the larger issues at stake. A tutor can also encourage revision and further conversation by telling the client that he is welcomed to send in a later version of the paper, closing with a thanks for using our service. Below are examples of end-notes representing this wide range of possibilities for an end note:

I hope I have been helpful, and look forward to seeing a revised version of your essay.
======
**I guess that's it for now. Feel free to send in a revision, or if you'd like to talk about anything I've just written, I'd love to hear back fromyou. Bye for now!:-)
======
*Okay!:-) That was very interesting to read. Your writing is nice and clear, so you're in pretty good shape there. All you need to do is work on focus—and concentrating on organizing and elucidating the various definitions of religion (I numbered 'em as I came across 'em), and showing the inherent conflicts between them is your best bet. Be sure to be systematic about it, though—right now

things are a little jumbled, like the part about culture/reincarnation. I think that once you've got a clear focus and organized structure, though, that those things'll just naturally smooth out. . . .

======

Mary - I'm glad you sent in your paper and I really enjoyed reading it.

I made a lot of comments, which I hope don't seem overwhelming. You expressed a lot of good ideas in your paper, so I didn't want to see grammar errors get in your way of getting a good grade and expressing yourself as clearly and as well as possible. If you have any questions, feel free to send them back to the OWL or come into the peer tutoring center in 444 C Angell Hall. We're open 7-11 Sunday-Thursday. Thanks for flying OWL!!!

OWL AS SITE OF EMERGENT LITERATE PRACTICES

On the face of it, our OWL is simply an email service based on an "asynchronous, 'epistolary' interaction" (Blythe). This technical model might be viewed as simply promoting a print literacy that places primary value on the production of "papertext," "a technological-epistemological product which locates the writer as a rational, stable subject and presents the text as a coherent, printed totality" (Johnson). While we originally conceived of our OWL as simply adjunctive to our f2f program, it quickly took on a life of its own. The point of divergence between our f2f program and our OWL is, obviously, the method of delivery. An OWL conference is delivered through a network, and that fact fundamentally changes the nature of the client/tutor interaction.[4]

For our OWL conference is not just an interaction between a tutor and a client. OWL tutors are subscribed to a mailgroup,[5] which itself becomes a rich conversation among tutors about writing, about how they and others think and talk about writing. And the OWL mailgroup affords tutors themselves a space to write and be literate in new ways. For the winter term, 1997, for example, the OWL generated over 2000 messages, only about 350 of which were actually client conferences. Tutor trainees were also subscribed to that list, saw the rich interaction of that network of tutors, and in turn, brought those conversations back into our seminars. As OWL tutors now themselves, they are enacting and encouraging new discursive behaviors with their clients and with each other.

Our OWL, then, is not just an online tutorial service, but a site where meaning and value are shared, contested and negotiated, a site that provokes and promotes new literate practices, both online and in print. An OWL conference that a client receives re-presents one end-point of that dynamicism. While an OWL conference is a written artifact, it is an electronic artifact, unstable and ephemeral, shot through with typos, jumbled formatting, and white noise.[6] As an artifact, the OWL conference challenges the ideologies of print and of academic literacy. As a dynamic process, OWL conferencing conflates and reconfigures the pedagogies of the top-down classroom and of the one-to-one conference alike, enacting a kind of many-to-one pedagogy, a new animal altogether, with a look-and-feel of its own.

NOTES

1. While I quote the work of many tutors in this article, I would like to acknowledge and thank three tutors whose work and online personas have profoundly influenced the evolution of our OWL conference pedagogy: Marion Wilderman, Gordon Smith, and Robert Way, otherwise known archetypally in our program as The Warm, The Witty, and The Blunt.

2. All names of both clients and tutors throughout this article are fictitious. This conference, as well as subsequent examples, is cited with permission from the students involved. Here and throughout this article, the caret sign (>) indicates the client's original submission. All comments preceded by *** indicate the tutor's remarks.

3. All my examples are taken from a single month of conferences in our OWL archive for the winter term, 1997, in an attempt to locate what is normative, but at the same time, to represent a range of tutors' personas and conference styles. Generally, I have not included the clients' writing that tutors are responding to, in part to save space, but in larger part, to focus on the tutors' work. When I cite more than one example of tutors' remarks to show variations, I use a double line ==== to separate those examples.

4. I am echoing Blythe's (1996) words here. Blythe outlines three theories of technology, the second of which is "a substantive approach" which suggests that "technology fundamentally changes the nature of student/tutor interaction."

5. What I describe here basically reflects how we administered our OWL mailgroup from 1994-97, during which time our OWL conference evolved into its current form. As of the winter term, 1997, we changed our subscription policy and mail-handling procedures. Only two faculty advisors and two student "dispatchers" belong to the OWL mailgroup. The two experienced cybertutors dispatch the mail, assigning and forwarding each request to a specific tutor on duty for the evening. When a tutor sends his response (the "conference") to the client, he also sends a copy back through owl@umich.edu, and the two dispatchers know that the client has been taken care of. If the client has given permission to use her conference for training purposes, a dispatcher removes the client's and tutor's names and addresses and forwards that conference on to the mailgroup for tutor-trainees. This new administrative policy is not just a matter of efficiency but also of ethics: tutors were concerned that clients may not be aware that their submissions to OWL were going to a mailgroup and were therefore public. We now ask clients' permission on our mailform to retransmit their work anonymously for training purposes. About 50% grant that permission. Our Web mailform page also lets clients know that OWL is a mailgroup and therefore an OWL conference cannot give them the confidentiality of a f2f conference.

6. I have editorially "cleaned up" all the examples in this article for the sake of readability.

CHAPTER TWO

Email "Tutoring" as Collaborative Writing

David Coogan

IN THIS ESSAY, I PRESENT AN EMAIL "TUTORIAL" BETWEEN MYSELF AND A GRADUATE student enrolled in our master's program in Technical Communication and Information Design (TCID).[1]

The student, Ruth, works full time as a technical writer and pursues her graduate degree in the evenings at the Illinois Institute of Technology. During the last year, we have generated over 200 email messages about her thesis. Sometimes we exchange posts rather quickly; sometimes not so quickly. Long lulls of inactivity are suddenly punctuated by a rapid volley of ideas.

> Not just our two voices here, either. Others interrupt us with commentary, obiter dicta, humor. All writers hear voices, but here [I've] made the convention/al choice to amplify those voices that inform us (or contradict us). (Spooner and Yancey, 253)

Vacations come and go. Semesters end. We write to each other from work, from home, on weekends, in the evenings. As I sit here writing this essay, the "tutorial" is still going. So if I seem fragmented or not quite in control . . .

Ruth[2]: Hi Dave, Joe [Amato, a professor of English at Illinois Institute of Technology] said he spoke to you and told you that I needed your help. It's true! I need help! I didn't have any guide-lines, (other than it should be a couple of pages long) so I am at a loss for what to give you.

Dave: That's ok! I just wanted to hear from you, in your own words, what your project is about.

R: The other day I gave Joe a couple of pages explaining what I wanted to talk about in my paper and he told me to write 8 paragraphs containing subdivisions of my primary thesis, taking care to ensure that each paragraph flows into the next.

> So email is like a letter, a personal letter that allows both cognition and affect: is that it? (Spooner and Yancey 259).

D: Well, yeah. That will be the ultimate goal. Eventually, we'll boil down the sap and make the syrup.

R: Your challenge is great. I am mostly sap.

Ruth and I communicate often—at least once a week. Because of her schedule at work and my interest in extended email conferences, we only communicate online. Though we feel like we know each other—at least, we know what to expect from each other online—there is a good chance we might not recognize each other if we passed on the street.

R: What I am trying to do in this paper is highlight the descriptions of hypertext that claim it to be democratic (by blending boundaries) and better than linear text because it is in the structure of memory, and its information is accessed how we access information in our brain.

D: ok, if I were to translate that it might sound like this: "In this project, I will investigate the claim that hypertext is a more democratic method of storing information, and the related claim that hypertext allows writers to externalize thought more intuitively than with print."

R: Yes.

D: huh!! So you agree with my characterization. That's good. We're on the same wavelength, then.

R: I want to explain that what society values is reflected in their rhetoric. In western culture today we value technology and democracy (democracy meaning all people are equal). I feel that some people even think that if all people are equal, then all people are the same. Very Cartesian. (That's why they make claims about other people's memory.)

D: hmmm, do I hear a hint of skepticism?

R: Yeah. Those are big claims that hint at optimism about technology. Fine, but why is everything measured in terms of democracy (especially technology)?

A good question—one that I'd like to respond to with an analogy. Not too long ago, General Electric ran a television commercial that depicted the first-ever night football game. The scene—shot in browns and greys, depicting a pre-NFL era—switches back and forth between the players, the fans, and the nervous engineers who are getting ready to throw the switch on their new lighting system. Of course, the lights go on, the game picks up speed, and everyone congratulates each other on the wonders of technology. Then, surprisingly, the lights go out, the players begin running into each other, the fans grow worried, and the engineers sigh—obviously disappointed. Years later, in a scene from a modern stadium, which concludes this commercial, G.E. redeems itself by throwing the switch on a more powerful, intimidating, lighting system. It appears we had nothing to worry about, after all! ("G.E. brings good things to life.")

If we could film a commercial for writing centers, or rather, the transformation of the writing center, would we choose the same role for technology that this company (understandably) chose? Do we imagine ourselves—directors-cum-engineers—with our hands on the switch, ready to boot those computers? And do we imagine our tutors and students on the field, our colleagues and chairs and deans in the stands, while the experiment dissolves into chaos?

Perhaps there isn't much difference between the wiring of sports arenas and the wiring of writing centers. Great expectations abound in both places. However, in the world of stadium lighting, G.E. delivers: with a flick of a switch, folks are saved from the night. Although I am, admittedly, and perhaps unreasonably, excited about the potential for interactive written communication in the writing center, that excitement has more to do with what Nancy Grimm (1996) refers to as "the re-articulation" of the writing center.

D: One thing I'm a little confused about, Ruth: Are you planning on focusing this project on an experiment? That is, are you going to DO anything to prove that hypertext is/or is not more democratic?

R: Good grief no!

D: (smiling) . . . ok, then! That much we can rule out for your proposal.

R: Yeah. Is that OK? I am a technical writer by default. I completed a biology degree in college because I wasn't encouraged to pursue literature (and *everything* language related) like I wanted to. I learned to *de-value* it. Technical writing discourse encourages support of technology in every way. I really like computers and technology, (very cool stuff) but I have found my suppressed sensibilities and wish to question, not condemn. I want to reveal, not prove.

The suppressed sensibility that Ruth talks about in relation to her undergraduate education could very well be applied to our own training in English departments where, until recently, collaboration had to do with tutoring or mentoring, but not so much co-writing. I have come to see this "tutorial" with Ruth as a form of co-writing that, in many ways, transcends the idea of the tutorial. This is not about deciding who holds the pen. Obviously, we both hold keyboards. Likewise, this is not about who sits where, or body language, or intonation. In so many ways, this is not a writing tutorial. But it does seem like a writing center activity.

R: Dave, Sorry I have been out of touch. I had to leave early on Friday. My father-in-law was hospitalized (he is seriously ill with MS).

D: I'm sorry to hear that, Ruth.

R: Anyway, I'm having a problem incorporating a contemporary angle to my critical investigation.

D: Huh? What do you mean by a contemporary angle? Why wouldn't a study on hypertext and information storage, itself, be contemporary?

R: You said you wanted me to "try and identify some contemporary angle on these debates and isolate it, say, in the form of a question." I thought you wanted me to create a statement so that I could filter those debates through something . . . ? But maybe I didn't understand you?

D: Wow. you caught me red handed with my own words! I don't even remember that.

R: You gave me the example: "Is the main use of hypertext going to be for information storage and online access or will it become a new form of writing to rival the printed book?"

This is an important exchange, primarily, because that which appeared insignificant to me has become very significant to Ruth. The interpretive process of reading and writing has entered into her process of drafting the proposal. Would my question have been funneled into her drafting if I had I uttered it face to face? Possibly. But how important is it that I am NOT present to diffuse, amplify, or spin my question? How important is it that Ruth has to imagine "me," or invoke "me," as she responds to this question?

R: I do know that I want to investigate the claim that hypertext is a more democratic method of storing and retrieving information, and that technology is part of that democratizing force (to use some of your words). So . . . it seems like I am naturally interested in the storage and retrieval aspect of hypertext, but what is my angle? I am truly frustrated. I don't want to specifically bring technical writing into it, however, I wouldn't mind addressing writing (and or language) issues. But this might be too big already?

It is no longer feasible (or even sensible) to separate "writer" and "audience" in the way it once seemed so natural to do. I also feel that the categories Lisa and I tried to describe/taxonomize (addressed and invoked audiences) are stretched to the bursting point. But it's those "invoked" audiences, whether online or off, but especially online, that are intriguing us here. Let's hear more! (Andrea Lunsford, 7 Sept. 1997)

D: hmm. I guess I have a few questions, then. First: what language issues or writing issues are you imagining?

R: Well, I was still thinking about having a filter through which to discuss the claim that hypertext is democratic. I was thinking about how writing will change because of the medium. How will fiction and non-fiction evolve because of the way the text is accessed. For example, Goethe was the first to write confessional literature. Will hypertext also create such styles?

D: A very good question, indeed! Now we're getting somewhere. And this is what I was hoping you might do: limit your question, say, to fiction writing. Then limit it again to the question of reading, or access.

R: Exactly, that's what I'm working on now.

D: I mean, it is quite reasonable to ask if the genre will create new styles. Do you think the medium is the message, then? —as Marshall McLuhan once said?

R: I think for awhile this will be the case—with multi-media, TV (and MTV!) It's like we are drawing on cave walls all over again.

D: Or do you think certain kinds of writers will have to do very particular kinds of things WITH a new medium before a new style can emerge?

One thing we do agree about is that email offers new ways of representing intellectual life. This is one way. (Spooner and Yancey 254)

R: I think as sensibilities change and writers (the real ones) figure out other ways to express themselves (as artists) they will come up with those styles. I mean, that's what the humanities are all about . . . new ways to interpret and express signs.

What Ruth says of hypertext we might also say of email tutoring. To paraphrase: as sensibilities change, tutors might find other ways to express themselves with students online. We have a chance, with email, to blend the boundaries between "writing" and "tutoring"—to do something different with students in the writing center. In so doing, we might begin to make a different claim about peer tutors. Instead of imagining them as people who demystify the university, who make it hospitable to write for professors, who make the expert/novice "caste" system seem natural or inevitable, we might go on to imagine peer "tutors" as readers or interpreters—people who work with undergraduates to create new knowledge in writing. In this way, we might re-articulate the idea of the writing center, creating, instead, something closer to a knowledge center, or what I think of as an interpretive framework for writing that contradicts the idea(l?) of unfettered "service."

It's not like no precedent has been established. It's not like networks haven't already been set up to challenge the relationship between publishers and writers and teachers and students. On the listserv for the Alliance for Computers and Writing (ACW-L), for example, Russell Hunt describes the way networks can transform peer-review groups in a writing class:

> If we can put our students in a position of writing for audiences . . . audiences who aren't helping them with their writing but are acting as dialogic partners through it—that is, who are literally, actually, and visibly being informed, confused, amused, impressed, persuaded—we can then begin to give them experience of audiences at greater distances. But if they haven't had the immediate experience, I think it's harder to imagine the, shall we say, virtual one. I think a potential web page audience "out there" isn't as close (or as powerful) as a colleague at the next computer; but it's certainly better than none at all. (5 Sept 1997)

What Hunt emphasizes in this passage is the social construction of meaning online. The dialogic partner is not "out there," beyond the footlights, in the darkened audience, passively receiving the text. This person is "actually and visibly" reacting to the text. In "Evolving past the Essay-a-saurus: Introducing nimbler forms into writing classes," Beth Baldwin makes a similar point about networked writing. Her challenge, which seems applicable to centers as well as classrooms, is to lay our theory money on the table—to enact, physically, methodologically, what we claim too easily in theory:

> In general, the academy now holds to theories of the social construction of knowledge. We promote the Bahktinian notion of the "dialogue" of texts. Yet, the kind of writing we ask students to engage in is monological. It's often an individual voice making some kind of claim. It's written to an imaginary audience, generally speaking (no matter what kind of pretending we ask students to engage in), it's written for the purpose

of assessment (again, generally speaking), and the content (generally speaking) pro-vokes no genuine response. In other words, where's the dialogue? (25 January 1996)

And again:

What amazes me is how so many of us seem to be trying to use the new technology to do the same old thing with students, albeit in new ways, rather than in using the tech-nology to totally transform our teaching. In other words, why are so many of us still slavishly committed to the monological essay as a model for teaching rhetoric through writing? Now that we can have real audiences who offer real responses, why not use the interactive capabilities to teach rhetoric through conversation? (25 January 1996)

These passages, like Hunt's passage, are at once familiar and strange when placed in the context of writing centers. On the one hand, writing centers know—and have known for some time—about the power of "real audiences" offering "real responses." Before networked classrooms made this type of student-to-stu-dent communication obvious and exciting, writing centers were quietly encour-aging students to talk about their writing in an informal setting. In fact, as I have already argued (1995), the decentralized writing classroom often resembles the traditional writing center. In both environments, students help students with little or no awareness of some Teacher or Director in charge.

Yet in another way, this transformation of the classroom seems utterly strange to writing centers, not just because they have grown accustomed to face-to-face conferencing, but because writing centers have never known the kind of power that Baldwin and Hunt know—that any classroom teacher knows. One of the rea-sons that writing centers remain "slavishly committed" to the monological essay is because other professors continue to assign it. Let me just admit then that I still assign monological essays in my classes, however often I supplement them with collaborative, networked writing. The point is not to deny the essay in the writing center. The point is to seek out alternatives to essay writing that invigorate the very idea of composition.

How can we, in writing centers, create such opportunities for tutors and stu-dents to forge new intellectual partnerships online? It's not a rhetorical question. The situation at hand—my correspondence with Ruth—is, unfortunately, too convenient to be much use as a model. Ruth is not an undergraduate and I am not a peer tutor. Ruth is already committed to working on her writing. She did not respond to an anonymous advertisement for online tutoring in the center. She was referred by her thesis advisor, Joe Amato, who explained to me on email (8 Sept 1997) why he referred her:

on the one hand, I sent Ruth to you b/c she was, as Odin and Elias, engaged in a long-ish piece of writing (tres long in her experience) and b/c I see the writing cen-ter as an institutional aid in such activities . . . but on the other, I realized when I sent Ruth to you that she would need more sentence-level assistance than I could manage alone . . . and it so happens that you are somebody who understands the issues at stake in writing and computers, and can lend some structural and content input, as well . . . that is to say: both your understanding of the writing process, in tutorial terms, and your nterest in writing *about* computers and writing seem to me to speak directly to Ruth's needs, which are as much to do with feedback, and with feedback of a sort that might help her in her writing process, based on your talents as a tutor and as a scholar-writer yourself.

Ruth, as well, projects a larger role upon the writing center, or upon me, than we might otherwise expect. Or rather, considering the circumstances—a graduate student working with the director of the writing center—her projection of a collaborative partnership seems entirely appropriate. I become, in this sense, an unofficial thesis advisor, not "just" a writing tutor. The point is that Ruth and Joe re-articulate the writing center just as much as I do. To be sure, there are elements of the conference that seem typical of most conferences. We peddle up hill when it comes to syntax. But this sentence-level work is not removed from her thematic work, as Joe anticipated. In Figure 1, for example, I interject my comments in between the sentences of Ruth's draft. In this way, I create a dialogue with the draft that imitates our regular dialogue over email.

Figure 1
Open-ended commentary on Ruth's proposal

> The aim of this study is to examine claims made by hypertext theorists that compare hypertext to human cognitive structures, including the claim that hypertext structures are inherently democratic compared to traditional linear texts and are accessible via technology. These

—> not sure I follow "and are accessible via technology."

> claims are important to investigate because they rely on scientific knowledge to determine the way the mind works, yet acknowledge an individualistic approach to the acquisition of that knowledge.

—> An interesting tension. Are you saying that the claims want to have their cake and eat it too? — that they want to posit a universal "Mind" but also want to posit individual minds?

> Specifically, I will examine those claims that compare the associations that form a hypertext document to human cognitive structures, structures which have definitions from computer programming.

—> So is the "science" that you spoke of earlier really just the discipline of computer programming? or were you really referring to another science like psychology?

> Because these claims raise epistemological issues, the second part of my analysis will also question institutional practices that relate to knowledge (Paulson, 178).

—> What does epistemology have to do with institutional practices? I mean, it seems like it does. But you state it here as if it were a matter of fact. Why do you assume so?

> Some of the claims include statements about the methods that people use to acquire knowledge. For example, linear type was believed to produce linear thought. This particular aspect is interesting because it demonstrates a continued belief in the Aristotelian concept that form follows function andthat technology promotes democracy.

—> I like this effort to explain the relationship between linear thought and linear type (or print literacy). But I'm not sure how it relates to the Aristotelian concept that form follows function. Couldn't we say that hypertext claims ALSO rely on this concept? Also, I feel like the gesture toward democracy comes too quickly. Perhaps you could elaborate that one in a separate sentence?

> This exploration aims at a more thorough understanding of those claims that emphasize hypertext's ability to facilitate knowledge acquisition more naturally that traditional linear texts. These definitions include a postmodern concept that hypertext has the potential to blend institutional boundaries as well as distinctions between author and reader and thereby envisions a distilled Marxist voice.

—> these are great sentences . . . all but that last part about a distilled marxist voice. How did you get there? what does that have to do with postmodernism?

> The final aspect of my analysis proposes that hypertext is an expression the way abstract art is (Hocks, 153) Further investigations of hypertext would have to examine how writing itself will be effected in the newest writing space.

—> are you saying that further analysis would have to consider hypertext as abstract art?

There seems to be nothing unusual about this exchange. All I've done is draw attention to that which appears nonsensical in Ruth's draft, to help her clarify her meaning. If it had taken place in a writing center, the scene would be easy to imagine: the two of us hunched over her text, me asking questions after each sentence, her taking notes or responding in some way, or just absorbing my comments. But it didn't happen that way. There was no phatic interplay. What we see is what we get. (What I see in Ruth's writing is what I see in Ruth):

D: these are great sentences . . . all but that last part about a distilled marxist voice. How did you get there? what does that have to do with postmodernism?

R: This aspect of my writing/exploring drove Joe NUTS! I like how you just say "wtf Ruth." For some reason I have a concept in my brain about what I want to say and something pops into my head to use as a description/marker that will remind me to explain it when I strain it out in a real explanation. Sometimes it remotely makes sense . . . other times not. I'm very grateful that you follow everything I'm shagging your way! Your comments really help me identify what I want to say even if they seem obvious to you to say.

This problem—in many ways, the old problem of distinguishing the author from the person—becomes especially problematic online. Andrew Feenberg (1989) refers to this problem as the "management of identity," or the textualization of a person's character. In an online environment, individuals have the impression—real or perceived—that they can control their presentation of self in ways that are not possible face to face.

The lure of increased control in online environments has interesting implications. Feenberg uses Irving Goffman's work on the sociology of interaction to explain the management of identity in more detail. He takes Goffman's (1950) double definition of the self as "image" and "sacred object" to show how CMC alters their relationships to one another. In face-to-face communication, the self-as-image is constantly modified according to the dynamics of group interaction. A self emits a line of behavior, receives feedback from the group, and either modifies the line or maintains it in consonance with the "sacred" qualities of self. However, by writing oneself instead of speaking oneself, one gains time—perhaps too much time—to then consider and reconsider one's image. "By increasing the individuals' control of image, while diminishing the risk of embarrassment," he says, "computer talk alters the sociological ratio of the two dimensions of self-hood and opens up a new social space" (25).

R: Dave I swear to God I'm trying to talk myself out of an all out allegiance to Marxism and fully *embrace* (wow, I really hate that word I can't believe I used it . . . I don't like the word *afford* either. I think J.F.K Jr. used them both 100 times when Dan Rather interviewed him at the democratic convention) Jameson because I'm so irritated with that smug academic G.P. Landow.

D: ooo! Good, good. I've been wondering what this was all about. I, too, found Landow a bit smug when I read that book. But I think . . . well, when you work at Brown and you're working with expensive equipment, smart students, and a strong literary/elitist framework for education, it's EASY to be smug.

R: He's pretty quick to criticize because he doesn't want anyone noticing his (and his superfriends') agenda. Landow has this totally pompous introduction to the last chapter of his book "Hypertext and the Convergence . . . " Anyway, I'm looking for specific applications because the theorist's general use of application encourages my own generalizations and I am looking for something more literal, less diluted. I realize this is all so abstract and reflexive (I'm in my own little hell here). Let me see if I can sort some of this out and make this activity of tooth extraction more organized.

D: Ruth—I actually think that your little hell makes a lot of sense.

R: And it's because you always understand that allows me to sleep at night!

D: You feel Landow's somehow not being quite honest, or rather, he's too quick to generalize his theory in order to create a discipline out of it to be with his superfriends? to align himself with theory, etc.)

> The purpose of conversation is relationship. (Baldwin, 25 Jan 1996)

R: Well, let's just say we are pretty clear that he lectures a lot at "Ivy League Campuses"—barf—He has this way of describing stuff using really prissy words and conservative phrases when he's pretending not to be critical—it *feels* like reading Jane Austen or Henry James. It's hard to describe but he describes a university in the "Deep South" or " a younger academic, concerned with . . . "

D: So noted. It seems to me like we can't separate his personality/persona as an author from his theories, as much as he may want us to.

R: Also, interestingly, his first observation was that: "a distinguished historical scholar worried aloud (see doesn't that sound like a novel?) in a conversation with me that the medium might serve primarily to indoctrinate students into post-structuralism and Marxist theory." I think this is an attempt to take emphasis off of the fact that his *theory* would send people running for Marxist theory!

D: Good point. It's a well known strategy. Diffuse the conflict by admitting it AND then ignoring it.

R: Then, he says that someone worried that: "hypertext would necessarily enforce historical approaches and prevent the theorizing of literature." i think hypertext needs more theorizing to make sure no stone is left un-turned to keep these guys in check. i just think the 2 examples he chose were so inverted.

D: This being the case, let's imagine a scenario: what would happen if you were to test Landow's claims against the actual reading practices of students or (I don't know, co-workers?). Would they be liberated by hypertext? Would they revel in the free associations? Why do you feel they would or would not? What would Landow say? Does his theory work outside of Brown University?

R: Hmm. Can you explain a little more?

D: Well, what I means is this: if you want to expose Landow somehow, why not put your money where your mouth is? That is, if you think his theories only work for him and his gang, how would folks outside the gang react? A bald example: how would a student from Malcom X college, on the west side of Chicago, experience hypertext as a writing medium? how would he or she experience it as a reading medium? and would this experience differ from a sophomore's experience in Professor Landow's class at Brown on hypertext and literature? One more note: What I'm saying is that I like the energy of your critique. It has more drive to it, now that you've taken off the gloves. But let's think through some creative way to funnel that drive into a sound research design. (So that it goes beyond Landow bashing...)

R: Oh, I know. You gotta understand that I was on the last chapter of my last Landow book... obviously the guy is super smart and ivy league institutions are outstanding. I realize that some of my comments were pimpy and immature, they were strictly off-line. As Mary Ann Eiler puts it when referring to Edward Tufte (and normally, we were agreeing with Tufte) *after awhile* we are aware that we are not breathing the rare air that they are. Besides, they don't have to write to everyone if they don't want to.

D: True enough. And you've got your own air to breathe, which relates to my point about the hypothetical experiment. what would happen if folks who don't breathe Landow's air (non-ivy air!) were asked to do so?

What interests me about this exchange is the transformation of Ruth's textuality, if I can say it that way. Gone are the measured, interiorized sentences of Figure 1. In their place, I don't think I find "pimpy and immature" sentences, but I definitely find something with a sharper, critical edge: a distinct opposition between herself and Landow that is based, in part, on the idea of class: "we" are not in the Ivy League. "We" cannot afford the same interpretation of hypertext in this context. What seems noteworthy, then, is this emphasis on "we"—the fact that I corroborate her rebellion.

It is tempting to think of our email exchange as a "grass roots" critique. But what we've said of Landow we might also say of ourselves. There is, in other words, a privileged side to our email exchange. Spooner and Yancey:

> Truth is, we lead our social lives primarily in conversational modes. This is where the grass roots social construction of knowledge and meaning happens. (Baldwin, 25 January 1996)

> The material conditions of the late 20th century have enabled a group of generally well-educated, relatively affluent people to communicate in a new medium. Many of these people believe that this form of communication is new, is different, and that it enacts new relationships between authors and readers. There is, in other words, an ideology already at work here, and it entails social action ....One could argue that computer literacy lives within an even more elite socio-economic hierarchy than does print literacy. But this is often quite forgotten by the users. (268, 270)

At this point in the conference, Ruth and I have been working for about six months. Clearly, her financial security and my workplace productivity do not depend upon her finishing this thesis in a timely manner. As well, I am not obliged (officially) to work with Ruth at this level, yet I have chosen to do so, answering email in the evenings and on weekends, checking up on her after long periods of silence. Email, I would contend, does not create this social space. Rather, it is Ruth and I that create it. The issue, then, is not whether it is possible to work with students online. It's not a matter of "if" but of "why." Why would peer tutors and students prefer to work with each other online? What position would they have to be in—as writers, as students, as thinkers, as technologists—to engage each other on an intellectual level with email? This depends upon what position we want to be in. It depends, that is, on the idea of the writing center.

Although writing centers, by many accounts, have "made it" in the academy, the work is still misconstrued, or easily aligned with notions of functional literacy, minimum competency, and basic (pre-college) skills. "What is it that writing centers do?" asks Muriel Harris (1990), in her best imitation of the academic community.

> Are we running only remedial centers, places to salvage some of the "boneheads" that have been permitted to enroll (for however brief a tenure) in our institutions? Are we band-aid clinics offering clean-up service for papers about to be handed in? Such questions persist with the tenacity of barnacles. We seem forever to be countering these and other equally limited notions. But why do we perennially have to keep explaining ourselves? And why do we keep doing it from a somewhat defensive posture? (17)

These questions sting anyone who has ever worked in or supported a writing center not just because they can be insulting but because they seem perennial. What seems, however, like a simple misunderstanding or miscommunication, is in fact more profound. As Lisa Ede frames the problem, "as long as thinking and writing are regarded as inherently individual, solitary activities, writing centers can never be viewed as anything more than pedagogical fix-it shops to help those who, for whatever reason, are unable to think and write on their own" (7). Ede does not defend the "fix-it shop" ideal. Rather, she argues that we can, and should, begin viewing writing as a social process. Only when we reconceive the nature of writing will we be able to reconceive the idea of the writing center as something more than a fix-it shop.

While working in a different context—the networked writing classroom—Baldwin nevertheless makes a similar point about the problem with traditional writing in the university:

> Essay writing is a particularly solitary activity (even when we do great peer review) and the point is to make your point. There really isn't any dialogue, not on the level

of ideas and not on the level of genuine responsiveness. We expect responsibility, but do not provide response-ability. (*Conversations*)

To be a responsible writer, she seems to say, one needs to cut short others' reactions, anticipate their objections, and in other ways isolate oneself from that which could become contentious. To be an effective email correspondent, however—in the center or in the classroom—one needs to share authority and cultivate responsiveness.

R: Hi Dave, I was just thinking about writing you . . . I need some feedback soon. I'm starting to feel anxious and alone while I write, but I wanted a chance to mold my paper into something so that I would make a commitment to an idea. Even so, I still spend too much time editing the rough draft.

What Ruth confronts here, ironically, is the very limit that hypertext supposedly destroys: the inevitable closure of paperbound writing. Walter Ong (1982) relates this sense of closure to the technology of writing, itself. "More than any other single invention, writing has transformed consciousness" (78). Writing, he says later, allows the self to distance itself from itself, allowing for greater introspection and reflection. Although this claim can be controversial, especially when it is applied wholesale to entire civilizations, or even to the activity of writing, which Ong tends to do, it is nonetheless a provocative claim: Who hasn't felt the anxiety that Ruth describes above? Who hasn't helped writers try to become more responsible? Yet at the same time, isn't it fair to say, as Baldwin says, that responsibility is at odds with response-ability?

D: ok, Ruth. Now that you've finished the proposal, let's get to work on the actual study!

R: oh, thank the Lord you are gonna see this through with me! I love the word "let's" (it does mean let *us* doesn't it??).

D: oh yeah. "Let's" does mean let US see it thru! I'm glad we finished up before Thanksgiving break, too. The skies are clearing up.

R: yes, but more important to me, I'll feel a sense of security knowing that you'll be working with me. Thanks so much!

D: hey, think of me as the reader inside your computer :-)

Clearly, Ruth and I have invoked each other as audience in this session. But exactly what have we invoked? What is the relationship between our mutual e-space and Ruth's private writing space? When she talks about "a sense of security," on the one hand, and feeling "anxious" on the other hand, what are we to conclude about the aims of writing? The problem, in many ways, is methodological. Is it our purpose to establish online the conditions for, what Belenky et al. (1986) have called "connected knowing"? Or is our purpose to relieve those tensions that one feels when one is alone, writing. Is email conferencing, itself, a form of intellectual life to rival solitary writing? or is it a handmaiden to traditional writing?

R: Hi Dave, This post [Figure 2] contains the first portion of my paper. It's hard to know what the paper says anymore, or if I'm contradicting myself in places. I'm sure you'll once again feel like you've been dropped into my notes in places . . . I feel like I need feedback from this portion to finish where I'm going with the rest because I need help with the organization (big time). I'll continue writing while I wait to hear from you.

Figure 2
Draft of Ruth's thesis

Reading and writing certainly involve cognition. However, the recent response to hypertext has prompted scholars to posit theories that have positioned reader's Gnostic mechanisms at the forefront of this new textual space. Hypertext theorists are claiming that since the hypertext reader (some say reader/writer because the reader chooses their own texts to become writer) links texts together choosing from multiple pathways, it has the potential to blend boundaries and is therefore a democratic activity. When there is an active participation of the reader in the making of meaning, political domination seems less possible (*The Experience of Reading*, 3).

Hypertext theorists, such as Brown University's George P. Landow, advance that hypertext units (sometimes called nodes or lexias) make up individual blocks of texts to perfectly represent what philosopher/theorist, Jacques Derrida meant by the de-centering of text. Since hypertext is non-sequential writing it (de)composes the original texts and the reader/writer is responsible for creating their own textual experience. As a result, Landow claims that hypertext goes beyond philosophy and language's sensory explanations to fully represent a political ideal. He claims that this form of writing exceeds language sensitivities to work the same as human thought processes. Hence, hypertext has more in common with natural brain determinism than with writing. "It is customary to think of literature as an expression of the mind, the psyche, or the imagination, but not as a record of metabolic intelligence." (*Open Form and the Feminine Imagination*, 194-195)

Claims suggest that movement from one textual unit to the next is how hypertext demonstrates democracy. Therefore, for hypertext, democracy lies in its movement. "Speaking and writing are physical activities, things our bodies do to express themselves and things which are physically recorded, as visible signs on the page." (*Open Form and the Feminine Imagination*, 195) But *Dictee*, in addition to being a book of feminine power, is a book about the body. Instead of thinking of *Dictee* in terms of its moral/intellectual content, she draws our attention to the actual moment of speech—to the lungs, throat, mouth, tongue, teeth, and lips. After presenting a diagram of these organs that shows how they produce physical sound, she describes the concrete act of words being spoken. (*Open Form and the Feminine Imagination*, 195)

To deconstruct even further . . . [snip]

D: Ruth—Well, obviously you've been doing quite a bit of reading! How this read-ing relates to your evolving sense of purpose, though, is unclear to me. The feel-ing I got was that you were rapidly condensing another person's work, skipping over the logical connections (what led you to that quote), in order to hurry up and finish the paragraph. Then, you start the next paragraph with little reference back to the ideas of the previous paragraphs. In short, I felt like I was reading a series of hypertextual lumps or snippets that *could* relate, but didn't really relate or work as a narrative.

So, you asked me to help you organize. And I'm thinking that the kind of lin-ear organization I have in mind might be inappropriate for the work you are doing. Do you want to present this narrative as a hypertext instead?

R: well, yeah. that pretty much sums up my structure (or lack of). if you recall, I told you that some of what I write represents to me a marker of some thought that remains undeveloped, yet important to my next attempt to exhume (remember the first scrawling of my proposal—I'm sure you didn't know what the hell I was talking about).

D: Fair enough. But what body do you want to dig up in this text? What is inside that grave that you so frantically scratch at? What do you hope to find down below?

R: well, to put it as plainly as I can, in addition to my issues with claims of human cognitive structures . . . I disagree that hypertext changes our view of what text does . . . that it will redefine text outside of the computer culture. Landow suggests that writing itself will move away from previous expressions and supports his argument with people who view text as accessing data.

D: I don't get it. What does this last sentence mean? (What are the "previous expres-sions? And what does "text as accessing data" mean?)

R: I'm arguing that he disregards the thought process for inspirational writing and takes offense (or defense) to a particular thought process (including Marxism . . .), yet makes claims that the hypertext method is more democratic.

D: So then: are you claiming that "inspirational writing" is more democratic? Or are you saying that we shouldn't even bother with this kind of one-upmanship. Power is power, so to speak. Or democracy is democracy. It has nothing to do with particular forms of writing. Is that it?

R: The irony of what I've presented to you so far, is that I wrote to you hypertextually.

D: See, I don't know about that. Or rather—I'd grant that you may have intended to do so. But I don't see anything in Landow or Bolter or any of those essays I gave you that says hypertext has to be incoherent. In fact, my main beef with Landow and company is that they are ultimately afraid of courting real incoherence.

R: I'm *totally attracted* to what you say here!!!

D: Good! Then you probably wouldn't find it difficult to write it THAT WAY in your paper. Since I am, it seems, a sympathetic audience, maybe you could write your argument with me in mind? Maybe that would get you into the direct style that I find so persuasive in your email?

R: Can you explain what you mean?

D: I'm trying to say that your writing seems to avoid creating a central focus. In some ways, this could be construed as liberating—perhaps more for you than for the reader. The centering affect of democracy, though, depends upon a certain confidence or shoulder rolling swagger that is ultimately, exclusive. You have to decide what will be suppressed, what will be featured, and so on. You can't talk about everything. You have to choose.

R: But I'm trying to steer clear of scientific descriptions of "new ways of thinking" when discussing writing, because writing should include exchanging ideas . . . even if those ideas are presented by an *author*. associations can be powerful, but supporting a method doesn't have to be undermining authorship.

D: Again, this depends on what you feel you have at stake. I mean, why do it? What kind of authority would you be undermining? Your own? or some other authors?

R: Dave, I'm sorry to subject you to my incessant free writing. but I would rather not do this if my outcome is obvious (implement SGML, the values of relevant searching)—no matter how well written or supported it is. But, I also might discover that I'm not qualified to support anything beyond that, but we can address that when/if that happens.

D: Well, I understand your dilemma. Honest, I do. But I don't think the situation is as stark as you make it out to be. Situating your study within a technical writing context, for example, would not mean kissing the theory good bye. You could, for example, put Landow to the test by revealing how institutions limit the ways hypertext is used. (If they didn't, wouldn't we expect immediate transformations in the workplace? a surge of democracy?)

R: I know I need to do this, I'm currently searching for a comfortable method. In addition, I realize that I COULD NOT do this without you, and I can't express how fortunate I feel working with you.

D: Nice. But believe me—I wouldn't stick with it if I didn't think you could pull it off! Now try again to imagine your readers, Ruth. Think not so much about the theoretical issues and more about the story you want to tell. And give some thought to the idea of TESTING some theory with a real-live situation.

R: OK. Let me try this:

Hypertext theorists depend on mythical cultural beliefs about computers and generalizations of critical theory to support their claims that hypertext embodies democracy. These theorists rely on {stereotypic} associations between computers and the human mind as well as a desire to define and validate the writing process. Brown University's George P. Landow describes a writing process that is inherently natural and critically accessible by illustrating how he converges technology to critical theory.

This investigation examines why associations to critical theories are contra-dictory because critical theory traditionally places literature, while hypertext theories situate the literature to critical theory. By taking a closer look at these assumptions, we can gain a broader understanding of why such claims of democracy exist.

D: SEE, THIS IS WHAT I'M TALKING ABOUT. I JUST . . . WELL, I DON'T THINK THAT THIS IS A VERY EXCITING PROSPECT. TO YOU IT IS. YOU'RE PROMISING TO EXPLAIN IT TO YOURSELF. WHY SHOULD OTH-ERS CARE ABOUT YOUR PROCESS OF THINKING? WHAT'S WORSE, I THINK, IS THAT THIS SENTENCE BASICALLY PINS YOUR ENTIRE ARGU-MENT ON LANDOW-BASHING. NOW I'M NOT ONE TO DISCOURAGE A LITTLE LANDOW BASHING! BUT NOT FOR THE WHOLE ARGUMENT!

R: ouch, a little blood there.

D: oops! Sorry about that. I'll unclench my fists now :-\

R: No way! Don't be, I need it. I think the reason I'm having a hard time limiting my topic is because I don't understand how much freedom I have in supporting it. as I previously stated, I didn't think I wanted to do a paper where I use litera-ture that explicitly gives reasons for supporting a particular position and then reiterating that proof. I thought that hypertext literature was fluid enough to reinterpret a little. But, maybe I'm not understanding what I'm reading. Give me some interpretation boundaries.

D: Well, it all depends on what you mean—or what Joe means—by fluid bound-aries. I understand your reticence. You don't want to simply repeat what you've read. But so long as you remain hostage to your authors' arguments, you WILL be doing just that. Even if you end up discounting what you've read, you'll still be stuck in the theory loop.

R: I think the reason why I end up with Landow (and I don't want the paper about bashing Landow either) is that his claims are something I can easily grasp—so when I'm off in a place where I'm gasping for air, I always come back to what he's saying.

D: Not a good reason to use Landow. I mean, if he has become the dock or the har-bor, and your other authors have become like little ships making day trips . . . all we get, finally, are a series of day trips that inevitably come back to the harbor. What I'm trying to get you do is all together different: I'm talking about a jour-ney away from the harbor, in search of something new.

R: Ok, then. On that note, I'll tell you what interests me from what you've suggested so faR: the statement you made about hypertext not having to be about incoherence and that Landow was afraid of incoherence. (btw—what defines incoherence?)

D: Ha! you wish I'd define incoherence for you! Like I know? That's why I suggested it to you. I thought you might be able to help me understand.

R: I like it. BTW, I'm working with you *only* on this until I get a draft ready for pub-lic consumption. I've learned more from you about writing in the last year than I have in my entire lifetime. I don't want to be a selfish writer, I want to try and offer something. Everybody blah blahs the way I do (in other words, everybody's a poet)— I'm all about wanting to say something. OK? Man, I need to chill and take some days off of work!

D: Yes. And it's nice to hear you say that. It means we both understand what this is all about. I believe you have something to offer. And I want you to offer it. I don't want you to lose that feeling. Keep constructing your desire into ever more direct and honest expressions. It's a moral thing.

Although this exchange, with its intense back-and-forthing, resembles, to me, a viable alternative to f2f conferencing, it is an alternative filled with irony. Yes, in some ways this exchange illustrates what Baldwin means by response-ability. But look closely: this exchange is about responsibility (a moral thing). It would not take place if Ruth were not writing a master's thesis.

What Ruth describes as an unselfish way of writing, or what I describe as honest expressions, are more properly seen as writerly habits from the garret. When I push Ruth, IN ALL CAPS, to remember her readers—drawing a bit of pixel blood—she does not retreat, but thanks me for sticking by her.

D: Ruth, do you feel as if you've missed something or lost out, in some way, working with me online instead of face-to-face?

R: No, quite the opposite. I'm reduced to my writing so that everything I put down here I'm held accountable for. Meaning, everything I say to you-you have assumed contributed to my end goal (paper). At first it was frustrating because I'm so used to being able to express myself with myself. But slowly, I was grateful because it taught me an almost feminist voice because you forced me to be straight forward.

D: What aspects of our interaction via email do you find most useful? least useful?

R: I find it useful because of my previous answer. I don't think anything is "least useful", but sometimes I can get overwhelmed because I realize that *every sentence* is going to be addressed because I give you bits and pieces. It seems like your comments take me on tangents and I never commit to a specific path.

D: What have you learned so far about writing a proposal for an extended research project?

R: That it's going to change, but it starts the process of narrowing your focus, which for me is the absolute hardest thing.

D: If you think you're writing has improved in some way, could you describe, with as much detail as you can, what you think you learned?

R: I've learned that writing is my written self. Whatever I write, I must first think of my focus and my audience. I have learned that good writing is good ideas and hard work—really hard work. For me, the desire to define myself through words instead of my visual self has always been my goal—yet I never took responsibility for what I put down. I've always considered myself a sophisticated reader, but since I've studied the process of writing, (through this experience) I feel so at ease with the written word—I'm confident of my ability to understand practically anything that can be written. Because I've taken abstract thoughts that meant practically nothing and written them into something someone else could relate to, I've added profoundly to a mind set to nurture existing abilities and/or desires to know and express. In other words, I feel that I'm at the starting point to begin to write well. I also know that one of *your* goals for me is to allow my words to flow as well as my written conversations with you.

It's true. One of my objectives is to juxtapose the conversational rhythms of the conference with the more measured, tones of her academic writing—to mix responsibility with response-ability. Though it is true that this session "reduced" Ruth to her writing, this "reduction," finally, became an expansion—not just for Ruth but for me. Email allowed us to create an alternative writing space that was not, in my view, narrow or reductive, but was—and still is—filled with possibility. This implies, I think, a reciprocal relationship not just between print and electronics, or thesis proposals and email dialogues, but between two writers. What I find so rewarding about email "tutoring" is the chance to write differently, in the company of another. Isn't that something worth pursuing in the "writing" center?

NOTES

1. A note on mechanics: Although I have presented this exchange between myself and Ruth as a back-and-forth dialogue, readers should keep in mind that our exchange did not take place in real time: a question asked on Monday might not receive an answer until Friday. In between Monday and Friday, other questions or comments might have been made. To provide each other with some continuity, we made liberal use of the reply key, often appropriating each other's email into the new post. In order to make the session readable, I have excluded email header information, and I have condensed the repetitious material. I have not changed the content or style of any of these posts. However, I have omitted some material, most of it drafts of Ruth's essay and discussions of those drafts that did not, in my opinion, seem all that different from the material I discuss here. My aim was not to be true to "the record" but to represent the record as a tutorial.

2. The text of the email exchanges here as a way to retain the informal flavor of the originals. I left all typos and unorthodox stylistics in.

CHAPTER THREE

Reflection and Responsibility in (Cyber) Tutor Training

Seeing Ourselves Clearly on and off the Screen

Rebecca Rickly

DONALD SCHÖN (1983) DESCRIBES "REFLECTIVE PRACTITIONERS" AS THOSE WHO are able to do all of the following: read and write and think and theorize about their own practice. They take what they've learned, assimilate it, and then they are able to apply it in different situations, altering content and application as context demands. This is the goal that most of us have for our peer tutors: to become reflective practitioners as they learn, observe, and practice their skill. Yet how do we teach tutors to become reflective practitioners? Somehow, the acquisition of this skill goes beyond merely completing reading logs and reflective essays. At the University of Michigan, the peer tutoring program is a shared responsibility: when I joined its ranks, the three co-directors divided primary responsibilities for recruiting, training, and administering the peer tutoring program, and every semester we traded jobs so that each co-director participated in all aspects of the program. With the growth of our program, we now have the possibility of including two more co-directors, and we've experimented with training students to tutor not only university students, but also those outside the university, accepting clients from other schools (and other countries) in our Online Writing and Learning program, and from high schools in two successful pilot programs.

In thus building our program, we found that both tutors and teachers must take on the responsibility of becoming reflective practitioners, to see their experience as a process which must be stopped and reflected on regularly and seriously. Camp and Levine (1991) suggest in their discussion of portfolios that this kind of reflection "makes visible much in learning that is otherwise hidden" (197). Making learning visible became a goal for our training program, since these student tutors putting into practice what they'd learned in order to help their peers. But as directors, we, too, had much to discover about making learning not only visible, but audible and tangible as well. Ultimately, both the instructors and student tutors had to be willing to alter their current academic mindsets to see how their learning might affect their practice, might then be altered to fit a particular context—often, the rhetorical situation—so that a student's or tutor's needs are better met. In this chapter, I will describe how the peer tutoring program at the University of Michigan evolved, paying particular attention to how tutor training was conducted, re-examined, and altered as tutors and teachers became "wired."

At Michigan, the peer tutoring program began as many do. Since students were often under prepared for college writing, yet were uncomfortable seeking help from professors, we began to recruit and train peer tutors to give students a chance to get help with their writing from a less intimidating experienced peer. Our recruitment and training program is a rigorous one: students must be nominated by a former teacher (they can self-nominate as well), must have reached junior standing, and then they must fill out a detailed application. After the directors review the applications, we invite the best of these students for an interview. As we reflect on these applications, we look for more than expertise in writing, though students must be competent: we look for experience in working with others, experience with writing outside of English courses, "people skills," and personality/interaction style. Based on the interviews, we select the best students to participate in the required two-course sequence that all peer tutors must take: ECB 300, "The Theory and Practice of Peer Tutoring," and ECB 301, "Directed Peer Tutoring." The first course, which meets three times a week, includes readings, discussion, systematic observations, research, and a demanding array of writing and writing assessment to encourage reflection on a tutor's evolving theory of peer tutoring. The second course, which meets only once a week, allows students actually to tutor for course credit outside of class. Once they've completed this sequence, the students have the opportunity to tutor for pay—currently $8-$10 per hour, depending on the level of experience and responsibility. In order to get to this point where they're working for the university, these students must make a significant commitment to the program.

Yet such a commitment isn't just one-sided. The directors, too, have to make a significant commitment: they must prepare, observe, assess, solicit feedback, and evaluate themselves, the students, and the effectiveness of the program. We must keep accurate and ongoing records to constantly legitimize what we do, or to ask for funding for a larger program to help more students. Finally, unless we continually solicit feedback and reassess how the program is working and how it might be made better, we're in danger of stagnation. In this regard, the tutors have had a significant impact on the program itself and how it has changed and evolved. Perhaps the best recent example of this impact was the inception of our Online Writing and Learning, or OWL. The OWL came to be after I gave a demonstration on how to conduct research on the World Wide Web to an ECB 300 class. Afterward, one of the tutors, Jonas Kaplan, asked if I'd ever created anything on the web. When I replied no, he offered to teach me how to make a home page so that we might create a website for the peer tutoring program. I became the student, which was both frightening and exciting: frightening to give up the control and authority I had worked so hard to achieve, yet exciting to be learning something so dynamic, so creative. Jonas and I began meeting regularly, creating a Tutor Home Page, and as we did so, we came to realize how much more we could do. After going back and demonstrating the new pages for the class, I asked if anyone was interested in creating an OWL like Missouri, Dakota, and Purdue universities had, where students could send papers to "cybertutors" online. Several students expressed interest, and that summer, three tutors and I met twice a week to learn about the web, teach ourselves html programming, and see if we could, in fact, construct an OWL. First, we conducted research, examining the online sites at other universities, then we began to make decisions about what we liked and what best fit the existing program (such as an emphasis on interactivity and communication rather than the informational aspect of the web), and, after a lot of practice on our own home pages, we eventually became adept enough at programming to create the first version of the University of Michigan's OWL. After discussing our plans with the other co-directors, we decided to try the concept out. Barbara Monroe piloted an email-only OWL the fall of 1995 with three sections of basic writing, and by December of that year, we had both web and email service in a larger pilot program. The OWL was open for public business campus-wide the following fall, during the 1996-97 school year.

When we first conceived of the OWL, we saw it as an extension of our physical peer tutoring: students would send papers in over email from their dorms or public computer labs rather than bringing them in physically, and the responses to these texts would be, we thought, quite similar. In both situations, our goal was to engage writers and tutors in a dialogue about the text, encouraging the writer to take primary responsibility. We did not proofread texts, but we did teach writers this skill by helping them to identify strengths and weaknesses by analyzing patterns and addressing directly the clients' concerns. Ultimately, we wanted to create better writers rather than better texts. We felt that we could maintain the close, dialogic nature of the tutor conference on email. After all, the peer tutoring program itself wasn't housed in an English Department or any other such departmental building. Rather, the tutors at the University of Michigan operate where writers are writing: in the largest public computer lab on campus. What used to be a library is now filled with over 300 Macintosh and DOS-compatible computers, and this expanse of technology is known as "The Fishbowl" (probably because there are windows on three sides of the open space, and glass skylights in the ceiling). The peer tutors hold consulting hours in one of the university's computer classrooms adjacent to The Fishbowl. There, every Sunday through Friday evening, six undergraduate tutors are able to address the immediate writing needs of the student population in the location where they are actually doing their work. Along with the ECB peer tutors, the Computer Science department houses graduate consultants in the same computer classroom, so nightly, the room is filled with students coming in from the fishbowl, working on their writing or programming while waiting to be helped, getting help on their work, and incorporating the advice they've received into their work as they remain in the classroom or finish up on one of the computers in The Fishbowl.

With the conception of the OWL, however, instead of merely moving from place (such a traditional "writing center" located within the confines of a writing department) to space (such as The Fishbowl where students are actually writing), we moved from space to medium (actually using the same media that students are using to write with). Since the University is technology "rich," all student having access to numerous computer labs both in and out of their dorms (as well as free ethernet connection from their dorm rooms if they brought their own computers), we realized that more and more of them would be writing online. Our newest goal was to go beyond simply being in the same physical space with the writers; we wanted to provide online writing help, using the same medium the students were using to compose, taking advantage of interactive aspects of the internet.

GOING ONLINE IN TUTOR TRAINING

While our undertaking seemed to be a logical one, since undergraduate students (and our tutors are all undergraduates) seemed to be composing more online, thinking more online, and communicating more online, none of us had really thought the concept of "going online" out completely. As computer users who are part of a larger professional community, we based our hypotheses of what would happen in the tutor training classes upon our own experience teaching writing using computers. Too, our tutoring program has been able to use this "wired" space so effectively to tutor (we've been located in The Fishbowl since our inception) that we believed that by going online more ourselves, both with our training and our services, we'd be doing the tutors and students a real service. Finally, we assumed that face-to-face (f2f) training and tutoring and online training and tutoring would be based on the same theoretical principles, just as we had based our writing classes on theories of collaboration, the social construction of knowledge, and process, all of which seemed to be enhanced by the computer. Therefore, both types of training, we felt, would necessarily be quite similar.

We'd already begun to integrate computers into tutor training as a means of community-building and knowledge-making—we meet the two required courses peer tutors must take in the computer lab where the students will be tutoring—and we continually evaluate our progress. When we first began, this integration of electronic media in tutor training meant email announcements (normally by the instructor to the list of tutors), mirroring a top-down informational structure that we came to realize we weren't completely comfortable with. Once we moved into a classroom equipped with networked computers, we used the Daedalus Integrated Writing Environment which was installed on all of the machines. Our first application was to post a class assignment: students came in and immediately logged on to see what the itinerary for the day would be. A typical example follows:

Tuesday, January 16 . . . Welcome back!

Today we'll be spending some good time on the reading, since I think what we read might be helpful to come back to. Before we begin our discussion, I'd like you to write down three questions you have, either about the reading or how it might affect what you do as a peer tutor.

Next, let's situate ourselves as far as the required observations—perhaps even schedule them. Don't forget, you've got to observe six conferences, and you need to schedule both ECB and peer tutoring observations. You'll be taking field notes, and we'll talk about that, too.

Finally, we'll have a "mock" peer tutoring session. I asked you all to bring a work-in-progress today, so one of you will get some extra help on a paper. Afterwards, we can discuss what went on.

The tutors seemed to appreciate the fact that we were all on the same wavelength by the beginning of class, and the specific, step-by-step instructions made them feel comfortable in what was, for many of them, a new classroom environment. The instructor had laid ground rules in much the same way a client might expect the tutor to control a conference. Yet as the co-directors met to discuss the program, then stepped back and examined this practice, we felt that, by itself, it still reflected the "top-down" format we were trying to change.

The next application we used in Daedalus was Mail. Almost every day, the first item on the class assignment agenda was a "reading response." Formerly, these reading response discussions had been both written and oral: the students, who'd been assigned a reading or two the previous class meeting, were expected to jot down notes and questions about what they'd read, then come prepared to discuss problems and possibilities they saw with it, and how they might apply information from the reading to our situation. This kind of reflection on their reading was an attempt on our part to create situations where students had to think not only about what they'd read, but about their own thinking process, and how this process might eventually affect their practice as a tutor. Sometimes we'd ask students to consider specific questions about the reading in their reading response journal or in the class discussions, often asking them to "reflect on the ways in which they learn and fail to learn" (Mills-Court and Amiran 1991, 103). Unfortunately, the oral discussions of reading responses, while sometimes quite lively and informed, were often dominated by only a few individuals. Because of our successful experiences using synchronous and asynchronous conferencing in our writing classes, we decided to move these reading response discussions online, using Daedalus Mail in order to give each class member a visible, public "voice" in the evolving community. Once we integrated more varied electronic communication into tutor training, classes might go something like this: As students wandered into the room before class, they immediately took a seat and logged onto Daedalus. Upon successfully logging on, they saw the class assignment, which the teacher had posted earlier. Here, the students were told that the first thing they'd do was to engage in a response to what they'd read on Mail, so the students got into the specified Mail files. There, the instructor had posed a question based on the reading material, and students then took all the time they needed to reply. They knew from the prompt that they were then expected to read the replies critically, and question, respond, or problematize them. An example of such a class assignment appears below.

Stardate: Tuesday, January 23

Welcome once again to the wonderful world of online communication. Today we'll be doing a number of things:

1. Posting reading logs to the MAIL conference WHO WE ARE. To do this, simply choose ACTIVITY above, hold down the mouse button and select MAIL. Then, to join the conference WHO WE ARE, go up to MAIL on the menu and select JOIN A CONFERENCE. There you may post your reading log #2.

2. After we've posted and responded to Log #2 on Mail and responded to at least three of your colleague's posts, we'll come back to the main table and have a f2f discussion about what we've just talked about online.

3. Then we'll form our WAC groups and set up dates for WAC presentations.

4. If there is time, we might try a role-playing exercise to start you thinking about WHO WE ARE as tutors.

The level of critical reading and honest reaction we were asking the tutors-in-training to engage in would be similar to the kind of directed reading and responding that they'd be expected to do once they began tutoring clients. The reading response on Mail generated some thoughtful, insightful commentary, but it also created some problematic situations. Because the commentary was public, if someone chose not to participate, their absence was also be public. Similarly, the responses made it clear for everyone to see who had read and thought critically about the assigned reading, and who hadn't. There was simply no way to "hide" or to "slack off" here if the reading hadn't been finished: students were responsible for completing the reading, reflecting on it, and responding to what others had written publicly. In a traditional classroom, a student who hadn't done the assignment could depend on someone else to carry the load—not so online. Some of the students found the public nature of this discourse troubling; a few were worried that they'd be seen as un-intellectual if they took risks, so instead of "responding" to the reading, as they were directed to do, in the first few sessions many students chose to summarize first, something they felt more comfortable with. Some did then go on to problematize views or venture suggestions as to application. The interactive capabilities of Mail proved to be distressing for some; while they often found the comments of their classmates informative and interesting, many later said that they felt pressured by the performance aspect of the public, online discourse. They were all known for and hired at least partly because of their verbal ability, hence some of them saw the Mail forum as a place to display verbal prowess and flex academic muscles. So while the instructors viewed the online reading response entirely as a collaborative discussion—a "group-think" forum where the students could reflect and respond to their reading and their classmates' ideas, which it was to an extent—some of the students felt they had to compete with their classmates to sound like they belonged in the program.

A few students reacted to the new context by responding in a "safe" manner, by simply intellectually reiterating what they'd read or what others had said. For example, Duncan first summarized the reading, then cautiously responded:[1]

Duncan:
The piece on minimalist tutoring basically sums up everything we've already discussed about getting the student to take control of her paper and not doing the work for her. The author suggests ways this can be done, which we've covered in class as well. A good point the author makes is that the primary goal is to help the student become a better writer, not to improve the student's grade on a specific paper.
The second piece, Collaboration and Ethics argues that active collaboration with a student (which may include proofreading) is productive. Though she brings up some good points, I feel that the tutor must deal with each situation on a case-by-case basis. I don't think it is ethical to proofread a student's paper for her. However, I would be compelled to help an ESL student with grammar and sentence structure because English is not her native language.

After these rather "safe" observations, Duncan ventured a personal experience based on the reading, incorporating some questions as his thinking became visible:

In high school, some of the best English teachers I had would tell me that certain sentences were awkward, or cross out words and replace them with better vocabulary. I often found myself incorporating these words into my own writing. Since so much of writing is imitation, aren't we just ripping off other people's work when we write anyway? I know that I incorporate a lot of what I read into my own writing. It really is difficult to figure out where to draw the line. I don't think tutors should make up sentences for the tutee, or supply factual evidence to her, but if a tutor finds a sentence awkward, I can't see why she shouldn't tell that to the tutee.

This honest, straightforward commentary prompted a lively discussion about the students' own experiences and how they felt about recreating these experiences with their clients.

Several students rebelled against the initial intellectual tone and became chatty, using humor and self-deprecation to express themselves. Ironically, this behavior seemed to enhance the level of discussion. These students began to take risks—first with their tone, their online "persona," and later these students were often more likely to take risks with their ideas:

Gary:
Hey Sports Fans!!!!! I am coming to you live from the classroom 444C in Angell Hall. I'll be your commentator today for the tutoring session with Julie Grammar. I did not quite understand or agree with the idea of the tutor being commentator which was suggested in Harris. I think it would be hard to tell how all of it is related to the student's growth or improvement in writing skills". I understand the coach aspect and the counselor/listener aspect but I would find the commentating a little hard. I was also opposed to the idea of the teacher-centered conferences. That is not the environment that we are trying to create here at the University of Michigan.

Interestingly, here Gary has not only attempted to engage his audience cleverly, but he's beginning to wonder how this reading fits into the context of tutoring at the university. This kind of realization requires multiple levels of reflection: the student must not only reflect on his own thinking and learning, but he must also begin to see how these concepts will be affected by context. Such multi-layered thinking prepares the tutor for responding to a wide variety of clients and papers. One reading, later in the semester, encouraged tutors to do some thinking about the context they'd be working in, and Garth responded enthusiastically:

Garth:
Well, the battle cry is sounded! I really enjoyed Stephen North's article "The idea of a Writing center." Someone finally engaged with the subject we have been dealing with for six weeks—tutoring—with passion and fervor, and not as if composing a dissertation intended only fro FOR other professionals specializing in the same area.
North's central thesis—that the writing center should not be merely for mechanical mistakes, but should be a center for writers who care about their work, no matter what their level of expertise—is excellent. However, he is not so concerned with propounding his thesis that he ignores the realities of the college academic environment. He acknowledges that student/teacher

relationships should not be undermined by a tutor, and that tutors should, in fact, set their allegiance on the side of the teachers, or as North puts it we are not teacher advocates either—the instructor is simply part of the rhetorical context in which the writer is trying to operate . . . all we can do is try to help the writer learn to operate in it. (pg 30) This is a great idea. It doesn't whitewash the issue of teacher involvement in text, and make promises about a pressure-free writing environment or anything like that: it is a perfectly frank statement of purpose. Further, North responds to teachers who criticize tutored texts which aren't perfect by saying we aim to make "better writers not necessarily better texts."

After this insightful summary, Garth posted a more personal reflection on his recent experience. He includes it because he feels it has significance, though he can't yet articulate why:

Garth:
I had an interesting experience last night that I can't help but feel fits into our discussion (although I'm not sure why). In my fiction writing seminar, I had my first story workshopped, and I had to sit there while people talked about the strengths and weaknesses of what I had written. Then, I got about twenty copies of my story back from the class in their comments, words crossed out, things circled with NO written nearby (interestingly enough, some people would mark something NO, and others would mark the same thing GREAT—a good argument for the subjective nature of criticism). All I have to say is that I have never felt such a lack of control over my own work, and I have to admit that I found myself shutting out some critiques because they were phrased in such a way that they did not respect my authority over the text as its creator.

The ability of a tutor to read and listen carefully, then indicate that something is important, or even not quite right, even without being able to articulate why is nonetheless a valuable skill to have in the writing center. Simply reacting honestly and pointing things out to a client can serve as the start of a valuable shared negotiation of text.

Finally, on more than one occasion, some of them complained that while they knew their classmates well according to their comments, they really didn't *know* them: their faces, their voices, their personalities:

Dustin:
I was just wondering . . . Are we ever going to discuss things in class face to face instead of online? I am getting to know who some people are, but there is no way that I could match many faces with names. Also, I tend to get bogged down reading for so long that I loose all inclination to respond by the time I am caught up. I like the online thing, but I feel like it is being used a bit too much.

As a result of the frequent online discussions, students felt an intellectual kinship with one another, but they also felt disembodied, physically separate from the evolving classroom community. It was time for us to pause and reflect on tutor training.

A REFLECTIVE PAUSE

Was it wrong to use the technology so frequently, especially when it required the students to be publicly accountable for the assignments? After all, they accepted the responsibility to participate fully in the program when they signed up. And their experience online with their classmates and instructor paralleled in some sense what they would eventually come to expect from those they tutored: that they would take the responsibility to help themselves, rather than wait to be told what to do, what to "think." Whose standards were being challenged when the students "rebelled" by being silly or informal? At first, it would seem to be the rigorous academic standards of the program and of the university; yet the instructors were all flexible in what they considered "good thinking" both on and off the screen, much more so than the students seemed to be. These students, the "best of the best," had been immensely successful at the university because they had bought into the traditional academic system—in this class, perhaps to the point that many were threatened by anything that appeared to skitter out of the realm of their immediate control and their known, safe experience. A few of the tutors continued to hide in the "safe" traditional academic safety net and responded publicly primarily by regurgitating information. Most, however, began to think critically not just about the readings, but about how they might be applied, and these were often the students who pushed boundaries. Similarly, we should now ask: what is the instructor's responsibility in this training program?

Part of what I perceived as my responsibility as an instructor was to engage these students in critical reflection—on common course materials, their impending practice, the peer tutoring community, and their own unique, evolving identity as tutors—which I saw facilitated (although problematically) in the computer lab. Throughout the course, the tutors were creating portfolios of their experience.[2] The portfolio included a writing autobiography, their email reading logs, field notes from their observations and practice peer tutoring, email, OWL, and other electronic participation, a WAC (Writing Across the Curriculum) collaborative presentation and handouts, a seminar paper based on primary research, and a reflective essay. While we weighted the final paper more heavily in this course (since it also fulfilled the junior/senior writing requirement), we also encouraged them to include all of the text they felt displayed their growth as a tutor, from student evaluations to field notes. This less formal, inclusive representation of themselves broke new territory for many of these students, who had become accustomed to turning in only polished final performances. Instead, I was asking them to portray the messy process of self-discovery as they began to see how their education was evolving, and perhaps even take an active part in establishing goals and constructing themselves within the new context of peer tutoring. Rather than ensure that the student tutors were comfortable, I chose to place them in situations that would be different from the courses they'd taken and succeeded in to this point so that these students might see themselves, their thoughts, and their practice in more than one context. I hoped that the uncomfortableness they felt might cause some reflection of the situation, their feelings, as well as who they were becoming.

The co-directors met several times a semester, sharing syllabi and experiences, and eliciting ideas and support from their peers. As a result of these meetings, we opted to introduce yet another electronic medium in tutor training: Daedalus InterChange, a "chat"-like program which allows all students to "speak" at once (students type in responses and comments, and when these comments are sent they appear on everyone's screen). Initially, we used InterChange for topical discussions. In these InterChange discussions, for example, students responded to what they'd seen in their required observations, a topic in peer tutoring they were engaged in and wanted to learn more about, or a continued, focused discussion on what they'd read for class, mirroring the type of student-centered discourse we valued. In these discussions, more so than in any other, students began to test boundaries—by changing their personas, by taking on chatty personas, and by flaming. Trying on these "voices" in the safety of the tutor training class allowed the students to experiment with a tutoring personality that would "fit" as they began their practice. In the following excerpt, I asked students to examine the "multiple universes" they brought with them as they embarked on the journey to become a tutor:

Mary:
Well, I'm a woman, which could (or could not) have implications on the way I interact with people, depending on how deep you want to go. It annoys me when people hype gender up so much that it permeates every aspect of a discussion, but in some cases, I think its valid. I think its possible that I could be intimidated by an assertive male tutor. Not necessarily intimidated, but hesitant to assert my own opinions. But in the opposite sense, I think that being the stereotypical "feeling" woman enables me to elicit comfortable conversation between people. Obviously, that's not just because I'm a woman, but I certainly think it plays a role.

Evan:
Hey Mary, are you a woman or a "womyn?"

In the same discussion, one of the students described herself as liking "the guy from ER," which prompted a rather long thread about the merits of a recent movie he was in. Sometimes, just as in actual tutoring sessions, these tangential comments generated a more interesting discussion based on what the students were feeling:

Julie:
Off the topic, but do you think your friends since you have come to college are more diverse or less diverse than in high school?

This seemingly off-topic comment was in response to the discussion about new people they had met—and could possibly be biased toward, or have difficulty communicating with—at the university. Sometimes, however, the tangential commentary simply deflated the entire discussion, as when one person's innocent request for Advil spawned a lengthy examination of headaches and their causes. The experience of staying on topic, exploring valuable tangential topics, and wasting time by going off topic all helped to prepare the students for focusing on a clients' needs in the limited time of a tutoring session.

Despite the fact that we engaged in only a few InterChange discussions (at least partially because of the difficulty these students had staying on task) I didn't see them as failures. Instead, I saw the students beginning to reflect on who they were as tutors and students, on the course, on the material, on the university and tutoring context, and on their own evolving practice. Interestingly, we also used InterChange (this time the students all chose pseudonyms) to evaluate the course at midterm and at the end of the semester. Here's what the students found when they logged on:

Andy Warhol:
You've done a lot of work for this class, and the end product is the portfolio you'll be turning in on Friday. Ok, now it's YOUR turn to evaluate this course. What did you like? What did you find helpful? What did you NOT like, or NOT find helpful? What would you change? Why? How would you do it differently?

The responses were extremely detailed and well thought-out. Following are some excerpts:

Ralph Wiggum:
The most important change I'd make would be to begin actual tutoring earlier. The rhetoric/theory was useful for a while, but after a certain point, the only way we can really learn anything is by doing it.

Snickers:
I, agree Ralphie, that we should have begun actual tutoring earlier. I really have learned a lot through my practice tutoring. Also, I like everyone in this class— interchange is the best—-I like hearing everyone's thoughts . . . I'm going to miss this aspect of the class.

woody allen:
I also think that we should have begun tutoring earlier. Arguably the best experience I had was the tutoring sessions. However, I do not feel at all prepared for ESL conferences. I wish we had had some training in this area. If such a large component of the tutees are in fact ESL students, a large part of our training should have been also. I had one ESL student during a practice conference, and while it went ok, I did not feel qualified to help him.

topgun:
I think we should workshop the WAC presentations because its important to get some hands on experience before we actually tutor. I think there was

unnecessary pressure going into those practice sessions because we didn't have confidence in our skills because we had never tried them out.

Owen Meany:
My biggest suggestion is less computer work and more conversation. I didn't even know people's names and faces in here until like two months into the class. Seeing how this is my smallest class, and probably will continue to be the smallest one I ever have, it seems a shame to spend so much time staring at a screen instead of talking to each other. Why not discuss readings and ideas around the table instead of on the computer.

Jackie Chan:
I liked using the computers, it was a neat experience, but I still feel like I don't really know everyone.

These InterChange discussions became instrumental in how we reconceived the course. The tutors, then, took the responsibility to reflect critically on our practice and to offer specific suggestions for change. The co-directors, in turn, shared these among themselves, and, after much discussion and reflection, incorporated some of the ideas into our revised courses.

A MARRIAGE MADE IN HEAVEN?

After the introduction of InterChange in class, most of our discussions were online, either in InterChange or Mail, and the students once again began to complain vehemently about the lack of human contact in their classes. As a result of this reflection, we began to consciously integrate oral and online discussions into the training program. As we began to make these changes, a typical day might go as follows: After logging onto Daedalus and reading the class assignment, students might respond online to what they'd read using Mail, then we'd gather around the table for an oral discussion on some of the key points raised. Or, after reading the class assignment on the computer, we might forego the online reading response to have an oral group "norming" session on a sample student paper, then have an oral presentation by a group of tutors on a WAC issue. This balance of oral and online activities seemed to work better as the course progressed, but I noted some interesting general results: the Mail discussions continued to generate summaries first and then reflections; the students still tended toward safety here. The oral discussions (and, later, the InterChange discussions, which "feel" more oral than the Mail interaction), however, tended to be based more on personal experience and views—students were more likely to risk sharing their feelings, experiences, and individual viewpoints orally. These more personal discussions didn't occur in a vacuum, however; they appeared to have been fueled by the critical thinking and reflecting the students had done for their reading responses in Mail. Students tended to situate themselves and their thoughts in the text online, and then they applied this "construction" of thoughts and experiences orally. In effect, the combination of online and oral classroom activities seemed to complement each other in a way we hadn't expected: the computers seemed to clear their heads and the oral discussions cleared their hearts. Yet I would venture to guess that, without the computer experience, we would have had fewer students participating orally, and their participation would tend toward the summary style we saw initially in Mail.

TAKING THE TUTORING ONLINE

While we included various types of computer-mediated conferencing in tutor training to help make visible the social construction of knowledge, the creation of a classroom community, and a means of reflective thinking, electronic media had originally been included in order to train the peer tutors to work f2f with clients in the "space" where writers were writing: the computer lab. But when we opened the practice to online tutoring, via email and the web, we decided that this training would work perfectly for OWL tutoring, too. Up to this point, while we had a class email list which students used outside class, most of the work for the course was done in a networked computer lab. We wanted to "initiate" each of the tutors into internet use so that they'd be comfortable with the OWL, and to do this we first signed all the new tutors-in-training up for the OWL email list. Everyone who was subscribed to this list received everything that came to the OWL in their private email accounts. When the OWL began, the directors and a few students who were involved in its construction were on the OWL list; the other students, who tutored only f2f, were not involved. During the pilot year, we subscribed only volunteers to the list; once again, the f2f tutors weren't involved. We soon decided that OWL training might actually benefit f2f tutors, and vice versa, so we made both mandatory. For a four-week period during tutor training, everyone in the class was signed up for the OWL list.

The first and most compelling problem that arose for the tutors was time and email management; most tutors, though familiar with email, were not able to handle the large amount of mail the OWL email list generated (for instance, a tutor might receive five student papers for the OWL on a particular day, then five more messages "claiming" the paper which had been cc'ed to the OWL, followed by five more messages cc'ed to the OWL with detailed responses to the original five papers). Most students only checked email once a week or so, and they were overwhelmed when they had 75 or more messages waiting for them. We tried to teach a "skim and delete" pattern, but students complained it took too much time out from their schoolwork and personal time. We directors were forced to think about *our* responsibility: Was it to teach email management? Were students learning skills that would help them as tutors? Based on this experience, we decided the answer was "no," so we compromised by asking students to join the list long enough to do a "reader response"/participant observation analysis of three OWL conferences which they then included in their final portfolio. Once they were finished with these observation reports, they could get off the list. From that point, the instructors (who were all subscribed to the OWL list) would forward interesting or intriguing conferences from the OWL to the class list.

When students had reflected on three OWL conferences on their own, we began discussing papers and responses from the OWL on the regular peer tutoring email list. However, students were still so overwhelmed with email that they often missed the discussion, or simply did not participate. What had been a somewhat lively list at the beginning of the semester dwindled to almost nothing toward the end. Once again, the co-directors were forced to reflect on what might be more pedagogically sound for the tutors. Finally, as with the f2f training, we opted to more fully integrate both electronic and f2f interaction with the OWL training. Interesting OWL conferences were printed out (with identifying material such as names, schools, email addresses stripped), and we analyzed them orally in class. First, we might look at a student paper from the OWL, standardizing on it: what did the student request help with? What kind of help did the paper need? How would you go about addressing this student? Next, we handed out a tutor's response (once again, stripped and printed out) and asked them to assess it. Did the tutor meet your expectations? How about the student's? What was the tone like? Was there enough help? Too much? Finally, I forwarded some actual OWL papers to the tutors and asked them to pair up with someone in the computer lab during class and respond to the paper as an OWL tutor would, keeping in mind all of the criticisms and praise they'd heaped on the papers we'd looked at before. Instead of sending the responses to the entire OWL list or to the student, they sent responses to the class list where students had the option of reading and reflecting on each one. I then stripped the headers from three of these, printed them out, and during the next class period we discussed these sample responses orally. What worked? What didn't work? If you were a student, how helpful would this advice be? How could it be more helpful?

Just as a combination of oral and online work seemed to help the students reflect more easily on their f2f reading and practice, so, too, this integrated approach seemed to work when training tutors to respond online. As the OWL grew and training switched to high gear, the co-directors met frequently to discuss the OWL and its service. Despite the emphasis on computer interaction, we were all amazed at how difficult it seemed to be for the students to develop an internet "online persona" who could both address the students' requests and do so in a tone that was neither condescending nor directive. The students were all developing into competent tutors, yet many of them had great difficulty putting this skill into practice in an accessible, friendly manner online. As a result of this observation, we began to question our initial assumption that f2f tutoring and online tutoring were the same; in fact, initially the pendulum swung a bit too far in the opposite direction, and we concluded that f2f and online tutoring were completely different. Yet after one more semester of refining our integration of online and f2f training, we drew in to the center, seeing online and f2f tutoring as cousins who shared many familial traits, but who nonetheless needed to be treated as individuals.

REFLECTIONS ON TUTOR TRAINING

Can the computer—or the integration of electronic and oral communication—provide a more reflective environment for the evolving tutor? How can we encourage students to become "reflective practitioners"? And how can we be more reflective in our teaching and practice? In our experience, it would appear that such reflection requires similar situations for the co-directors and the tutors. Based on this experience, I've outlined below a necessarily brief list of suggestions concerning experiences that might encourage reflection and responsibility in tutor training.

Collaborate With Colleagues

Take advantage of colleagues with administrative experience, with interpersonal experience, with theoretical and pedagogical experience, and don't limit your interaction to those in your field. As co-directors of the peer tutoring program, we met regularly to discuss the peer tutoring program, shared ideas about how it might be improved, and when conflicts arose, we compromised our views. Most programs, granted, don't offer a co-directorship, but that doesn't limit opportunities for collaboration. If you have access, you can explore the descriptions of peer tutoring programs around the country via the World Wide Web (starting with the National Writing Center's home page at http://www2.colgate.edu/diw/NWCA.html), and for those with internet access, lists like Wcenter (information about how to subscribe can be found on the NWCA home page) provide interaction with colleagues from around the world.

Collaborate With (and Among) Students

Our program would never have evolved at the rate nor to the extent it did without frequent collaboration with the students. The OWL is the most outward representation of that collaboration; without student input, the OWL would likely not exist. Similarly, the content of our peer tutoring program is greatly influenced by the feedback we get from students, both during and after the course. Finally, we found it helpful for the older tutors to meet with the tutors-in-training at least a few times a year to share their insights and experiences.

Be Flexible With (and Within) the Curriculum

It's important to base a tutor training curriculum on sound theory as well as specific university concerns. But allow students to determine curriculum within the context of the classroom. For instance, in one InterChange discussion, it seemed to be more important for students to express their concerns about their impending tutoring rather than discussing the reading for the day. If students need to reflect on an issue at length, don't be in a hurry to move on. Alter the curriculum as needed.

Become a Learner Yourself

Those of us who work with technology soon realize that we need to become comfortable with "not knowing." Because technology changes at such a rapid rate, if we don't become learners over and over again, we miss out on ideas and abilities that could supplement our practice. It's easy to become comfortable in our expertise, in our "knowing." But by becoming learners, we not only open ourselves to new experiences and ideas, but we also realize how difficult it is to reflect on these and assimilate them successfully into our practice. This realization can only help to make us more effective, empathetic teachers.

Determine Needs and Ask for Resources

In order to expand a program or increase participation, detailed records must be kept to justify requests. For instance, when the OWL was finally open university-wide, we needed to convince the university to increase our funding so that we could employ "cybertutors" to populate the OWL while still maintaining out growing f2f program. Our records helped us to write proposals and grants, our positive public image throughout the university helped build our ethos (the OWL was linked directly to the university home page, and several tutors wrote articles about the OWL), and by consulting each other and other experts, our specificity impressed "the powers that be" to give us what we asked for.

Take the Time to Reflect

Evaluation shouldn't come only at the end. Take the time to reflect on what goes on daily, and how it fits into the mission of the program, of the school, and of the larger theoretical framework. If a particular practice isn't working, then solicit feedback and offer an alternative. Examine the theory, the practice, and the outcome of the training program on a regular basis.

When Using Technology, Have a Plan

Initially, we expected our use of technology to mirror our own positive experiences personally and professionally. We began with a sound theoretical foundation, but we weren't prepared for the differences context and audience might cause. The corollary to this axiom is, of course, also true:

Don't Be Afraid To Change That Plan

Be aware when the plan is too rigid or isn't working, and try to rethink how it can be revised. In our situation, that meant a conscious integration of electronic and oral interaction as we trained students to tutor both f2f and on the OWL.

CONCLUSION

Ultimately, we found that the ability to go back and forth in a text, to see thoughts made visible on the screen as a tutor wrestles with ideas, concepts, and applications, does, in fact, help the tutor reflect on what he or she is doing and becoming, just as it helps the instructor to "see" the thinking going on in the classroom. Yet the tutors also seemed to need the physical reality of human contact to ground that reflected image and synthesize what they'd learned in a community of like-minded peers, just as the instructors needed to meet regularly to discuss and assess the program. Too much of either environment seemed to limit the tutors in their classroom interaction and in their subsequent practice: those who were exposed only to oral classrooms had difficulty getting past their own definition of "school" and academic discourse as it appeared in student papers. They tended to be a bit more top-down in their thinking and with their clients, following and modeling the example they'd been successful with to this point in their lives. However, with the inclusion of computer-mediated discourse in the tutor training program, students became uncomfortable but began to take risks, to push boundaries, to try on new personas. More importantly, they began to see beyond the physical text—even when the "physical" text was online—to seeing writing as ideas generated by someone in a specific rhetorical and physical situation, rather than a simple, new-critical text unto itself. In both cases, the tutors take responsibility for their own work; in the latter instance, however, they are able to reflect more often, more fully, and from different perspectives about who they are, what they do, why they do it, and what it means to others in the writing center.

NOTES

1.   All names of tutors have been changed, but the excerpts have been cited with permission.
2.   A copy of the syllabus for this course can be found at <http://www.lsa.umich.edu/ecb/ECB300.html> and <http://www.lsa.umich.edu/ecb/ECB301.html>. For a description of the peer tutoring program at the University of Michigan, go to <http://www.lsa.umich.edu/ecb/peertutor.html>.

WAC on the Web
Writing Center Outreach to Teachers of Writing Intensive Courses

Sara Kimball

INTRODUCTION

A SEARCH WITH THE ALTA VISTA ONLINE DATABASE FOR THE KEYWORDS *WAC* and *curriculum* reveals that many writing centers and writing programs now use the World Wide Web to communicate with faculty involved in Writing Across the Curriculum (WAC) programs. Larry Beason of Eastern Washington State University also provides a web page with a long list of links to other universities' WAC web pages (http://ewu66649.ewu.edu/WAC.html). These pages range from simple sites offering descriptions of programs and requirements to the impressive sites at Northern Illinois University and University of Kansas that offer faculty short essays on aspects of writing instruction, sample syllabuses, templates for assignments in various fields, information on grading and on using journals, and handouts for students, in addition to program information.

Publishing on the web has obvious practical advantages for a writing center involved in WAC outreach. It's an efficient way to store documents and disseminate them to a wide audience. Users can browse and download documents at their own convenience, and electronic documents take up less space than paper. But the web isn't simply a bulletin board or library: it was invented as a workplace technology, and it is widely used in work and recreation for interactive communication. Although mass media coverage of the web has tended to emphasize its more individual self-promotional, recreational, or spectacular aspects, the coverage in the mass media masks a quiet revolution that has taken place in the lives of many computer users for whom the web has become an increasingly common and convenient tool for gathering information for business and personal tasks and for online transactions[1]. Few writing center WAC sites, however, fully exploit the potential of the web as a workplace technology and vehicle for interactive communication with a faculty audience. A presence on the World Wide Web also has obvious promotional advantages, and many commercial and academic websites—including writing center sites—serve at least in part to project a public image of the entity that sponsors them. Again, this is an aspect of the web that could be better recognized and more fully exploited by WAC sites.

In this chapter, I describe revising UT–Austin's WAC website to make it more useful as a workplace site, giving the reasoning behind specific decisions about content and design. A website is like a writing project that is constantly in progress, and many of the decisions involved in designing or revising one are rhetorical: a site has goals and an audience, it is situated within a specific social context, and its designers should pay attention to ethos. The UT faculty site is intended as a resource that faculty across the university will visit, explore, and make use of often. To that end, it is designed to function as a publicly-accessible intranet. An intranet (modeled after *internet*) is a private network, not necessarily connected to the internet, that functions within an organization to provide services like those on the internet, such as web servers for the distribution of information within the organization. The site's primary audience—faculty at a large state university without a centralized WAC program—is fairly sophisticated technologically, and it is large and diverse, both in fields of specialization and in acquaintance with composition pedagogy. The site also has secondary audiences, including high school teachers in the state of Texas and elsewhere, and members of the general public. One additional goal of the site is to provide models, both for UT faculty and for the site's various secondary audiences, of progressive, professional teaching practice.

THE WEB AS A WORKPLACE TECHNOLOGY

UT faculty have some experience with a semi-public intranet, since the university's home page and web pages linked to it function in this fashion. Campus users can, for example, now visit the Provost's office's home page to view and download guidelines for preparing promotion cases, use email to request official forms, or send a question to the Provost's staff. UT's Office of Human Resources maintains a website that provides a searchable database of job descriptions, employment applications that can be completed and submitted on the web, and downloadble templates for employee performance reviews. Prospective students can not only visit university websites to get information about departments, programs, and the admission process, they can now submit applications electronically. Enrolled students can view an electronic version of the university's course catalog, and they now have web-based access to evaluations of faculty teaching the courses they might be interested in. Campus users can even apply for a parking permit online, navigating through a series of maps to make selections. Each of these services has its public and private sides. Much of the information on these sites is unrestricted, but financial transactions and confidential information are protected. The transmission of credit card numbers is protected through encryption, and services restricted to people affiliated with the university require an electronic id number.

THE WEB AS INSTITUTIONAL DISPLAY

The difference between the university services described above and a private intranet is that the university's sites are semi-public. Although the information they provide is intended for campus users—or for prospective students and their families—much of it is freely accessible to anyone with a web browser. These sites present an image of the university to the rest of the world and expose some of its workings to public view, an aspect of work-a-day use of the web that is perhaps not yet fully appreciated. While there are some obvious disadvantages to conducting one's business in public, there are potential advantages if the documents on the site reveal the institution as responsible, innovative, and professional.

Mostly, a website used for work purposes establishes its parent institution's ethos passively, allowing visitors to come to their own conclusions while browsing. It is possible, however, to take a proactive approach by displaying some information prominently or by drawing the public's attention to particular content. UT's home page, for example, has a section at its top entitled "Spotlight" for links to items of current interest. Shortly after a serious fire in one of the chemistry labs last spring, a link to an online version of the university's laboratory safety manual appeared in this section of the home page. It has remained there ever since, perhaps less a document that users routinely access than a visible sign that the university is committed to laboratory safety.

Like many public universities, UT is often viewed with skepticism by the state legislature and members of the general public. A publicly-accessible website that demonstrates a commitment to undergraduate instruction is one way of demonstrating accountability to these audiences. The UT writing center is supported by a student fee, a method of funding that provides an unusually generous budget but also demands high levels of accountability. An additional benefit of a WAC website is that it offers a concrete example of how the writing center is using its funding productively.

AUDIENCE AND INSTITUTIONAL CONTEXT

As an audience, UT faculty vary widely in their sophistication about writing pedagogy. Some have for years used writing both effectively and creatively in teaching in disciplines as different as Finance and Astronomy. For other faculty, however, the idea that writing can be viewed and taught as a process is still news. A great many people who fall somewhere in the middle appreciate information about matters like portfolio evaluation or desire advice about adapting their classes to include a writing component without sacrificing subject-matter teaching.

The diversity of faculty interests and expertise is in part a function of the university's size and in part a function of WAC's on campus history. With a total enrollment of about 48,000, including slightly over 35,500 undergraduates, and a faculty of approximately 2,000, UT is one of the largest universities in the country. It has fourteen colleges and professional schools, eleven of which offer undergraduate programs in humanities, arts, science, social sciences and various professional fields, including Architecture, Engineering, Pharmacy, Nursing, and Social Work. WAC courses are offered in each of these fields.

UT does not have a centralized WAC program, but students are required to take four writing-intensive courses, called Substantial Writing Component (SWC) courses, two at the lower-division level and two at the upper-division level. Historically, the SWC courses have had varying fortunes, and WAC outreach has to contend with a certain amount of distrust and cynicism. The SWC requirement, initiated in 1983, was intended as part of a university-wide program to include both general writing courses taught within the English Department and specialized, discipline-specific courses taught by faculty within other departments (Kinneavy 72-73). Key parts of the program, however—support for advising faculty about using writing to teach and a junior-level collegewide course offered by the English Department in four generic WAC areas—were never funded. Any initial enthusiasm for WAC had waned by the early 1990s. There was no particular incentive for faculty to teach SWC courses, and some departments offered few of them. Until recently, it was not uncommon for students to experience difficulty in fulfilling SWC requirements with courses relevant to their majors or interests. The rarity of SWC courses also created disincentives for faculty, since they ran the risk of having their SWC courses fill up rapidly with students not especially interested in the subject matter.

Two years ago, however, the administration announced an innovation in computing faculty workload credits that awards more credits to SWC courses, allowing many faculty members to teach two classes per semester rather than three, if at least one counts as SWC. The result has been a predictable radical increase in the number of SWC courses offered. The site's potential audience, therefore, has undergone a rapid expansion. Many of the people teaching these courses, however, have little familiarity with modern composition pedagogy, and they have widely varying levels of commitment to using writing to teach their subject matter.

The UT writing center and the Division of Rhetoric and Composition of which it is a part are fairly new entities on campus, having started in the fall of 1993. Part of the writing center's mission is to advise faculty teaching SWC courses, and given the history of WAC on campus, it has been important to establish an atmosphere of trust and goodwill in our dealings with faculty. The writing center and Division have also worked hard to establish themselves as visible and respected entities on campus.

In part, the website is intended to complement and extend workshops about various aspects of teaching writing that the writing center provides. In these workshops, we try to speak to faculty as colleague to colleague, respecting their disciplinary knowledge and trying, through collegial conversation, to help them develop approaches to teaching writing. In practice, however, given the size of the university, the diversity of its faculty, and the history of WAC on campus, it can be difficult to establish connections across colleges, though barriers to communication are as much intellectual and social as physical or geographical. A website designed along the lines of a corporate intranet is one approach to overcoming geographical barriers to communication across a large campus and perhaps some of the social and intellectual ones as well.

DESIGN ISSUES

According to the *Yale C/AIM Web Style Guide* (http://info.med.yale.edu/caim/manual/interface/interface.html), the differing goals of external and internal (intranet) websites and the differing needs of their users lead to different design principles. While external sites try to capture an audience, drawing visitors deeper into the site with entertaining information or presentations, an intranet should be designed for users who want to move into and through a site quickly in order to retrieve information. Since our site functions as an intranet, even though most of it is open to the public, it opts for ease of navigation and clarity of design rather than elaborate lures. Since it is an open workplace site, however, it also has to show a public face to visitors not connected with UT Austin.

Figure 1

Undergraduate Writing Center Faculty Pages

These pages are intended to help UT faculty members teaching Substantial Writing Component (SWC) courses and anyone else using writing to teach academic subject matter. They contain suggestions, strategies, and short pieces of writing by members of the Division of Rhetoric and Composition and by others, as well as links to online resources and information on how the UWC can assist faculty and students. We would like these pages to provide a wide variety of approaches to designing writing assignments, responding to drafts, evaluating final drafts, using computer technology to teach writing, and other issues in teaching writing-intensive courses that faculty can adapt to their own pedagogical goals and teaching styles. We therefore welcome contributions from faculty across the UT campus. Please feel free to adapt material here for your own purposes. We do, however, ask that you give appropriate credit in quoting signed material and that you retain information identifying the UWC or any writing center we are linked to if you download handouts and distribute them to students.

Sara E. Kimball
Director
Undergraduate Writing Center

About UT Austin's SWC courses	Planning and teaching a SWC course	Working with students	UWC services for students and faculty	Communicate with the UWC	Online resources for teachers

Return to:
Undergraduate Writing Center
University of Texas at Austin
Send comments or suggestions to: writing@uts.cc.utexas.edu
Last updated August, 1997

The first page that greets visitors to our faculty site is a "front door" or "cover page" (also called an index page) designed to give anyone who visits a clear sense of what the site is about. (See Figure 1 for a draft version of our site's cover page.) The cover page is roughly analogous to the public foyer of a large corporate office building. It needs to provide enough information for visitors to orient themselves, and since the site is open to the public, it should clearly identify who we are. Our site's cover page opens with a message signed by me as director explaining the site's purpose, inviting colleagues to use and contribute to the site, and describing our policy on materials use. I would like colleagues to use samples in much the same way people in a department might share syllabuses and assignments, using what they find relevant and adapting material to their own needs, and part of the message is an invitation to do so. Since the site includes signed material and handouts that teachers might distribute to classes as well as links to other writing centers, however, we request that faculty retain identifying information on material they distribute to students unadapted[2].

The content of the cover page is broken into six general categories that correspond to the site's goals. Each category leads to a separate menu page. This design tries to strike a balance between providing a clear overview of what the site has to offer for regular users and for visitors who happen to wander in and providing a detailed map of the contents for users who want to find information quickly.[3]

The categories on the cover page are simple and direct. "About UT's SWC courses" links to official information about SWC requirements and includes a brief history of WAC at UT. "Planning and teaching a SWC course" is the rubric for practical advice and sample assignments. "Working with students" presents information about how to hold individual writing conferences with students and about teaching writing to students with special needs (e.g., returning students, ESL students, speakers of non-standard dialects, and learning disabled students). It also includes a page discussing the challenges that all students face in learning to write college-level academic prose and trying to persuade faculty to understand (or remember) the struggles of college writers from the student's point of view. "UWC services for faculty and students" provides information about how our writing center works with students, including a FAQ file with answers to questions that tend to come up in responses to surveys our writing center sends out to faculty. "Communicate with the UWC" links to a message form and a description of how to subscribe to our electronic discussion list for teachers of SWC courses. "Other subjects of interest to teachers" is a catch-all category that includes using computer technology in teaching, resources for communications scholars, online bibliographies, and links to other sites.

The cover page has a *mailto* form soliciting comments and suggestions about content, and it links back to our writing center site's main index page. At present, the cover page simply has a set of links arranged in a table. Eventually, however, it will include a simple image map or navigation bar.

The menu page for "Planing and teaching a SWC course" (See Figure 1) breaks the process of incorporating writing into a syllabus into clear categories that replicate the process: "Current views on teaching writing and using writing to teach" (designed to provide an intellectual framework for the rest); "Incorporating writing assignments into your syllabus"; "Designing writing assignments"; "Responding to student drafts"; "Evaluating and grading student writing"; and "Managing the workload." These divisions were planned with future expansion in mind; each category functions as a conceptual "bin" into which documents can be dropped as they are created. The categories are loose enough to be appropriate for diverse content, but they still provide a conceptual and organizational framework.

The organization of this site section serves pedagogical ends, functioning as a cognitive map to the process of incorporating writing into a course. The page presents the user with the idea that using writing to teach can be viewed as a process involving discrete but interrelated steps and that teaching writing involves ordering one's priorities astutely. For example, the menu has separate headings for "Responding to drafts" and "Evaluating and grading," in order to reinforce the idea that a thoughtful response to works in progress is more effective than a summary judgment on a final product. Headings also highlight matters of special concern to the audience. Although the information and advice under "Managing the workload" could belong conceptually under "Responding to drafts," "Managing the workload" appears as a separate category because it addresses one of the audience's biggest fears: that they will be buried under unmanageable loads of student papers if they introduce a writing component into their courses.

TECHNOLOGICAL ISSUES

UT faculty are a relatively technologically sophisticated audience. As the result of an administrative initiative, most faculty have computers that allow them to access the web, and many work in buildings that have been wired for Ethernet access. Some also have computers at home and presumably access the internet through dial-up connections. Although the site's primary audience uses sophisticated technology that allows access to sites with graphics, multimedia, frames and image maps, the most technologically sophisticated presentation is not, however, necessarily the most appropriate or the most useful for all of the people who might make use of the site. Like many corporate intranets, a WAC site has little intrinsic need for a graphics-rich presentation or for multimedia[4]. Relying heavily on images to organize such a site, for example, may put off some users who turn off image loading in the interests of obtaining textual information quickly.[5]

A technology-heavy site—even on a campus with state-of-the-art high-bandwidth technology—also excludes some potential off-campus visitors. In addition to its primary audience our site has other secondary audiences, one of which is high school teachers, whose access to the web may be limited. Our writing center does outreach to a few Texas high schools, and some of our material may be useful to high school teachers in teaching their own classes. At the very least, the site could give teachers some sense of the kinds of writing their students will do in college. While there are initiatives to introduce computer technology into all Texas schools, the results so far are uneven. Some, for example, only have Lynx, a text-only web browser available with a UNIX shell account, and many schools only have slow, dial-up connectivity. By providing at least a version of the site that is accessible to low-bandwidth technology, its value to this wider audience can be increased.

CONTENT

An attractive site with a sophisticated presentation will not be very successful if nobody reads the material on it, downloads documents, or interacts with the writing center because the content is dull, thin or not very interesting to faculty. In designing a WAC site, it is important to distinguish between content of interest to composition professionals and content of interest to faculty. The site's audience is by and large more interested in the practical than the theoretical. Although there is a rich literature on the theory and practice of WAC, including studies of writing in particular fields, much of it is aimed at an audience of composition professionals. Faculty who are busy juggling the demands of teaching, scholarship, and service, however, are more interested in concrete advice, and our site focuses, therefore, on providing samples, models, and practical advice rather than academic references. Nevertheless, bibliographic information and pointers to online bibliographies about WAC, can lead colleagues to items of potential interest and make the point that the practical advice our writing center gives comes from a rich intellectual background, and we link to online bibliographies[6]. In this way, the site can serve as an interface to more complex discussions of literacy for those members of its audience who are interested.

Most WAC websites—our own included—offer information about their school's WAC program, such as requirements for designating a course writing-intensive, a description of the course approval process, copies of relevant forms, and perhaps a program history. Northern Illinois University's site, for example, has a page entitled "A Short History of WAC" describing both the origins of the WAC movement in the 1970s and the history of the program at Northern Illinois (http://www.niu.edu/ acad/english/wac/histwac.html). Such information locates a program in a historical and intellectual context, and presents a public image of the program and its sponsoring institution to a wider audience. Historical information is also often useful in understanding present realities, and it might be of interest to some faculty for that reason. Faculty members who do not receive clear information from their departments find a review of general information about requirements helpful. Information about the program, however, has little lasting value for a local audience and probably does little to attract and hold this audience's attention.

The sample syllabuses and assignments the site provides represent diverse approaches and points of view. Although some fundamentals are important to emphasize to those members of the audience that have little or no training in teaching writing—for example, the idea that focus on sentence-level concerns at the expense of invention and organization is misplaced effort—there are many ways to put the fundamentals into practice. Some approaches fit different personal tastes or training better than others; some are more appropriate to some fields than others. For example, our site includes information on formalized, visually-oriented methods of teaching invention because they work well for some teachers and some students, even though this approach is not congenial to all styles of writing and teaching.

Members of our writing center's staff have produced a number of paper handouts on aspects of teaching writing to distribute at faculty workshops, and these provide an obvious starting point for content. In some cases, we have adapted handouts designed for paper into formats more appropriate for the web, for example breaking them down into short, linked segments, and adding links to related documents. We have two types of paper materials for students and faculty: most are unsigned references on matters of general interest, and their voice tends to be anonymous and corporate, though not bland. Often they are written as a collaborate effort. Occasionally, however, someone on our staff has put considerable time and effort into writing a piece that is more complex than a simple handout and is written from a discernible personal point of view. For example, several years ago one of our graduate consultants wrote a set of guidelines for students that ran to several pages about how to read literature in order to write about it. It's appropriate to acknowledge the time and thought that goes into writing like this by publishing it with the author's name. We will continue this policy in publishing on our faculty website. We are also actively soliciting signed contributions from colleagues in our writing program and in other departments, both to emphasize a variety of points of view and to encourage faculty outside the writing program to realize that they are authorities on writing in their fields.

Links are also content. An obvious practical advantage to linking to other sites that offer information to WAC instructors is that we do not have to write all of our site's content. Our site links to such sites such as those at Northern Illinois and the University of Kansas that provide material about teaching writing. In some cases, however, for example when a site concentrates on material specific to its own program and institution, it makes more sense to link to a specific document on another site than it does to link to the site's index page. For instance, Ray Smith of Indiana University Bloomington's Campuswide Writing program has written a clear, useful essay describing minimal marking, (http://www.indiana.edu/~wts/cwp/quickguide.html). As a signed essay, it fits in well with our site's design, and some UT faculty who are concerned with mechanics and style in their students' writing may be interested in using this technique. Linking in this way does raise some issues of etiquette and clarity. It's necessary to get permission to link and to identify the document's source in annotation that goes with the link, and it helps if all of the other site's pages also offer clear identification.

INTERACTIVITY: PUBLIC AND PRIVATE SPACES

The simplest way to use a website for communication is to put a *mailto* tag on each of the site's pages that enables a visitor to send email to the site's author or sponsor. Our writing center site already uses *mailto* tags, and we do, in fact, receive several email messages a week from visitors to our writing center's web pages. These messages are not usually from faculty, however, suggesting that to encourage faculty to use the site for communication part of the site needs to be identified explicitly as a forum for communication.

At present, the communications forum is a separate page linked to the description of services for faculty with a *mailto* tag accompanied by a message inviting faculty to send us questions or suggestions, make arrangements for class visits from writing center staff, or schedule workshops or presentations. Eventually, however, the site will extend the individual consulting we do with faculty by providing a form that would allow instructors who wanted advice to paste in and send us syllabuses or assignments.[7]

Eventually too, we would like to use the interactive capabilities of the web to encourage communication among faculty, for example, by providing comment forms for dialog about particular documents, proposals or approaches to teaching. The online version of *The Chronicle of Higher Education* has such a service, called "Colloquy," that invites visitors to its site to comment on articles it publishes. Many of these on-going commentaries attract a number of participants with widely diverging views on issues of common interest to academics, such as tenure, treatment of graduate students, and the role of technology in teaching. Some of the classes taught in UT Austin's Computer Writing and Research Lab use message forums constructed of message forms linked in a thread to continue class discussions online. (See Figure 2 for a discussion question posed by the instructor in one class.) Technology of this sort creates collaborative texts that can bring together diverse points of view and sources of knowledge in addressing a common concern and, in doing so, create sense of community. The collaborative potential of hypertext is perhaps better known to some in composition in its application to literary studies, but using collaborative hypertexts to address common concerns and solve problems may become increasingly important in progressive businesses and industries (Johnson-Eilola and Selber).[8]

Simply offering a message forum for the campus at large would probably not be very successful at UT Austin at present. To generate responses, a forum probably should address a particular group of users with clear common interests or a clear sense of community, and teachers of SWC classes don't form such a community on the UT campus. Eventually, our writing center would like to offer summer seminars for faculty, and a message forum might be a way of keeping participants in such a seminar, who would form a discrete community, in touch with each other and with the writing center during the school year.

Figure 2

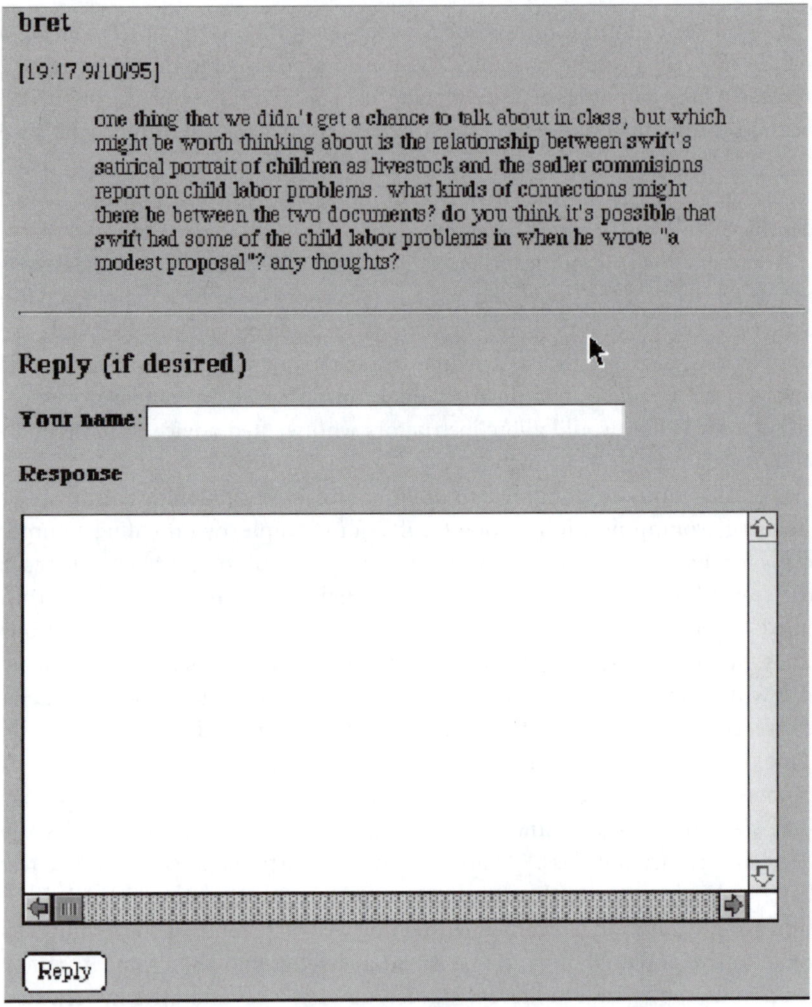

bret

[19:17 9/10/95]

one thing that we didn't get a chance to talk about in class, but which might be worth thinking about is the relationship between swift's satirical portrait of children as livestock and the sadler commisions report on child labor problems. what kinds of connections might there be between the two documents? do you think it's possible that swift had some of the child labor problems in when he wrote "a modest proposal"? any thoughts?

Reply (if desired)

Your name:

Response

[Reply]

Interactive technology like message forums raises questions about public and private aspects of a website. A conversation about teaching or writing accessible to anyone over the World Wide Web puts institutional practice and attitudes about teaching in the public view. Practically speaking, there is no way to exclude visitors who are not members of the campus community from participating. Message forum discussions in classes in the Computers and Writing Research Lab do, for example, sometimes attract participants from outside. A public discussion of teaching might have advantages if, for example, it displayed to a wider public some of the common concerns of faculty or it allowed members of the community to communicate their concerns to faculty. It also has some obvious disadvantages; it seems likely that some people would be unwilling to participate in a discussion open to the whole world, or that participants in such a discussion would feel inhibited about expressing opinions frankly. If the faculty website is intended as a workspace, then an analogy to real-life workspaces is appropriate: the cover page is a public foyer that greets visitors and provides clearly marked doors to work areas (the various informational pages) through which anyone may wander at will. A few areas, however, should function as "backstage areas" in the sense of Goffman (1950, 111-134)—places where regular site users can speak to other users and "reliably expect that no member of the audience will intrude (113)." In the interests of preserving a sense of community, for example, a web-based discussion among participants in a seminar should probably be kept private by restricting it to users with an authorized password.

CONCLUSION

UT–Austin provides an example of one particular institutional context for WAC and a writing center WAC website. Some decisions about site design and content appropriate for UT may not be applicable to other institutions and programs. Faculty teaching WAC courses at UT do not, for example, form a discrete community. A WAC website on a smaller campus with a more coherent WAC program, however, such as one in which faculty shared the common experience of attending an orientation seminar, could help to sustain and strengthen an already existing community. A website could also, for example, serve as central information source and communication forum for faculty from several departments teaching a common WAC course. Unlike some writing centers, the UT writing center neither evaluates nor approves proposals for WAC courses, but a center with this responsibility could provide online versions of official forms and enable faculty to send completed applications to the center. It could also use the web's interactive capabilities to advise faculty writing course proposals and applications, making the process of designing WAC courses a collaboration between faculty and the writing center.

Some decisions made in designing the UT website may be more generally applicable. The intranet model seems feasible on a technologically sophisticated campus in which many faculty are accustomed to using the web for professional purposes. The increased use of the World Wide Web for commercial transactions, research, and recreation by computer users in and out of academia, however, suggests that this is a model with which potential audiences at a wide variety of institutions will be increasingly familiar. Given our funding and the history of the UT WAC program, we find it important to pay attention to our writing center's ethos both within the university and in communicating with the general public. Our web pages, both for faculty and for students, help establish a desired ethos. Given the current political climate for higher education and the tenuous position in which many writing centers find themselves in trying to obtain funding and institutional support, however, our concern with ethos is hardly unique. If a presence on the web can contribute to establishing a positive ethos for writing centers and their parent institutions, then we should all pay attention to ethos in planning for the future.

NOTES

1. The surveys of World Wide Web users conducted by the Georgia Institute of Technology Graphics, Visualization, & Usability (GVU) Center since 1994, for example, document use of the web for general business purposes and ways in which users find and make use of the information they obtain through browsing and searching.

2. See Gaskin (1997, 241-275) for a discussion of intellectual property issues and copyrights for a corporate audience. The acceptable use policy for materials on our site assumes that conventions established among colleagues for sharing paper materials still hold: syllabuses and assignments are not normally accompanied by information citing sources of inspiration, and faculty are welcome to download and adapt such material to their own purposes, while sources for signed works should be cited or preserved.

3. The *Yale C/AIM Web Style Guide* (http://info.med.yale.edu/caim/manual/interface/basic_interface2 .html) points out that intranet users tend to prefer menus with a minimum of five to seven links and experienced users in particular tend to prefer a few menus with a dense selection of choices over many layers of simplified menus.

4. See the intranet design guidelines presented by the Yale *C/AIM Web Style Guide* (http://info.med.yale.edu/caim/manual/interface/basic_interface2 .html). Graphics and multimedia can, however, be central to the goals of some work-related sites. For example, a site maintained by a hospital or medical school might present slides or video to illustrate a discussion of disease diagnosis.

5. Close to 14% of the respondents to the 1997 GVU survey report turning off image loading at least some of the time (http://www.gvu.gatech.edu/user_surveys/survey-1997-04/bulleted/use_bullets.html). A site that relies wholly on images for navigation or doesn't offer a no-frames alternative also excludes blind users and others who use alternative software (UT Team Web).

6. The Campuswide Writing Program at Indiana University at Bloomington, for example, provides an extensive bibliography of articles available in its library (http://www.indiana.edu/~wts/cwp/cwphome.htm).

7. The barriers to offering a web-based consultation service are organizational rather than technical. We cannot offer this service until it is clear that the staff members involved will have adequate time and support.

8. Webchat programs that enable real-time communication could also be used to make a website interactive. Although our writing center is exploring the use of such software for online consultations with students, real-time conferencing seems less likely to work with a faculty audience for whom one of the advantages of a website is the ability to access it and communicate with the writing center at their convenience.

CHAPTER FIVE

Have You Visited Your Online Writing Center Today?
Learning, Writing, and Teaching Online at a Community College

Clinton Gardner

ALTHOUGH THE PHYSICAL WRITING CENTER AT SALT LAKE COMMUNITY College (SLCC) has allowed us to reach many students and instructors, we still believe that a writing center is a "place without walls"; it is an idea; it is a place for discussion, for seeking, for sharing, and should not depend on particular physical locations. We like the idea of being "wall-less" because it posits that what we do in a writing center represents a better way to write, and should occur anywhere writing occurs. To fulfill this notion, we established the writing center at several physical locations throughout our multicampus community college with the idea that it could be a resource for both students and faculty. Nonetheless, we were concerned that the program was not reaching its largest possible audience. To reach students and faculty more effectively, we introduced the SLCC Online Writing Center.

The motives for broadening our outreach were based on several key assumptions about community college faculty and students. Both groups lead complex lives that preclude them from full participation in a writing center. Many students, for example, hold down a full-time job, or multiple low-paying part-time jobs[1]; attempt to take a full load of classes; often have parental obligations; and have to commute to work, day care, and (since many community colleges like SLCC do not have student housing) to school (Vaughan 1995, 18). Simultaneously, they struggle to make economic, personal, and academic ends meet[2]. George Vaughan from the Academy for Community College Leadership and Advancement, Innovation, and Modeling (ACCLAIM) describes the typical community college student as a "citizen-as-student" who ". . . is concerned with paying taxes, working full time, supporting a family, paying a mortgage, and with other responsibilities associated with the everyday role of a full-time citizen" (17). Vaughan differentiates the community college student from the traditional four-year college "student-as-citizen" who is "customarily perceived as being in a holding pattern, waiting until graduation to assume the rights and responsibilities that accompany full citizenship" (17). Unlike so-called traditional students (right out of high school with few obligations), we believed that on- and off-campus pressures make it difficult for community college students to take advantage of services like peer-response tutoring.

Community college instructors have similarly unsettled lives. Of the roughly 190,000 part-time community college instructors in the United States (Vaughan 19), most teach only one course per quarter (Vaughan 21; Spear, Seymour, and McGrath 1990, 23), yet lead, as Eugene Arden writes, " hectic lives, on killer schedules. Many . . . hold a full-time job elsewhere or . . . [manage] a household, in addition to moonlighting as adjuncts" (1995, A44). Nevertheless, George Vaughan shows that a substantial group of "dependent" part-time instructors "may teach at more than one community college during the same term, [and] depend upon the community college for much of their income, their professional contacts and, to a degree, their social life" (21). Even if the instructor attains full-time status, she often teaches five three-credit-hour courses per term (Vaughan 21), works on committees, oversees programs, and coordinates part-time faculty (Palmer 1992, 6062). Likewise, faculty often strive to keep current with their field, yet have little time to share their ideas, fears, or course goals with fellow instructors (Spear, Seymour, and McGrath 23-26; Palmer 1992, 62).

Still, when contemplating the difficulties students and faculty face, we saw that a community college provides exceptional benefits to both groups. For example, due to smaller class sizes and the higher number of instructors with several years of teaching experience, students can have a focussed and personalized educational experience that may not be available at other institutions. Likewise, because of economic constraints or previous performance in schooling, many students would not even have the chance at higher education without the community college(El-Khawas and Carter 1988, 20 and 22; Medsker 1960, 4). Furthermore, because of community colleges, it seems, many students change their view of their role in the community. Rather than seeing themselves as "remedial," many students grow to see themselves as critically astute citizens in a community of learners. Our experience has shown us, however, that students received fewer benefits from their college experience without the opportunity to make contact with instructors and fellow students.

Instructors benefit through having greater exposure to teaching first and second year students than is available at large research universities where scholarship is usually required, and graduate students teach most first and second semester composition courses. Because of their exposure to teaching, community college instructors can develop an experienced insight into first and second year composition that cannot be achieved through outside research alone (Palmer 1990, 33). Collaboration with colleagues enhances the instructor's insight. As with students, we know that if instructors do not have the opportunity to collaborate, their academic development will suffer.

Indeed, besides the hectic nature of their lives, community college faculty and students have few opportunities to share their experience and knowledge with colleagues either on or off campus. Furthermore, outside the writing center and the classroom, chances are rare for community college students and faculty to collaborate in *nontutorial, nonteacherly* setting with readers who are their *respondents* rather than their *instructors.*

The assumptions about the benefits community college faculty and students receive and problems they face lead us to the notion that a writing center could be the place to enhance community college educational opportunities. The community college mission privileges the notion that education should be available to those who seek it, and upholds the belief that learning derives from a collaborative, community effort.

The positive effects of collaborative education shaped our model writing center; yet, if we were not reaching a fuller audience, and if the people who were supposed to be collaborating could not share in the writing center, then would that paradigm really affect how individuals write and think about writing? To be beneficial to such an audience, a writing center must attempt to bring them together in ways that take into consideration the complexities of their lives. Our audience's constraints motivated us to figure out how we could better reach them.

A COMPUTER-BASED OUTREACH

We presumed that to reach more people, we would have to reduce the effects of time and space—the most complex aspect of their lives. In the late eighties and early nineties, SLCC instructors began to distribute information through computer networks. Initially this was only through a local area network, but, because of its universal conventions and accessibility, instructors began to use the internet. By the early nineties when we first used such technology in the writing center, teachers had been using computers for several years to connect students via email, electronic bulletin boards, or news lists. These resources were available at locations other than our writing center computer lab. Public libraries in the surrounding cities offered access to bulletin board systems like gopher, or collaborative sharing programs such as news lists. SLCC's campus labs offered those services as well as email and real-time chatting software. These electronic services, we supposed, might reduce the limitations of time and space.

Since instructors were using these resources already, we felt that using them in the writing center would bring our services to more locations and people. In these early stages we set up email tutoring, experimented with electronic bulletin boards, shared in news lists, and investigated some primitive real-time "chatting" software.

Nevertheless, during these early experimental stages few students and even fewer instructors used our resources. We conjectured that students and teachers did not know about the services available, did not know how to get to them, did not know how to use them, or, as the profile of their hectic lives suggests, did not have time to go to campus labs or the library to get to them. After considering our audience more fully, we came to the conclusion that the greatest obstacle for our audience was the lack of home access.

Impact of the Web

The World Wide Web has been one of the most important developments on the internet, since it spurred the desire for internet connectivity in the home[3]. It provided a unifying medium for our service and the impetus to develop our resources. The web is easy to use, is graphical, presents multimedia, and supports the easy distribution and linkage of information. Likewise, the web integrates many internet resources such as email, FTP, or Telnet. Because of its appeal, easy use, and its comprehensive application of internet protocols, the web gives writing centers an excellent outreach medium.

Electrifying the SLCC Writing Center

Our first web pages, created in 1994, merely offered information about the physical writing center: how people could make an appointment and where we could be found. This simple "bulletin board" approach revealed our rather unenlightened notion that the site could only advertise our physical writing center. After understanding our audience's need to contact the writing center from off campus, we soon replaced this bulletin board approach by broadening the pages to include information that related more to writing issues than schedules and locations.

The Next Step: the Online Writing Center

Soon after we posted our first web pages, we realized that there were many possible uses of this new medium. At that point we searched the web for other writing centers. We were particularly inspired by Purdue University's Online Writing Lab (OWL), one of the first attempts to bring a writing center to the web. At the time, it presented a variety of handbook-like resources about writing, as well as links to online tutoring. Through observing other early OWLs, we soon expanded our web pages to offer comprehensive writing center resource designed for our diverse audience.

We fashioned the SLCC Online Writing Center home page (see figure 1) to be a simple-to-use writing environment (Gardner 1997, "Welcome"). All information is succinct in order to make the site easier to read. A table of contents remains constant throughout the reading of the site because of web-based HTML frames[4]. The frames split the screen into two independent pages: the table of contents, and a space for viewing selected web links. To enhance readability further, a forthcoming index of the site will allow readers to find information by subject or keyword.

When the user selects a link in the table of contents, the reading frame switches to the linked document, but the table of contents remains the same. This constancy gives readers a point of reference so that they do not easily get lost. Many novice web users find the lack of connections between sources on some web pages frustrating. They will search the web, find a link that seems cogent, go to that link,

Figure 1
SLCC Online Writing Center Home Page

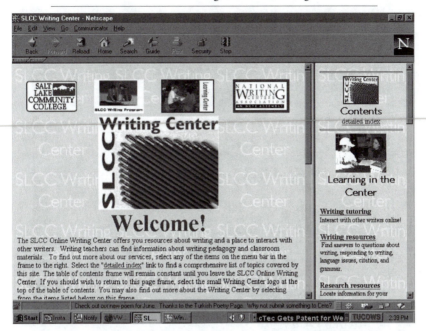

yet not know the purpose of what they are reading, or cannot go farther because of inconsistency in the web page. This experience often baffles the novice reader. Maintaining constant templates provides the reader the consistency of format they need to find their way through a site[5].

We keep the pages graphically simple to speed loading on slower internet connections and to lessen any confusion do to "graphics overload." Our images remind readers where they have been, help them track their way back, and hint at what the links associated with the graphics are. Such reminders are very important for new internet users, who lack experience using web browsers. Graphics also help the reader to identify sections of the online writing center without having to refer to manuals or help screens. We also want to make the SLCC Online Writing Center as human as possible; thus our graphics are mostly digitized photographs of people working in or around our physical writing center, or people in writing and learning situations (see figure 2).

The Frame is divided into three sections (two of which are visible). Note the use of icons to suggest the purpose of the sections. The icons used also serve to "humanize" the site by showing people in writing situations.

Keeping the Audience in the Center

The division of the table of contents into three major sections that represent our diverse audience enhances the readability and the relevance of the pages:

Figure 2
Detail: Table of Contents Frame

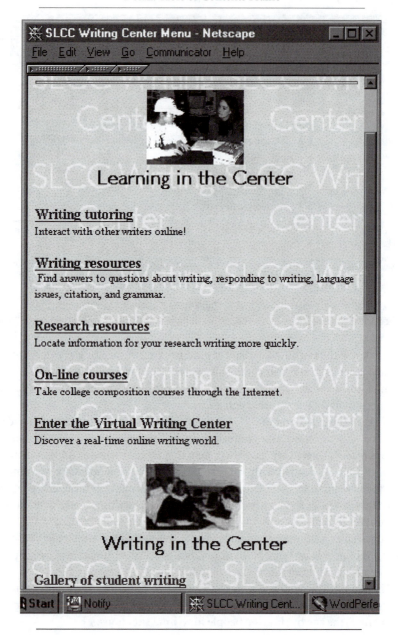

- Learning in the Center (for student writers);
- Teaching in the Center (for instructors);
- Writing in the Center (for both audiences, and others interested in writing).

Rather than segregating the readers by making one series of web pages for students and another for teachers, we mesh their endeavors by crafting one multipurpose, clearly-organized site. Unifying the site for students and faculty emphasizes that writing and learning are inseparable—that both groups engage in the activities the online writing center promotes. (See figure 3 for the architecture of the SLCC Online Writing Center. For more detailed information about the site, point your web browser to <http://www.slcc.edu/wc/index.html>.)

Reading the online flow chart (figure 3) from top to bottom, the reader "hits" the main page with the table of contents and can select her way through the site. The table of contents (see figures 1 and 2) remains constant throughout the navigation of the site, but disappears when the browser displays pages that the SLCC Writing Center does not maintain.

Learning in the Center. The first major subsection of the SLCC Online Writing Center, "Learning in the Center," offers student writers online tutoring, hypertext links to resources about writing and research on the internet, and specific pages and computer programs for the SLCC Writing Program and its courses. These services present a broad spectrum of ideas about writing, and offer different methods of writing response. For example, we offer links to writing and research information from a variety of other OWLs exemplifying different theoretical perspectives. Furthermore, we offer online tutoring both asynchronously through email and synchronously (in real time) through our MOO server, the Virtual Writing Center MOO (VWCMOO). We provide easy-to-understand online guides for both types of tutoring, and student writers may choose the system they feel the most comfortable with.

Writing in the Center. "Writing in the Center" is the SLCC Online Writing Center's core. It provides a place for students and faculty of a community college to share their writing with each other and the world through such resources as online student-edited community "E-zines" (see Hall 1997), or archives of instructors' writing (Gardner 1997 "Teachers Writing"). Generally, the writing represented is as diverse as the community it supports. We also offer a web "bulletin board" and real-time discussions on VWCMOO. On these systems writers share their writing, and discuss issues with others.

Teaching in the Center. The "Teaching in the Center" pages support writing instruction at Salt Lake Community College. Through resources ranging from weekly online discussions of computers and writing on VWCMOO (Gardner 1997, "MOO Discussions"), to course resources such as syllabi and curricular

Figure 3
Flow Chart

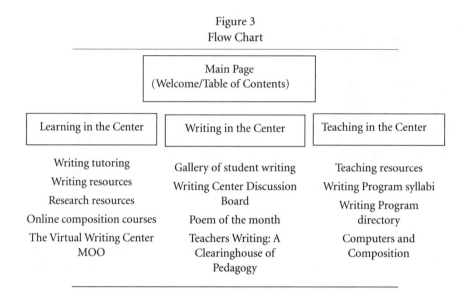

Main Page (Welcome/Table of Contents)		
Learning in the Center	Writing in the Center	Teaching in the Center
Writing tutoring	Gallery of student writing	Teaching resources
Writing resources	Writing Center Discussion Board	Writing Program syllabi
Research resources		Writing Program directory
Online composition courses	Poem of the month	
The Virtual Writing Center MOO	Teachers Writing: A Clearinghouse of Pedagogy	Computers and Composition

guidelines for writing courses, the writing center offers a place for instructors to collaborate with their colleagues at the college and from around the world.

A writing center's purpose is about writers and the complex process through which they create writing. Encouraging writers to submit their work and share in a broad discussion of writing, promotes the notion that a writing center (online or not) is a place to think about writing, to share writing, and to develop as a writer. Such a site is unique for many students and faculty at a community college since few publications are dedicated to their work and the discussion of that work. Moreover, for our audience few places exist, except the classroom or the physical writing center, that stimulate such writing and discussion. Although getting community members to submit their writing is difficult, students and faculty are beginning to submit their work as the SLCC Online Writing Center gains more attention.

As in the physical writing center, the SLCC Online Writing Center fosters a place to write and to discuss writing. Moreover, the online writing center provides different opportunities for sharing than can be found in the physical writing center. For example, because of spatial constraints and general inconvenience, collecting and sharing texts with a variety of people in the physical writing center is very difficult, whereas such an archive is readily attainable online.

CONCLUSION

Online services allow the SLCC Writing Center to reach students and faculty who might have previously felt marginalized because of their busy lives. Though the number of people currently using these resources is not overwhelming[6], use has increased as more students and faculty discover the Internet[7]. Centering the

SLCC Online Writing Center on the specific concerns of its community college audience encourages continued growth. A community college online writing center provides a place for overwhelmed students and faculty to center themselves on academic work in the midst of very complex lives.

Through developing the online writing center, we have gained an important insight: the SLCC Online Writing Center is not merely a transferal of our "real" writing center to a computer mediated setting. Online services shape how we view the physical writing center and broaden what it has to offer. In a sense, our assumptions about audience's demography have become less important. While we believe that busy students and instructors have fewer chances to use the physical writing center, an online component is becoming essential to what we do with *any* student, not just the ones who cannot come in person. Going online has given us fresh insight into the role of the writing center and what happens in a place that has fewer physical constraints to it. We built our physical writing center around the idea that a writing center is, in essence, wherever writing occurs. The SLCC Online Writing Center realizes that idea.

NOTES

1. According to U.S. Census data, nearly 51% of community college students have a full time job. The same data indicates that roughly 10% of traditional four-year college students have full-time jobs (Vaughan 1995, 18).

2. Recently, our assumptions were corroborated through a writing center survey. We found that 40% of the surveyed students who have heard of our services, but did not come in, claimed that they were "too busy" to visit the writing center (Thompson 1997) We surveyed 145 Salt Lake Community College students in composition courses English 99,101, and 102 at the beginning of Summer Quarter 1997. 114 (76.3%) of the students had heard of the writing center prior to being surveyed (Thompson 1997).

3. Like many online writing labs (OWLs) on the internet today, the SLCC Online Writing Center exits primarily in the web (Pegg 1997). Through these pages we have integrated our offerings, and they are presented seamlessly to the web user. The web pages reflect the services we wish to offer our patrons. To ensure our pages respond to our audience, we put together a faculty advisory committee that oversees the general direction of the online writing center. I am chair of that committee and am editor/implementer of the online writing center. I have regularly polled online writing center users to gain their perceptions of the readability of the site, and how it might be improved. Both response from the advisory board and information from the polls have shaped the direction that the takes.

4. An excellent site to learn advanced HTML coding is *A Beginner's Guide to HTML* by The National Center for Supercomputing Applications (1997).

5. Since some web authors are wary of using frames, other OWLs will often create a similar "menu bar" by using a common format and appearance for all of their pages.

To forgo problems for users with less powerful systems that cannot support frames, we have created a "no frames" version of the SLCC Online Writing Center which contains the same information as the frames version (Gardner 1997 "No Frames"). A fine example of a repeating format is at the University of Michigan's *Online Writing & Learning* (1997). This page presents a common interface throughout its various pages.

6.   Although it is difficult to account for usage of the resources, we do collect several statistics: the online writing center home page, for example, has approximately 800 page hits per month, but our other pages average approximately 100 hits per month. A hit is counted whenever a web browser reads the pages. Our email tutoring was about 2% of our total tutoring effort during the 1996-97 academic year. This usage seems low, but it has increased from .5% the previous year.

7.   As the previously mentioned writing center survey showed, 45.9% of the sampled students claim to have internet access at home, and 76.4% of the respondents claimed to have a computer at home (Thompson 1997). This rather surprising percentage indicates the potential internet access of our audiences. Because the prices of appropriate computers are dropping, internet access is fairly cheap, and the general appeal of the World Wide Web, it seems likely that soon most of the students with computers at home will also have access to the internet.

CHAPTER SIX

The Other WWW
Using Intranets to Reconfigure the Who, When and Where of Network-Supported Writing Instruction

Kurt P. Kearcher

*T*HERESA, A HIGH SCHOOL SOPHOMORE, SITS AT ONE OF THE DOZEN OR SO computers in the common computer lab of her school. There is a sporadic clicking of keys as the three other students in the room, none of whom Theresa knows, work at computers. Theresa sighs; she is nowhere near having a draft for tomorrow's peer review session. She does have a couple of paragraphs and a page of brainstormed words and phrases, but she wants something that at least resembles an essay—title, thesis sentence, five or so paragraphs, double-spacing, one-inch margins—by tomorrow morning so her teacher will give her credit for it.

She sighs again, lays one hand on the computer's mouse and stares into the screen of the computer monitor. The computer's desktop has several icons lined up in a neat row. Among these are icons for standard computer programs: a word processor, a spreadsheet, a graphics program, and a World Wide Web browser. Theresa deftly uses the mouse to place the on-screen cursor on the browser icon. She clicks the mouse button. As she waits for the program to open, she glances out the window and thinks about the after school pep rally she's missing. She sighs again.

The browser finishes loading and her school's home page appears. She moves her cursor past the lunch menu and sports schedule links and clicks on the link titled "Write to Know." Her school page disappears and a new one appears. It has just a couple of graphic images, so it loads quickly. Dull, thinks Theresa, but fast. Theresa enters her username and password when she is prompted to do so and then clicks on a button to submit this information to the network server. A new page appears on the screen with the following message:

Hello, Theresa! Glad you dropped by. How are things today?

Theresa mumbles a response and reads further.

Here's what's going on at Write to Know right now:
At Plato's Place of Pondering, KarenK, Overide5, and Bomber3025 are chatting.

The Teachers' Lounge is quiet, and the lights are off.
In The Writing Center, MsMullin is sipping coffee and waiting to talk with someone about writing. *Watch for the new video conferencing link coming soon!*
The Commons is featuring Poetry 4 Reading, a collection of poems written by members of the Write to Know intranet community.
You can also connect to other Writing Related Resources:
Writing Basics—A Searchable Collection of Information on Writing
Essays of Interest—A Searchable Collection of Essays

Theresa reads through the list of these and other links that use the internet to connect her to any of these sites that, together, constitute the Northwest Ohio Writing Education Consortium intranet. She is inclined to go to the "3 Ps" to talk about her writing assignment with the people logged onto that chat room, but the last time she went there, she spent her time talking about music instead of writing. MsMullin is logged onto another chat channel, "The Writing Center." Theresa doesn't know much about MsMullin, except that she helps people with their writing—at least that's what Theresa has heard from some of her friends. She considers checking to see if anyone has posted a comment about the poem she published on "The Commons," an electronic bulletin board system for student writing, but she reminds herself of the task at hand and clicks on the "Writing Basics" link instead. The following text appears on a new page:

Welcome to Writing Basics
A Source for "How To" Information About Writing
Please select the kind of writing you are working on and what part of the writing process you want to know How To do. Click the Go button when you are done.

- Planning
- Writing the First Draft
- Revising
- Editing and Proofreading
- Writing with a Computer
- Writing on the intranet
- Poem

- Writing in General
- Essay
- Research Paper
- Journal
- Letter
- Book Review
- Story

Well, Theresa thinks, I have some ideas, and I really need to have my first draft for tomorrow, so. . . . She clicks the "Writing a First Draft" and "Essay" boxes to select them and then clicks on the "Go" button to begin the search. As she waits for the computer to process her search request, Theresa leans back in her chair and stares at the screen, which is quickly filling with links to information related to her search items. "Man!," she exclaims, "this could take a while."

VIRTUAL WRITING PROCESSES AND EVERYDAY WRITING PRACTICES

Theresa's writing task—preparing a rough draft of an essay for peer review—is part of a widely shared process approach to writing. Her responses to the task—jotting a few items down, making some tentative starts at paragraphs, waiting until the night before to compose the draft—are recognizable as fairly typical student responses to writing assignments. What is not typical about Theresa's writing experience is the access she has to computer network technology and a variety of online writing resources that have been specifically developed for her and other members of her online writing community. This centralized access increases the number of options Theresa can exercise at any given point in her writing process, requiring her to make decisions about her process. She is, in practice, designing a particular process to address a particular writing situation.

Theresa is still at work half an hour later. She finishes writing in her notebook and puts down her pen. The information she has found on using a thesis statement to focus her thinking and her essay has been very useful. She is pretty sure the thesis sentence she has written does a good job of tying together the paragraphs she had written earlier. She was also able to use some of her brainstorming ideas to begin writing two more paragraphs. A thesis sentence and four paragraphs—now she's getting somewhere, she thinks. But she wants to be sure what she has written makes sense. She grabs the mouse, moves the cursor to the "Home" button, and clicks. She is returned to the Write to Know homepage. Theresa anxiously glances at the list of current activities. Good, she thinks, MsMullin is still in "The Writing Center." Theresa clicks on the link and glances at her notebook while she waits for the computer to connect to the chat room. A new window appears on the screen. It is a text chat box, which will allow Theresa and Ms. Mullin to have a conversation by typing messages to one another.

Theresa: hi
MsMullin: Hi, my name is Ms. Mullin. What's your name?.
T: Theresa
MM: Hello, Theresa. How may I help you?
T: hi. i want to now if my thesis sentence and pargraphs go together
MM: Okay. Do you have a file I can look at?
T: ???
MM: Have you made a text file of your writing that you can upload to the Postmodern?
T: no
MM: Looking at the document would be very helpful. We can talk about your thesis sentence and paragraphs without one, but it will be more difficult. Do you want to go ahead and talk now or come back later after you have had a chance to type in your document?

Theresa looks at the clock on her screen: 3:47. She has to type the draft anyway, and she is pretty sure she's on the right track.

T: how late will you be in your room?

MM: I will be here online until six, but a consultant will be in The writing center until 10 tonight. We can work now, or you can make an appointment to work later. What would you like to do?

T: how do you make a file?

MM: For more information on making text files and sharing them on the network, go to "Writing Basics," select "Writing on the Intranet" and "Writing in General," and click on "Go." Find the link that says "File Sharing on the Intranet"—or something like that. It will tell you how to send a file to the Postmodern.

T: thanks. ill type my stuff and make a file you can look at. i should be done soon.

MM: It's almost 4 now. Would you like to make an appointment to come back at 4:30 or 5:00?

T: yes

MM: Would you like to come back at 4:30 _or_ 5:00?

T: 5

MM: I will talk to you then, Theresa. Bye.

T: bye

Theresa logs out of the chat room, follows the World Wide Web links to the information on file sharing, scans the information to get a basic idea of how to create the file she needs, prints a copy of the instructions for later reference, quits the web browser, opens the document processing application and begins typing. As she types, she adds a couple of sentences to each of her existing paragraphs. When she finishes typing, she spellchecks her document, saves it to her folder, saves another copy, according to the instructions she printed, to a public folder, and then transfers a copy to "The Writing Center" folder, where MsMullin will be able to retrieve it.

Theresa looks at the clock: 5:07. Oops, I'm late, she thinks. As she opens the interrelay chat application and makes the connection to "The Writing Center," she hopes her conference won't take too long. Maybe, she hopes as she clicks on "The Writing Center" link, I'll catch the end of the pep rally.

THE IDEA OF AN INTRANET WRITING COMMUNITY

The assignment Theresa addresses in her after-school writing session is familiar to those who teach writing. Marked by current writing theory, it is process-based and incorporates collaboration. Theresa's approach also evidences more "traditional" writing instruction: it emphasizes the formal characteristics of the essay—itself a traditional academic form of writing. This combination of contemporary methodology and traditional form creates an interesting tableau of secondary writing instruction curriculums, which must constantly re-invent themselves to respond to—and often conform to—the demands placed upon them by local, state, and federal governmental bodies, which are in turn influenced by business, industry, higher education, and other cultural institutions.

Amid this profusion of institutional structures, however, Theresa is able to put together an approach to her writing task that enables her to respond to conventional writing instruction through the exercise of her own, self-constructed, writing practice. Her practice, based less on the strategies of writing provided by theories and curriculums of writing instruction and more on the tactics of the student writer herself, takes advantage of the resources afforded her by her access to online writing resources.

Michel de Certeau (1984, xix) has defined strategy as "the calculus of force-relationships which becomes possible when a subject of will and power ... can be isolated from an 'environment.'" In this case, I am presenting schools that are organized in ways that are grounded in the regulation of locations and times of instruction—most schools—as the "subject of will and power." This isolation allows the "subject of will and power" to generate "relations with an exterior distinct from it. . . . " In other words, schools create their identities, or relationships to others, by regulating the locations, or spaces, of instruction and the times of instruction in ways that differentiate it from everyday life. In contrast to a strategy, a tactic is

> a calculus which cannot count on a "proper" (a spatial or institutional) localization, nor thus on a borderline distinguishing the other as a visible totality. The place of a tactic belongs to the other. A tactic insinuates itself into the other's place, fragmentarily, without taking it over in its entirety, without being able to keep it at a distance. It has at its disposal no base where it can capitalize on its advantages, prepare its expansions, and secure independence with respect to circumstances. (Certeau xix)

Tactics in education, then, can be thought of as being practiced by those who seek to construct their own approaches to learning within the teaching and learning structures of the institution. Teachers use tactics when they use classroom time in a manner not directly regulated by a curriculum-driven administrative structure. Students engage in tactics when they pass notes during a lecture or daydream while another student is at the board diagramming sentences. In Certeau's relationship between these two approaches to "everyday practice," a strategy relies on "a victory of space over time," while a tactic "depends on time" (xix). The result is that a tactic, when employed by a student, "is always on the watch for opportunities that must be seized 'on the wing.'" The tactic-practicing student must "constantly manipulate events in order to turn them into 'opportunities.'"

The result, or "intellectual synthesis," of combining the various information derived from these tactical opportunities is not to be found in something one can necessarily point to, but in "the decision itself, the act and manner in which the opportunity is 'seized'" (Certeau xix). In short, Theresa, as a tactician, took advantage of the fact that 1) she had the time to work outside the traditional constraints of the class period and 2) she had access to documents and people who, while working within the structure (and often the employ) of a strategizing institution, were separated enough from the "spatial or institutional localization" (Certeau xix) of that institution to create a number of "heterogeneous elements" that could be combined, on the one hand, to produce a draft of an essay that included a thesis statement and paragraphs—a discourse—and on the other hand, to produce a *critical* experience and a *critical* act recognizable as a critical thinking activity to be valued in and of itself.

This shift from institutionally-based writing instruction *strategy* to learner-based writing *tactic* is the result of providing access to the textual and human resources that comprise the everyday reality of the institution. The critical elements of this concern are who will have access to what features of writing instruction and where and when they will have it. The relative flexibility Theresa has in determining who will be involved in her writing process (peers, instructors, writing consultants, herself), where that process will take place (the classroom, the computer lab, her home, a variety of virtual electronic spaces, or elsewhere) and when that process will take place (during her English class, during other class time, before or after school) is made possible by using currently available *internet* technology to construct an *intranet* writing community, a learning community that supports a tactical rather than strategic approach to literacy education.

Certeau's account of tactic and strategy is interestingly echoed by two recent comments on how an intranet redistributes institutional authority. "From a user perspective," Michael Taylor (1997, 40) wrote, "an intranet provides more control over information, making it possible to get what you want, when and where you want it." And according to Glenn Haseck (1996, 65), "Unlike the internet, which typically involves a few individuals communicating to many people, intranets involve many people communicating with many people. This chapter presents the "idea" of an intranet community developed to facilitate secondary writing instruction by providing student-selectable alternatives to the traditionally managed classroom, a classroom whose identity is based on locating particular people in a particular physical space during a particular time period. Forming intranet writing communities allows opportunities to rethink how writing instruction will be managed by affording students, instructors, administrators, and others who belong to the intranet writing community (including students, instructors, and administrators from other traditionally-defined schools and people unaffiliated with traditional educational institutions) opportunities to make instructional or informational choices based more on a writer's need to have access to a variety of writing resources during a variety of hours and from a variety of locations rather than on the needs of the institution to organize and regulate such access to conform to a notion of the work day that may no longer serve people's educational needs.

What the technology and design of the intranet promise is a way to rethink the organization of writing instruction by challenging two critical determinants of instructional organization and management: location and time. The intranet provides the opportunity to move away from the concept of the classroom, the class period and the requisite class management associated with both. The technology necessary to make this next move is available now at a reasonable although not insignificant cost. But, like Theresa's uses of technology described earlier, this technology can be used in a myriad of ways, ranging from replicating the traditional English classroom to challenging the notions of writing as a skill best learned in those classrooms.

THE INTRANET: SOMETHING OLD, SOMETHING NEW

The intranet, a relatively new but fast-growing use of current internet technology, has been developed primarily to support intracorporate and intragovernmental communications. A "domesticated internet" (Trowbridge 1996), it uses existing internet pathways and platforms to provide corporate and governmental information and communication services, from lunch menus to video conferencing, once handled by costly and limited dedicated information systems. Because an intranet is developed to serve the specific needs of a specific community—large or small—it often stands in contrast to current perceptions of the internet. As Trowbridge has pointed out:

> On the web, the emphasis has been on "recreational surfing" in a setting that is often indistinguishable from anarchy. Organizational users enjoy a more organized environment and thus have an entirely different set of application requirements. The technologies of the internet can indeed be very useful in an organizational setting but they must be "domesticated"—integrated in a fashion that observes organizational realities. (52)

Trowbridge's touting the ability of an intranet to organize corporate (and educational) environments in a manner that "observes organizational realities" serves well as a promise and a warning. Intranets, like other technologies, both shape and are shaped by the more general cultures in which they exist. It is therefore important to carefully consider what type of community is to be connected by an intranet. An intranet writing community may or may not reflect the current organization of educational institutions into classrooms, grade levels, school buildings and school districts at the primary, secondary and post-secondary levels. An intranet writing community may or may not reflect the traditional hierarchy of administrator, instructor, student, and "general public." Theresa's experience, for example, contains many recognizable elements of current writing instruction associated with classroom teaching: approaching writing as a process; an emphasis on publication; support for collaboration, peer response and conferencing; and support for the connection between reading and writing. There are also obvious differences: Theresa is not in a traditional classroom; she can choose from a variety of approaches, resources and people rather than the one approach selected by the classroom instructor; and she is free to move from place to place, depending upon how effectively each place addresses her needs. These differences in approaches to the teaching and learning of writing are made possible by changes in 1) the technologies available to support writing instruction, 2) the use of these technologies to manage writing instruction, and 3) the rethinking of the writing classroom as a writing community.

AN ALTERNATIVE APPROACH TO TECHNOLOGY AND WRITING INSTRUCTION

Using current internet technologies to support intranets provides flexibility in determining what information will be made available to users, in what form (textual, graphic, interactive event) that information will be made available, and who will have access to all or some of the available information. Whereas the limits of computer technologies once determined how we could use them to support collaborative, process-based approaches to writing instruction, the new internet information and communication technologies challenge us to make full use of their potential to support writing instruction.

Many writing classrooms currently use computers to support student writers, but as the role of computers in writing instruction shifts from one of speeding up word processing to one of providing access to a wide range of writing-related information through email, the World Wide Web, and other online resources, writing classrooms will need to reconsider the role of technology in writing instruction.

When computers first began to be used as part of writing instruction, they were little more than high-powered typewriters. Their innovation lay in their ability make the writer's job of document management an easier one by offering the ability to cut, copy, and paste text within and between documents and to store many pages of writing on a single 5 1/4" floppy disk. One could also print copies of these files, which a student writer could spellcheck before submission to the writing instructor. Word processing became a commonplace activity in a student's preparation of a document for submission to an instructor. Whereas legible penmanship and minimal crossings out once had been indicators of careful editing, correct margins and properly placed page numbers became the marker of scribal abilities.

Stand alone computers were soon linked together by cables, and local area network (LAN) computer classrooms came into being. No longer did each computer have to monopolize a printer. Several computers could be connected to a single printer. In advanced networked classrooms, instructors at the instructor or teacher stations located at the front or back of the classroom could project samples of student writing on a screen using an overhead projector and a liquid crystal display. Others in the classroom could watch as the student or instructor revised the draft in front of the classroom members. Students could then submit their final drafts by having them downloaded to the teacher's computer, where the teacher could retrieve them for evaluation. The paperless writing classroom had been achieved.

At the same time computers were being used for word processing and file management, they were also being used to provide computer assisted instruction (CAI), which consisted primarily of drill tutorials and Socratic dialogues that assisted students through the writing process of prewriting, drafting, revising, and editing.

Fairly recently, computers have been connected to larger networks, including the internet, and students now have access not only to word processing but also to electronic mail, electronic bulletin boards, chat rooms, electronic mailing lists devoted to special topics, and research reference sources once available only in a library. The bookless classroom has come hard on the heels of the paperless one, and students can now conduct research from one location, their internet-connected computer terminal.

Marjorie Montague (1990, 100) has touted the promise of such a computer-assisted, process-based writing pedagogy to provide "a context where writing processes can be taught effectively and reinforced and where students become motivated and enthusiastic about writing." Montague, citing Daiute, has listed the following advantages of a "computer writing environment" (98) over the traditional classroom: the writing is more personal; the curriculum is student-centered; instruction is individualized; students have more practice in writing at all stages of the writing process; students are encouraged by computer-assisted instruction to participate more actively in the writing process; it reduces anxiety and increases risk-taking; reduces writer's block; and it facilitates both surface and deep revision. When Montague made her observations, "electronic networks" were equated almost exclusively with email, a mode of electronic discourse that had even greater promise than computers themselves to promote collaboration among student writers.

But even as the sophistication and flexibility of technology grew, writing instruction as a whole remained relatively unchanged. Instructors still chose the textbooks, made the assignments, and managed the classroom. As the technology changed, educators struggled with inventing new ways to manage the technologies, ways that frequently reflected traditional pedagogical approaches—particularly teacher-centered classrooms.

An intranet approach to instruction uses currently available computer technologies to support a more decentralized and interactive learning environment by simplifying the movement of information to the point where users can make use of the technology to support their writing without spending a great deal of time contending with the technology itself. Accessibility and usability lead to greater opportunities for participation and the formation of very real virtual, or electronic, communities. Such communities are defined less by the management of teachers and administrators and more by those who belong to them, particularly those who are expected to contribute the most—students. "Students," George Landow has remarked, "who frequently comment that they have encountered texts by friends and acquaintances, experience a particular kind of community with an ongoing history and culture" (Tuman 1992, 110). This community, Landow also notes, frequently extends beyond the time and place defined by a particular class or course.

In addition to extending the boundaries of the traditional writing community, computers can, Helen Schwartz has observed, "help us picture collaboration and its consequences differently, not as a metaphor or theory but as a new and tangible thing" (Tuman 112-13). An intranet, then, would help writing communities move current writing theories toward another practicable reality by facilitating the restructuring of instruction and learning time and establishing protocols for communicating among community members. In doing so, it would both enable and prevent members in their literate practices; it would be both responsive and resistant to community manipulation. In other words, it would behave like a technology—both passive and aggressive in its interaction with people. Not all educational institutions will be prepared to or interested in supporting the alternative literacy community promised by an intranet, but for those who are interested and able to make a commitment of technology, time, and personnel, there are benefits to be realized from community membership.

ESTABLISHING A CONCEPT OF THE INTRANET

Tobin Anthony (1996) has offered the following vision to potential intranet designers:

> I like to think of an Intranet as a concept, rather than a physical mass of network hardware and chattering computers. Your Intranet users will utilize services that you'll develop and nurture. These services will grow in scope and sophistication along with your growing administrative expertise. . . . I like to think of your Intranet as an amorphous information entity that encompasses and enhances the lives of your coworkers. (1)

But before investing in the hardware and software needed to achieve Anthony's "amorphous information entity"—or a more modest writing community intranet—it is essential that the intranet be carefully planned. This planning will involve rhetorical assessments of purpose and audience in order to better determine the technologies required to achieve the information processing goals established by such rhetorical analysis. In addition, purpose and technologies will need to be adjusted to reflect the realities of limited finances and technical support. If it is determined that intranet members who have modems connected to their computers should be able to connect to the server via those modems, then certain types of data transmission that are very intensive, like large graphics, audio, and video, may not be useful. Text-based data with minimal graphics would be a better choice in such circumstances. And of course, pedagogies would need to be adjusted to reflect these choices.

A school system- or consortium-sponsored intranet could provide electronic bulletin boards and chat rooms; email conferences and list services; online writing reference resources; online interactive tutorials, virtual communities (MOOs and MUDs) in which students and teachers could meet to discuss their writing; online workshops, including print materials, slide shows, and audio and video files for both student and teacher development; World Wide Web links to other internet resources related to writing and writing instruction; and other intranet and internet resources. These components could be combined to form a relatively modest information posting and exchange system using web pages, email, and file exchange, to sophisticated interactive communities using extensive use of audio and video technology. A single building could support an intranet, as could an entire school district or state school system. But the scale of the intranet has to be such that it is small enough to reflect the individual, perhaps unique, needs and concerns of its members while also being large enough to provide enough diversity to promote change and growth through the sharing of ideas and practices.

Planning the Intranet

Whether an internet-technology based network is used to facilitate the sending of text files for evaluation by an instructor or the gathering of several student writers to collaborate on a writing project, there are basic considerations in putting together such a network. Many writing-related computer networks have failed to live up to the visions of their implementors because of inadequate—or absent—planning. It is important that a comprehensive plan be developed in putting together an intranet writing community, a plan that carefully analyzes the community's purpose, population, organization, technology resources and finances.

The advice Cynthia Selfe (1990 "Computers") has provided for post-secondary English departments applies to any institution planning to support writing instruction with technology: make technology a learning community rather than strictly technological issue, thereby involving more people in the decision making process; make technology decisions reflect community goals; remember that the needs of people, not technology, should be emphasized; and place community issues before technological ones. John B. Dykeman (1997) has provided suggestions similar to Selfe's but tailors them to a business community. As the lines between education, business, and other institutions blur, it is important to plan technology use in a way that takes into account points of shared interests and points of contention.

Like writing itself, planning an intranet is a recursive and flexible process. While the following description of one approach to planning an intranet presents determining content type before assessing actual network resources, both factors, need to be considered together. Ultimately, the shape of the intranet will be formed through a sifting of the various factors into a coherent plan of action.

According to Bob Wallace (1996), the first consideration in forming an intranet is determining content type. Content type is different from content in that the former denotes the form that actual content will take. Content type affects the speed at which information can move through the intranet and the sophistication of the computer hardware and software needed to use that information. Small electronic files, such as text-based web pages, text files, and email files, move quickly along even "slow" network connections such as a dial up connection via a modem. Most computers in use today can also accommodate text-based communications. Likewise, interactive text-based communications like internet Relay Chat (IRC) work well with relatively unsophisticated networks. Large files, such as video and audio files, and large bandwidth communications technologies, such as video conferencing, however, require high speed connections to be effective. Matching the kinds of information and communication made available on an intranet to the capacity of the intranet to process and transfer it between users is critical.

Wallace has also suggested that procedures for posting information and conducting communications exchanges on the network must be established. It may, in fact, be in the best interest of the network community to limit the use of audio and video on the network, perhaps reserving it for special occasions such as one-to-one tutoring or conferencing. Providing widespread access to audio and video features can quickly tax the resources of an intranet network server, the computer that stores and processes the intranet information. If audio and video files are used, say to provide poets reading their works or an act from a production of *King Lear*, the systems administrator may well want to require that users first download a file and then play it back locally using the processing resources of the user's computer, rather than playing it in real time and using the intranet server's resources.

Content, according to Wallace, must also be controlled in order to guard against overloading the resources of the intranet server. It is important to note that Wallace is advocating control of content based on the total amount of information being processed rather than on a particular point of view. The format of the content file (text, video, audio) combined with the size and number of such files determines the amount of storage space and processing power required of the server computer. Determining who will select content is a matter of community concern.

Managing the Intranet

At this point it is a good idea to consider carefully who will be managing the intranet server or servers, the computer or combination of computers that store and process information for the intranet. This "webmaster" should be someone with considerable computer and networking experience. However, it is also important that the person responsible for managing the information on the server be someone who has a strong theoretical and practical grasp of the relationship between the construction and maintenance of the server, the content it provides, and the community it serves. This is also a good spot to insist that the manager of the intranet server be considered a full-time position. If a server is to assist a community in remaining dynamic and viable, then there must be someone available to facilitate that robustness.

Three models can guide the management of an intranet server. The first, managed access, restricts the access content developers and other community members have to the workings of the server itself. Centralized access, the second approach, places the server administrator in control of the installation of all approved content. The third model, distributed access, consists of a team of administrators managed by a central administrator .

Managed access allows community members to publish personal home pages in files they have been assigned by the systems administrator, but it would also deny them access to other parts of the server. Community members would be able to place content on the server with little or no restriction. In this model, the webmaster maintains the server hardware and software integrity and creates accounts for the intranet members but does not control content. The webmaster is essentially a technician in this scheme (Anthony 123-24).

A centralized access model places a central administrator in charge of all content changes to the intranet. Unlike the managed access approach, community members would not be allowed to directly upload files to the server but would have to have them placed on the server by the central administrator. While a centralized access model runs counter to the communal nature of the intranet, it may be a pragmatic approach to server management if the community is constituted by relatively unsophisticated users who do not frequently "post" information to the server. However, if the intranet is to be more than just an administrative vehicle for disseminating selected information, one prerequisite for community membership might be enough technological literacy to allow the intranet to operate at the level of managed access (Anthony 124).

The distributed-access strategy empowers a centralized team of developers to create intranet content. One administrator coordinates the actions of the other team members, who are responsible for editing, converting, and archiving information provided by the community members. This approach is often employed by large corporations who feel the need to carefully manage the information content provided by employees (Anthony 125).

While the management strategy adopted by any one intranet community will reflect the needs of that community, there is an obvious "sliding scale" of centralized control as one moves from managed access toward distributed access. Centralized and distributed access appear too tightly controlled to allow for the high level of interaction necessary if theories of collaborative learning and process writing are going to be realized in an electronic writing community. The greatest benefits of the these administration-focused approaches, their consistency and regulation, are gained at the expense of dynamism and collaboration. In a community constituted by technologically literate members, or in a community provided with technology that is relatively easy to use and guidelines for using that technology that are consistent and minimal, managed access provides the best opportunity to realize truly collaborative approaches to literacy development.

When community members are able to not only access information but to publicly post it for other community members, they are placed in a truly literate environment, one that demands they actively, and ethically, engage in constructing a language environment that is responsive and responsible to all members.

Connecting the Intranet

Once matters of planning content and access, as well as administration, have been addressed, attention can productively be paid to the specific hardware and software needs of the intranet. Obviously, the server computer must be connected, either physically through a wired network or via a cellular phone connection, to each of its client computers. It must also be able to exchange information with those client computers. This data exchange is facilitated through the adoption of protocols, or standard ways computers communicate with each other. The two most important protocols for internet connections are TCP (Transmission Control Protocol) and IP (Internet Protocol). These protocols greatly reduce the incompatibility problems associated with using different computer platforms (PC, Macintosh, Sun, etc.).

Since one of the appeals of the intranet is the fact that it uses existing internet protocols and network connections, it is important to plan how these connections will be made. Because most server computers will be connected to a local area network (LAN), which will then be connected to the wider internet, it is important to consider how the server, its locally connected computer clients and the distant clients connected by an ethernet or modem connection will be "webbed" together to form the intranet.

First, planners should determine how the various computers will be physically connected to one another and to the internet. Beginning with the intranet's connection to the internet and working "down" to each desktop computer, they will need to produce a comprehensive diagram of the intranet's wiring. With this information, they should reconsider how the intranet will be used in light of the speed at which it is able to transfer data from the server to each of the clients. The speed at which data can be transmitted to the various parts of your intranet will be a significant determining factor, if not the determining factor, in making pedagogical choices. It matters little that an instructor or student has a very fast desktop computer if the information traveling to and from that computer is crawling along a slow modem connection. Decisions regarding the location of network clusters should not be made without considering the impact of network speed on how the computers in those clusters can be used effectively.

If the intranet server is going to make use of an existing LAN (Local Area Network), such as a computer classroom, it will probably be wired together using a 10BaseT cabling system. While there are newer and faster cable configurations, 10BaseT should be fast enough to handle all but the most data intensive communications, like high quality video conferencing. If both the server and the client are communicating on a very high speed network and there is a desire to use high quality video conferencing, the faster 100BaseT, which can move ten times the amount of information moved by 10BaseT, might be warranted. Planners should remember, however, that content type requiring such high speed connections will be all but useless to anyone who must rely on a slower network connection. There are other cabling systems out there, both older and newer than the currently common 10BaseT, so the current network administrator should be consulted in order to determine what system will best serve the community's specific needs.

If the intranet server will be called upon to direct a great deal of network traffic to a variety of locations, planners should consider the use of a router to direct the information flow. A router, also called a gateway, can be a regular computer running routing software or a piece of hardware designed specifically for routing data to its appropriate destination of the network.

Once local connections are made to create local networks, those LANs will need to be connected to the internet itself. Since the intranet being promoted in this chapter may have to span significant distances in order to connect its community members, it will need to make use of the globe-spanning internet. This connection to the internet and its vast resources, however, comes at a cost to the community. Security must be carefully considered because gaining access to the internet means the internet also gains access to the information shared by the intranet community. Therefore, specific guidelines for accessing the intranet, including security measures such as a user identification and password combination, will need to be provided to all users.

There are many ways to connect to the internet. Most post-secondary education institutions and some secondary schools have their own high speed connections known as T1 or T3 lines. These lines can pass a great deal of data very quickly; therefore, the intranet server and any clients that will be used for intense information processing, such as video conferencing, should have such a connection. Some schools and most individuals use an internet Service Provider (ISP) to gain access to the internet via a modem that connects a computer to a standard telephone line. Compared to T1 and T3 lines, even the fastest modems are slow. In determining how information will be shared on the intranet, the disparity between connections must be considered. A user connecting via a modem, even a fast modem, will not be able to use intranet resources in the same way someone with a fast direct connection can.

One of the great appeals of the internet is its ability to serve a community that is not located within a limited geographical area. Planners may, therefore, want to enable their intranet community members to access their intranet from a remote site, a site not identified as a stable part of the network. Remote access enables community members to use intranet resources from any computer with internet access, providing high levels of mobility to community members. Two protocols that will allow a computer to emulate a TCP/IP connection, SLIP and PPP, enable community members to read their email or surf the net from any phone connection.

Selecting an Intranet Server

Once it has been established how the computers that make up the intranet are connected to one another, a server computer must be selected. This intranet server is responsible for providing a "home" for the software necessary to process information to and from the other client computers belonging to the intranet, as well as storing the various files that will be distributed to intranet members.

Selecting a computer to act as an intranet server requires planning that addresses the intranet's immediate and future uses. For most networks—those that receive limited numbers of hits, or connections, per day—any fairly new computer with a reasonably fast processor speed, adequate data storage space, and enough RAM will do. Typically, what slows networks is not the processor speed of the connected computers but the speed at which data can travel over the network wiring. Usually, the server computer can provide as many files as the network connection can handle. If all the server is doing is providing static web pages or other text files, little strain will be placed on the server—and most intranet servers will likely begin with such static text files. However, as community members want to make use of dynamic files like audio and video, the processing ability of the server becomes much more important. As users enrich online content with graphics, photos, and other elements that make text documents more visually appealing, the size of those document files will swell. A breaking point might be reached when the server is required to respond to dynamic content requests such as database searches, real-time video, etc. and must process tremendous amounts of information in order to serve up the requested data. Providing searchable content, forms, instructional processing, etc. is processor-intensive work. If the community has a need for this interactive and multimedia content, considerably faster, more powerful processors will be required. A separate server for special processing applications might be called for in order to support the work of the intranet server itself. An intranet can make use of several servers working together to process more data at faster speeds. However, relatively small intranet communities, communities that are purposely limited in numbers, should be well-served by a single, reasonably fast, server computer.

A server, however, is just another piece of hardware until it is configured to use the software that will allow it to process, organize, and move the data along the intranet. Various software packages are available to enable the server to handle World Wide Web services, such as publishing web pages and allowing connections to other WWW addresses; File Transfer Protocol (FTP), which allows the server to send and receive a variety of files; email; searchable databases; internet Relay Chat (IRC); electronic Bulletin Board Systems (BBSs); and video conferencing. They vary greatly in capabilities, costs, and ease of use, so understanding resources and goals is once again a prerequisite to making an informed choice.

In order to take advantage of the server's resources, planners must select application software for each client computer belonging to the intranet. Much of this client software is available now as integrated communications packages. These packages typically include a World Wide Web browser, an email manager, and some type of collaboration software that enables users to collaborate on projects by sharing files. Other internet software for other applications, such as video conferencing, is also available.

New Technologies, New Literacies?

Perhaps the greatest promise of using communications technologies (in this specific case, intranet technologies) to support secondary writing instruction is using it as a means of reshaping the traditional boundaries of literacy instruction in ways envisioned by critical educators. Intranets, by making possible redefinitions of institutional boundaries, learning populations, and curricular timetables, encourage what Daniel A. Wagner (1994, 319) has written about as life-span and life-space literacies, literacies that challenge traditional notions of how literacies are acquired, including factors of age (time) and locale (space). Wagner has asserted that "literacy is practiced in ways that can and should be understood *across the life span*, and *across life spaces*. . . . " More specifically:

> It is becoming increasingly clear that in a number of fundamental ways, a more literate society cannot be created in America or elsewhere without a more comprehensive conceptual framework—one that explicitly attempts to link children's acquisition of literacy with that of adults, and one that assumes that there is no single normative theory to literacy development.

Henry Giroux (1990, 32-33) has also asserted that current notions of literacy must change in order to create a literacy paradigm he has represented as

> a shifting sphere of multiple and heterogeneous borders where different histories, languages, experiences, and voices intermingle amid diverse relations of power and privilege. For example, within the pedagogical cultural borderland known as school, subordinate cultures push against and permeate the alleged unproblematic and homogenous borders of dominant cultural forms and practices. . . . Critical education needs to provide the conditions for students to speak differently so that their narratives can be affirmed and engaged critically along with the consistencies and contradictions that characterize such experiences.

An intranet community has the potential to provide the "conditions" for approaching thinking and writing in ways that address Giroux's theoretical stance through concrete practices. Such practices might include the uses of technology to create communicative opportunities not otherwise available due to distance, time, or cost; the uses of people other than professional educators to constitute the talk that leads to learning within this intranet community; and the dedication of professional educators to providing the institutional resources necessary for learners to engage with one another in constructing literacy communities that exist extra-institutionally. Whether students will be allowed to "speak differently" is a much more complex matter, one that is beyond the scope of a mere technological fix. The intranet writing community promises, however, to challenge its members to focus on establishing Giroux's "socially nurturing" pedagogy less through some material realization of grand theory than through tentative and frequently faltering establishments of conversations among community members—a community whose borders are constantly being defined in response to the influences of institutions outside of and within which they extend themselves.

CHAPTER SEVEN

Wiring a Usable Center
Usability Research and Writing Center Practice[1]

Stuart Blythe

I T'S NO SECRET THAT THE STUDY, IMPLEMENTATION, AND USE OF NETWORKED computers in writing instruction requires critical reflection. (Many writers, such as Cynthia Selfe, 1992, Christina Haas, 1996, and Ann Hill Duin and Craig Hansen, 1996 have made that claim.) We're still learning, though, how to reflect critically—how to examine the interactions of technology and humans in the writing process. We're still learning because the task is complex: To employ networked computers effectively in writing centers, one must be able to examine (at the very least) the writing process, human interaction, and sophisticated technologies. Each phenomenon, elusive and complicated enough by itself, becomes all the more difficult to examine in combination with the others. Nevertheless, we must attempt this complex task because "[t]o be literate in an age of electronic tools," as Jane Zeni (1994) writes,

> learners must act and then reflect: how the writing went; where they got stuck; when their tools helped or impeded the flow; what revisions the text needs; which tools will support the next phase of the process. (79)

If we are to help students develop electronic literacies, and to develop our own, we need to practice the kind of reflection that Zeni advocates. We need to develop research methods well suited to examining the interactions of networked computers and writing instruction.

To illustrate the challenge of researching and implementing networked computers in a writing center, consider the following scenario: A director has received funding to implement several networked computers in a writing center that offers f2f tutorials to the entire campus, and she wants to explore how email, the World Wide Web, and various synchronous environments (MUDs/MOOs and other types of conferencing protocols) might aid instruction. She reads the pioneering accounts of networked computer use in writing centers (e.g., Coogan, 1994 & 1995, Jordan-Henley and Maid, "Tutoring" "MOOving", Kinkead 1988) but discovers that these accounts often contradict one another. Such contradictions shouldn't be unexpected, she soon realizes, because the success of networked computers at any particular site depends on a wide variety of local issues, including existing technical support, administrative policies and procedures, tutorial practices, and prevailing theories of technology.[2] A MOO, for example, may benefit a long-term tutorial relationship where tutor and client have time to become proficient with the program, but such a technology may fit poorly at walk-in centers where most clients meet with a tutor once or twice during a semester. Students in the latter setting would lack the time to learn the technology.

Though accounts of networked computer use have a significant value, the writing center director in this scenario realizes that they aren't enough to predict what might ultimately prove useful in her center. So, perhaps she creates a questionnaire to determine students' and tutors' needs regarding writing instruction and networked computers. She soon discovers, however, that it's almost impossible to have anyone discuss something meaningfully without actually having seen or used it. How can someone guess at the potential of email, or a video conferencing protocol, without actually seeing how the technology works? A question such as "Would you be likely to use email to send papers" may get many affirmative responses on a questionnaire—as was the case for Muriel Harris when she first assessed student needs and attitudes at Purdue.[3] But will tutors and students actually use email for tutorials once they've tried it? Or will they even take the time to try it in the first place?

How, then, does one determine what's valuable in one's own center? One could purchase technology and experiment with it; however, most of us lack the time and resources to experiment randomly with networked computers (although some amount of trial and error is inevitable and beneficial). It also would be unethical to "experiment" with students who come to a writing center with pressing concerns. Like us, they often lack the time to take a chance on a networked technology. Nevertheless, we need to investigate our technology needs and to persuade others of the reasonableness of those needs. We need to be prepared to act when funding becomes available (in part because funding often comes with spending deadlines that prohibit critical reflection). What we need, therefore, are methods to determine when, where, and how networked computers may benefit writing center tutors and students, methods that help us consider not only what such technologies *can* do but what they *should* do (Zeni, 76).

Methods already exist for studying the interactions of technology and humans—methods that can be adapted to writing center practice. What I refer to here are usability research methods that have been developed in repeated attempts to design technologies that support humans' efforts to learn, work, and communicate. In this chapter, I introduce readers to (or perhaps remind them of) several of those methods, and, more specifically, I

- define usability research[4] and argue for its promise and ethical appeal for writing center practitioners,
- describe several of the most promising types of usability methods and relate some of my own attempts at them, and
- identify several resources for those who wish to pursue the subject further.

Though this essay cannot offer an in-depth treatment of usability research, it offers an introduction intended to convince readers to begin planning their own research projects, projects that can generate qualitative data suited both to informed change and to publication.

THE GOALS OF USABILITY RESEARCH

If we as writing center practitioners are to make informed decisions regarding the implementation of networked computers, then we need ways to gather meaningful data that will yield insights[5] into how people interact with sophisticated technologies. Moreover, we need to develop productive research strategies that bring about change. We don't need methods for what Larry Hickman (1990) calls "armchair inquiry" (24). Nor do we particularly need a way to establish Truth— e.g., to prove or reject certain hypotheses with a statistically "rigorous" sense of certainty. Rather, we must learn to examine networked technologies as practitioners, as people who each have "an interest in transforming the situation from what it is to something [she or] he likes better" (Schön 1983, 147). To do this, each of us needs to reduce the confusion and ambiguity that networked technologies introduce to writing center practice, to reduce that ambiguity to a point where we can take purposeful action in implementing such technologies. Usability research is a promising methodological resource because it enables such action.

Usability research and testing can enable researchers to gain insight into human/computer interaction. The most promising methods for writing center work see humans not as parts of a system, but as partners engaged in a dialogue with technology. When users engage a technology, they look to it for clues as to its intended use. The way a technology is configured—e.g., the options available in its design—sends messages to users about what can and cannot be done with that technology. "Through their structure and appearance," Paul Adler and Terry Winograd (1992) write, "designed objects express more or less effectively what they are, how they are to be used, and how they are integrated with the embedding context" (7). The icons available in an operating system, for example, set expectations for the type of work that can be done and even for who the appropriate type of users might be, as Cynthia Selfe and Richard Selfe (1994) have argued. (Think about a time when you first interacted with a technology, such as a new computer program, or a bread machine, or a VCR. Think about how you may have looked at buttons, labels, and other objects in order to determine the technology's uses.) A dialogic model places users in a position at least equal to technology because a "breakdown" cannot automatically be blamed on the user. A poorly designed technology, a technology designed with little consideration of users' needs and actions, may be at fault for sending poor messages.[6]

The basic goal of usability research is, consequently, what Lucille Suchman (1987) calls "studies of situated action," the purpose of such studies being "to explicate the relationship between structures of action and the resources and constraints afforded by physical and social circumstances" (179). In studying the relationships between actions and resources, one can gain enough certainty to change and refine the technologies that make up a writing center's networked resources. What usability research can yield, therefore, are insights into how writers interact with networked computers in order to complete writing tasks, and such insights can best be achieved through studies of writers interacting with technology, which is why I advocate usability research methods that draw users in from the start. To understand situated practice, one must observe users at work in actual settings because, as Pelle Ehn (1992) has argued, knowledge and skill is best understood in situated practice, rather than through some formal model (121). Therefore, insights for design—insights that can guide a writing center practitioner's decisions regarding the implementation of networked computers—must come from careful observation of, and interaction with, actual users. The next section describes several methods for fostering such observation and interaction.

PROMISING USABILITY RESEARCH METHODS

Usability research includes numerous types of methods, several of which can prove useful for writing center practitioners. In this section, I describe several such methods and recount some of my initial experiences in implementing some of them. Though I describe ways to examine the interaction of humans and technology, I do not offer an in-depth "how to" discussion. My intent is to offer an introduction rather than a complete guide. (See Table 1 for a summary of the strengths and weaknesses of each method.) Those interested in detailed planning advice should look at the resources listed in the section entitled "For Further Reading."

Interviews and Questionnaires

Interviews and questionnaires are familiar methods that can be adapted to the needs of usability research, particularly for determining subjects' current uses of technology. Through interviews or questionnaires, we may be able to find out how many people have computers where they live, how often they use computers, and general attitudes toward such technologies. Such methods have a significant limitation, however: They cannot predict future uses. You could send out a one-time questionnaire to students and tutors, for example, in order to discover what they might need and want from email, but you're likely to discover that one-time responses aren't very useful. It's difficult for questionnaire respondents to envision possible uses of networked computer technologies, especially if they haven't seen the technology in question. Without any network experience, how is a respondent to answer in any meaningful way?

Focus Groups

In focus groups, a researcher/moderator brings together a representative group of people and tries to foster several hours' worth of discussion. (Jakob Nielsen 1993, 214) suggests gathering approximately six to nine participants for about

Table 1

Benefits and Challenges of Four Usability Research Methods

Method	Primary Advantages	Primary Challenges
Interviews & Questionnaires	Researchers can easily assess a large group of subjects' current uses of, and attitudes toward, networked computers	Difficult to predict future uses if subjects are unfamiliar with the technology in question
Focus Groups	Allowing subjects to engage in dialogue together makes it likely that researchers will uncover unexpected issues	Requires significant effort in terms of bringing group together and moderating discussion
Think-Aloud & Question-Asking Protocols	Observing subjects at work with a technology allows researchers to discover the kinds of decision-making processes that people use when encountering that technology and to identify potential "breakdowns"	Requires significant effort because one researcher can observe one participant at a time
Self-Reporting Logs	Asking subjects to record certain types of technology use over time allows trends to emerge and also encourages subjects to reflect	Requires researchers to ensure that subjects understand how to use the logs and that they complete them
	Logs can be generated collaboratively between researchers and subjects	Quality of the completed logs depends in great part on subject's input

two hours.) One benefit of a focus group is that participants could interact with a technology and then take time to discuss with others the implications of that technology. For example, a writing center director could invite a group of first-year students to the writing center, introduce them to a set of conferencing protocols such as those included in Netscape Communicator, give them time to try it out, and then encourage discussion about its possible uses, their reactions to it, etc. This not only lets participants interact with the technology, but it also allows for the kind of discussion that may yield unexpected insights, thus overcoming some of the major limitations of questionnaires and interviews.

Despite their promise, however, focus groups present challenges. One faces not only the daunting logistical task of gathering people together at the same place and time but also of moderating the group in a manner that fosters discussion. For example, I wanted to assess the expectations and preferences of first-year writing students using networked computers, and I knew I'd have difficulty bringing a group of students together for several meetings. I thought, therefore, that a listserv might allow a number of people to discuss issues of computers and writing while eliminating the need to negotiate meeting times and places. To test the possible dynamics of such a dialogue via listserv, I invited students from a computer-based developmental writing class to participate in a listserv discussion during the month of November, 1996. I assured the students that their instructor would not read what they had written, and I encouraged them to raise issues as well as respond to questions. I had hoped to create a dialogue not only in which I discovered useful responses to my own questions, but also in which students raised their own concerns. However, the students stuck to a question-and-answer format. I would pose a question, and then a number of the students would respond to it. The students never raised their own questions or responded to each other. One person even responded directly to my email account, rather than to the listserv, thus keeping his responses from his classmates. (I never knew whether he did this intentionally.)

A face-to-face (f2f) session may have been (and may be) preferable for promoting dialogue, especially among developmental writers. Perhaps the need to respond in writing was too daunting. (A listserv may prove possible when working with people who are comfortable interacting in writing, people such as tutors.) Or it could be that I have to learn to moderate an online discussion. It is also possible that I recruited too many people for the study. (I had more than nine people participating.) Most likely some combination of the three factors affected the study. Despite these problems, focus group remain a promising research method for me because they can yield insights into students' uses of technology and their expectations for writing instruction. My first experience at running a focus group simply illustrated to me the importance of establishing a comfortable forum for dialogue.

Think-Aloud and Question-Asking Protocols

In think-aloud protocols, a researcher observes a participant as she uses a particular technology. The participant is encouraged to "think aloud," to articulate what she is thinking about, as she works with that technology. For example, a researcher wanting to test a website's navigability might ask a potential user to browse through the site and would encourage the participant to talk about his reactions to particular pages, about his decisions to choose particular buttons, about confusions, hesitations, pleasant surprises, etc. As the participant worked through the site, the researcher would take notes, including quotations, a record of mouse clicks, time spent on pages, etc. A question-asking protocol is almost identical, except that researchers often "intrude" on the user's work by asking questions as they use the technology. Or researchers may pose a set of questions at the beginning of the test for participants to address as the test proceeds. In my experience with think-aloud protocols, researchers have to prompt participants to give voice to their thoughts anyway, so the distinction between a think-aloud and question-asking protocol is blurry.

The benefit of such protocols is that they generate direct observation of a user working through a particular technology. This leads to several significant benefits:

- researchers get to see a user as she or he actually works with a technology, which means that researchers can discover the kinds of decision-making processes that people use when encountering that technology.
- Researchers can identify potential "breakdowns," points where the communication between a technology and a human fails.

The drawback of such protocols, however, is that they are labor intensive. A researcher can only observe and interact with one participant at a time.

I have used think-aloud and question-asking protocols in order to test how people respond to an online survey and to observe their navigational habits in the World Wide Web. By observing students as they tried to fill out an online survey, I could

- discover preferences for filling out text boxes or clicking on multiple-choice options,
- determine whether wording needed to be modified and when fewer or more instructions were needed, and
- determine how to where to place links between web pages

By accident, the tests also helped me decide to reject the use of video in a test using *Enhanced CU-SeeMe*, which I explain in the next section.[7]

Self-Reporting Logs

Using self-reporting logs, researchers can prompt participants to report and reflect on their uses of a particular technology over time. For example, a practitioner may ask a number of students and/or tutors to keep track for one week of such things as when they logged on to and off of a network, what they did while logged on, and their reflections on their experiences. This method has an advantage over others such as think-aloud and question-asking protocols because it could allow one practitioner to examine the work of a relatively large number of participants. (Because the logs are "self-reported," a practitioner need not be present when a participant logs on to a network.) However, the method's strength also can be its drawback. A practitioner must trust that a participant is reporting accurately. One also may miss such subtle things as a user's hesitancies at the keyboard, immediate reactions to certain things encountered on screen, etc.

Despite their potential drawbacks, self-reporting logs can be useful with tutors and other colleagues, especially if one is trying to prompt participants to reflect on their uses of technology. Because tutors have already been trained to reflect on writing and its instruction, they already possess a significant training and vocabulary through which to examine networked computers and writing instruction. Tutors may generate a rich set of data as a consequence. By prompting participants to log their activities with—and responses to—technology, self-reporting logs may prove useful by revealing certain patterns of technology use that had not been recognized previously.

I used self-reporting logs during the spring semester of 1997 with two groups of tutors, each from campuses roughly 90 miles apart. We used the logs to help us identify the potential implications for tutoring of the video- and audio-conferencing package, *Enhanced CU-SeeMe* by WhitePine. (The intent was not so much to decide whether to implement *CU-SeeMe* as to discover the factors that may be important when using such a package for distance tutoring.) The tutors from both campuses took turns serving as tutor, student, and observer, and together we developed research logs for each type of role. (The logs appear in Appendix A.) Consequently, each distance tutorial generated four logs (two from observers at each end and one each from the tutor and student). The logs prompted participants to report the time spent on tutorials and time spent on "technical" and "logistical" tasks such as logging on and working around technical glitches; to describe the tutorial; and to reflect on ways in which the technology may or may not have helped.[8]

Self-reporting logs generated a rich body of data on which all the participants could reflect. Moreover, the use of the logs made all participants significant partners in the research project because complete sets of the logs were shared among everyone in the study. Because of this, and because the logs were generated through group discussion, this project illustrates a democratic form of research in which all participants take a significant role in generating and analyzing data. Moreover, the data comes directly from observations of people interacting with each other and with technology. This method seems well suited to adaptations in writing center settings.

Each of the four types of usability research that I describe in this chapter have potential strengths and challenges, which are summarized in Table 1. (I label the third column "primary challenges" because they're not necessarily weaknesses.) A research project may benefit, consequently, from using a combination of methods in order to take advantage of the unique strengths that each method offers. Nielsen's book offers helpful advice on choosing and combining usability methods (see chapter seven). Also, as with any research project, there are a range of planning issues that one should consider before developing a project using any of these methods—issues such as setting goals, budgeting a project, and recording information. For example, a researcher should walk into a think-aloud protocol or a focus group session with a clear idea of the types of issues that he wants subjects to address; otherwise the discussions may digress to a point where comparisons across sessions become difficult. A researcher also needs to think carefully about gathering data. One may want to use written notes, audio tape, or video tape. Decisions about data gathering should be based, of course, on the goals of the research.

WHY PRACTICE USABILITY RESEARCH?

We are constantly learning to use networked computers to support what Adler and Winograd (1992) call "higher-order cognitive activities" such as writing and social interaction. Usability research methods can play a critical role in this learning process because, as Adler and Winograd (1992) point out, "there is often no substitute for direct user participation in the design process" when "the effectiveness of a system depends on how well it supports higher-order cognitive activities" (5). Usability research offers several promising methods not only because they engage students at various points in a design and decision-making process, but also because they can empower participants; they are theoretically informed; and they can yield data that is not only locally useful but potentially publishable.

Usability research merits our attention in large part because many of those methods were developed to meet productive aims. Because usability research methods have been employed in design and production processes, they are methods for generating knowledge that leads to changes in design and implementation. As is mentioned earlier in this chapter, usability research rejects "armchair inquiry" by going beyond mere description and interpretation of data. Such research also merits greater attention because much of it (especially the research of the Participatory Design movement; e.g., see Susanne Bødker (1991) and Ehn) has an openly political goal that writing center practitioners can easily accept. The goal of many usability research projects has been to empower users, in each case to design a technology that "supports the potential for people who work with it to understand it, to learn, and to make changes" (Adler and Winograd, 7). This desire for research methods that lead to human empowerment, rather than their subordination to technology, makes many usability research methods compatible with writing center practice. After all, most of us would rather empower than subordinate tutors and students. If we are to use technologies (and we're always using them) then we should use them to further democratic purposes and to enable students to learn in satisfying ways.

The approach to usability research that I advocate here meshes with many writing centers' long-standing emphases on student empowerment and echoes arguments by such writers as Stephen North (1984) and Christina Murphy (1994) that writing centers are uniquely suited to join current writing pedagogies in a student-centered setting. While arguments may appear in writing center literature over the means of empowerment, the purpose of encouraging students to become more engaged in discourse about writing and the academy, to become agents of their education, remains widely shared. By developing research methods that engage students in ongoing dialogue, we are asking them to assume an active role in determining what they want to accomplish in their education, and how they want to proceed. Not only do usability research methods make users equal partners in a dialogic act rather than the subordinated component of a larger technology, the inclusion of end users into the design process can give them a significant voice, thereby allowing their needs to be represented more fully. Students and tutors deserve this type of voice in our centers.

Usability research is theoretically informed and can therefore be "academically rigorous." Such research is heavily influenced by the work of Martin Heidegger, the later work of Ludwig Wittgenstein, and of other social constructionist theories. (See Ehn, Winograd 1995, and Winograd and Flores 1986 for detailed explanations of the theoretical grounding of usability research). In a purely practical sense, therefore, usability research can help us both as teachers and researchers. We not only generate usable data that affects design and instruction, we also generate qualitative data that can be reported in journals and that may prove compelling to others on our campuses. (i.e., a director of computer resources might find the results of a usability study more convincing than other types of evidence).

What usability research offers us, therefore, is the chance to do action research, to do teacher-initiated research that can satisfy the need both for change and for publication. "Action research by insiders, with a consultant linking them to outside perspectives, is well suited to studies of technology and literacy," Zeni writes:

> For the reflective teacher, action research is a way to solve problems, change patterns, and improve instruction. For the scholar, action research is a way to investigate something that won't sit still long enough for a controlled experiment. For the critical educator, it is a way to put educational decisions in the hands of the teachers and students who will live with them. (85)

Usability research methods, though not perfect, are adaptable to the study of networked computers and writing centers. They provide one way to reflect critically upon the interaction between users, environments, etc., not by helping us build abstract models by which to design networked technologies for writing centers, but by helping us to observe and reflect upon tutorial interaction mediated by networked computers.

FOR FURTHER READING

Those interested in learning more about usability research might consult some of the following resources (full citations appear in the works cited):

The Usability Methods Toolbox - This well organized website, compiled by James Hom, offers an overview of usability methods as well as an extensive, partially annotated bibliography. The URL (as of early 1998) is http://www.best.com/~jthom/usability/

Usability: Turning Technology into Tools - This collection, edited by Paul S. Adler and Terry A. Winograd, offers a variety of essays on usability. Some of the essays are theoretical, and some of them are accounts of actual tests. This book is a good place to start if you're looking for a thorough introduction to the subject of usability.

Handbook of Usability Testing: How to Plan, Design, and Conduct Effective Tests -Written by Jeffrey Rubin, this book offers practical "how to" advice. It can be read like a reference work.

Usability Engineering - Though Nielsen's book is intended for engineers and others working in industry, many of his suggestions can be adapted for writing centers. For example, he offers a series of useful questions to help plan a test—questions about the goals of the test, test subjects, necessary equipment, and testing methods (see 170-171). He also offers helpful reminders about test budgets (171-174) and pilot testing (174-175).

NOTES

1. I wish to thank Muriel Harris, William Hart-Davidson, and Eric Hobson for their patience in reading drafts of this chapter and for sharing their insights with me.

2. For more on the role of theory in conflicting accounts of technology use, see Blythe (1997).

3. Though the students that Harris surveyed during the early phase of Purdue's OWL expressed enthusiasm for using email to connect with tutors, few actually used the system once it was in place. This probably happened because the most common email programs available to students prohibited the insertion of existing files, such as text files from other word processing programs. Consequently, students at Purdue seldom used email to exchange papers. Instead, they used email as a kind of grammar hotline through which they posed short questions about such issues as punctuation, spelling, and MLA or APA documentation. For an account of Harris's early experience with predicting student computer use, see Blythe, Stuart, et al., (1998).

4. Patricia Sullivan (1989) differentiates between usability research and usability testing. Jacob Nielsen (1993) makes a similar distinction in when he refers to "usability testing" and "assessment methods beyond testing" (see chapters six and seven). I use the term "usability testing" to refer to a range of tests often conducted near the end of product development. Such tests are designed to ensure that a product is "usable" for clients and consumers. "Usability research," on the other hand, need not be tied so directly to product testing; rather, it is intended to yield insights into how people use tools in specific situations. The immediate goal of usability research is insight into human-computer interaction, while the immediate goal of usability testing is making humans fit in with, or accept, a technology. I am indebted to William Hart-Davidson for alerting me to this distinction between research and testing. Hart-Davidson is applying usability research methods to the study of teacher training for networked computer classrooms.

5. I take the distinction between "insight" and "Truth" from Duin and Hansen's argument for a "social perspective" in the research of computers and writing. Though Duin and Hansen argue specifically for such a perspective in nonacademic writing, their call for a social perspective, for studying "the ways writers apply their social, political, and cultural experiences to their interpretation and construction of audience; and the ways context inhibits or enables writers to form ideas and transfer them to others" (7) resonates with calls from others for situated studies of human-computer interaction. For example, see Ehn (1992); and Suchman (1987). The approach is equally relevant in writing center scholarship, especially because a sense of place is so important to a writing center's identity.

6.   When I discuss usability research, I am not referring to "human factors" engineering in which engineers attempt to "fit" humans into the design of technological systems. As Adler and Winograd point out, this more traditional form of technological design views users as parts of a mechanical process; a human is treated essentially as a component of a technological system. Such approaches reduce users to little more than cogs in a machine, and troublesome cogs at that. When breakdowns occur, engineering experts and their technological accolytes are likely to blame the user, rather than poor design. (Anyone who has tried to get help from a condescending computer lab assistant knows what it's like to be blamed for a technological breakdown.) This version of usability, with its emphasis on deskilling workers, subordinates humans to technology and "engineering experts" who, according to Adler and Winograd, are often "accorded the central role" in such approaches to design (4).

7.   Though I cannot claim to have studied a representative sample of users, none of the people I have ever asked have wanted a video link during distance conferencing. Though almost all users have appreciated having an audio connection, all have felt that the video link is a mere distraction. With the technology available to most people right now, a video link hurts system performance significantly anyway.

8.   The logs, when gathered, revealed a number of significant insights into such things as the difficulty of setting goals and the intricacies of turn taking online. One observer noted in her log, for example, that the student found it difficult to wait for a tutor's response. (Interestingly enough, the student didn't mention this problem in her log). The student's possible difficulty with waiting for a response seems reasonable because most students are anxious for feedback when a tutor reads their papers, but the lack of f2f contact online denies a student any chance to read the tutor's face for certain cues.

APPENDIX

The two logs included in this appendix were used by tutors during the Spring of 1997. They were used as prompts to aid reflection following tutorials mediated by the conferencing protocol, *Enhanced CU-SeeMe*, by White Pine.

The two-page observation log prompted observers to do two things during the tutorial: (1) to describe (as neutrally as possible) what they observed and (2) to reflect on what they saw. The log also prompted them to reflect on the tutorial afterwards. The one-page participant log prompted students and tutors to reflect on their tutorial after it was over.

The term "logistics" refers to tasks that were necessary in order to support the actual work of a tutorial, tasks such as calling up computer programs, copying and sharing files, and making sure audio connections were working.

Observation Log

DURING THE TUTORIAL

As you observe the tutorial, please describe what is happening and use the grid following to comment on what you see. The description should include only a reporting of facts, and the comments should include your thoughts on why you think things are happening as they are. Record anything that you think is important, but also be sure to pay attention to such issues as

- How tutor and student listen to each other and attempt to clarify what they're hearing
- How tutor and student take turns talking, listening, reading, and writing
- How tutor and student deal with silences

AFTER THE TUTORIAL

To help recap what you've seen, please respond to the following questions:

What was the tutorial about?

How long did the tutorial take?

How much time was spent on logistics versus tutoring?

What kinds of logistical tasks were necessary for the tutorial?

	Description	*Comments*
How did the session begin?		
How did the tutor discover the student's problem?		
How did the tutor and student set a task for the tutorial?		
How did they complete that task?		

How did the session end?		

Participants' Logs

After your session, please address the following questions:

What was the tutorial about?
How long did the tutorial take?
How much time was spent on logistics versus tutoring?
What kinds of logistical tasks were necessary for the tutorial?
What aspect of the tutorial worked best? why?
Which aspect of the tutorial could have worked better? why?
Which medium would you have preferred for this tutorial? why?

PART II

Critical Assessments
of Wired Writing Centers

CHAPTER EIGHT

Drill Pads, Teaching Machines, and Programmed Texts
Origins of Instructional Technology in Writing Centers

Neal Lerner

INTRODUCTION

A s someone who began teaching writing in Silicon Valley, CA, it seemed inevitable that instructional technology would interweave with my career, whether in the writing center or the classroom. My experiences, however, have made me skeptical about the relationship between writing centers and instructional technology, and this skepticism stems from what I have seen as several persistent and misguided ideas: the belief that "fundamentals" of language must be mastered before moving on to "real" writing tasks; the use of drill-and-practice exercises to teach those fundamentals; and the combination of that drill with higher and higher technology, whether that technology is in the form of a stimulus-response-reinforcement textbook or a beeping, blinking, if not talking, computer.

To many researchers, administrators and teachers, writing instruction and instructional technology—particularly in writing centers—have often seemed to be a perfect match, particularly when that technology was applied to "remediating" students not prepared for college-level writing. From the "laboratory approach" to teaching composition—first discussed at the turn of the century—to crises created by sudden large influxes of under-prepared students, to more modern faith in "scientific" solutions for persistent dilemmas in teaching students to write, American higher education has turned to technology to satisfy long-standing needs. Unlike technological innovations such as synchronous and a-synchronous environments, hypertext writing, and multi-media documents, the technology I present in this chapter did not (and does not) have the potential to fundamentally change the very nature of what it means to teach and learn writing. Instead, the historical practices I describe provided a means for sorting students and transferring responsibility from institutions to individuals, ultimately giving administrators a method to convey the impression that they were doing *something* about making their institutions more democratic, open, and accessible.

The historical analysis that follows is also not merely a quaint episode in our instructional past. In fact, the fundamental beliefs and the use of technology to pursue those beliefs are still with us (indeed, the specific programmed-instruction materials that I will refer to are still being published today). Our writing centers might focus on the writer and not merely the writing, but the lure of technology to offer "easy" solutions to complex problems is powerful. The tutor-less writing center does exist at many of our institutions. This type of center consists of a bank of skills computers administered by bored work-study students where faculty send students "deficient" in "essential skills." It is often a one-time capital budget expense and much more meaningful to some administrators than a more expensive and complicated tutor-staffed writing center. As we rush to embrace the high tech in our writing centers, our history with various technologies provides no small measure of caution. The problems of under-prepared students, crises in "standards," and definable "outcomes" are all persistent. It is easy to crave technological solutions, and in what follows, I hope to show that these solutions are never ideologically neutral, never without a history and an underlying belief in how students learn. This is true for "old" technologies and no less so for current ones.

TECHNOLOGY IN THE "MODERN" UNIVERSITY: THE WRITING LAB APPROACH

In his study of the uses of radio, film, and television in public school classrooms, Larry Cuban (1986) defines instructional technology as "any device available to teachers for use in instructing students in a more efficient and stimulating manner than the sole use of the teacher's voice" (4). For this chapter, I will slightly alter that definition to include not merely devices (e.g., blackboard and chalk, texts, computers), but pedagogical techniques. In other words, when those in higher education found themselves dissatisfied with the inefficiency and tedium of using lecture and recitation to teach writing, they "technologized" pedagogy by turning to the "laboratory method," a precursor of today's writing center (Carino 1995 "Early" 105). As early as 1895, John Franklin Genung of Amherst College claimed that "the best term, perhaps, by which to characterize the way in which the teachers of English at Amherst have met [the] challenges [of teaching composition] is *laboratory work*" (174). The influential Fred Newton Scott of the University of Michigan agreed with Genung's characterization, describing the English laboratory as a place where "the instructor can again meet his students as individuals and can have leisure for deliberate consultation and personal criticism" (180).

Throughout the early part of the 20th century, the writing lab approach was seen by many professionals as a solution to overcome the frustrations and failures of teaching students to write. In 1902, Frances Lewis recommended laboratory techniques for high schools and described the "revolution" in teaching methods: "Classroom work, once entirely recitation from a text-book,' is now often on the laboratory plan, with questions to lead the pupil to make his own discoveries and form his own opinions" (15). By 1912, an editorial in *The English Journal* asked,

"Why not give laboratory principles an adequate test, somewhere, for a sufficient time, to determine whether or not students can be trained to do certain things according to the standard of established present usage?" (48).

That final goal, the "standard of established present usage," provides an important theme that recurs throughout these pedagogical debates. For many critics, the laboratory method would provide a superior way to teach grammar and usage. Instead of comprehensive lectures on various aspects of mechanics, students would work through exercises under the one-to-one guidance of their instructor. This type of instruction was the common feature Genung described at Amherst: "Each of these courses is a veritable workshop, wherein, by systemized daily drill, details are mastered one by one" (174). However, as Peter Carino (1995 "Early") has pointed out, drill and practice was not the only model of laboratory instruction. In fact, work in the writing laboratory could often sound quite familiar and "modern," not so much a large room of worksheets and grammar drill, but instead a place where students wrote, responded, and revised. In 1928, E. L. Holcumb described her high school writing lab:

> Here my English students should write, and write for the joy of writing, each in his separate star. Here sometimes they should play word games and letter games and grammar games. Here sometimes they should give debates and make oral reports. Here they should even learn rules. But most important of all, here they should write. They should learn the joy of expression. This should be our workroom, our laboratory. (51)

Exceptions to the laboratory as merely for drill appeared in the literature from such diverse institutions as the University of Minnesota General College (Appel, 1936) and its College of Science, Literature, and the Arts (Grandy, 1936); Ironwood Junior College (Ferster, 1937); George Washington University (Colby, 1940); or the University of Florida (Wise, 1939). In the last institution, the writing laboratory was a two-hour weekly addition to the required freshman composition course and was a place where, in 1934,

> each student writes what he has to write, whether that be a letter to be mailed, a book report, an assignment from another course, or something of a creative nature. Whatever the case, the instructor is present to serve as a guide, a counselor, or a helper to enable the student to overcome his weakness, let the weakness be one of ignorance of elementary fundamentals or one of style. (456)

By the late 1920s and 1930s, however, those proposing these teaching methods in the laboratory came up against a powerful force. During this time, higher education enrollments increased greatly, tripling between 1910 and 1930 (Willey, 1937), as the children of the great immigrant waves of the turn of the century began graduating high school and pursuing college degrees. This influx of students with varied preparation presented a crisis of sorts. As one commentator noted in 1930: "It is now quite generally admitted by college authorities that deficiencies in students' previous preparation, especially in such tool subjects as reading, the mechanics of English composition, arithmetic, and spelling, constitute a rather serious handicap to academic success" (Arnold 262). Increasingly, the writing lab became associated with "the mechanics of English composition" and remediating under-prepared students (Carino 1995 "Early"). In H. J. Arnold's (1930) "remedial program" for English composition, "Self taught practice exercises should constitute an important phase of the work. If such helps are not available, provision should be made immediately for these teaching materials" (267-68).

Many professionals were upset over the "burden" of remediation and increasingly identified the individualized laboratory and drill-and-practice methods as best suited to deal with such students. In 1939 Alvin Fountain surveyed institutions nationwide and found "a writing laboratory for those in need of additional drill" (311) a fairly common practice. In the same year, W. Alan Grove (1939) of Miami University in Ohio described the contents of remedial course and lab work at his institution:

> Taking nothing for granted, but beginning with an explanation of the parts of speech—particularly of their functions—the work proceeds thoroughly but with surprising rapidity through sentence structure, punctuation, and grammar, although perhaps seeming to linger a disproportionate length of time over certain fundamentals, a perfect command of which, however, has proved itself valuable, if not indispensable. (231)

Regardless of whether or not the "perfect command" of fundamentals is desirable, drill and practice was also seen as a way to "individualize" instruction. If one student needed practice with verb forms and another on sentence boundaries, then drill-and-practice exercises could address both students in an efficient manner. As a 1925 *English Journal* editorial asked, "Will the 'individual instruction' movement furnish us the solution of the "difficult but inescapable problem of drill on grammar and mechanics?" (The Place of Individual Instruction" 329). That remarkable paradox—the difficult but inescapable problem"—continued to fuel the use of such pedagogy as writing laboratories flourished.

Ironically, attacks on drill-and-practice techniques are as constant in the literature as are their descriptions and recommendations. For instance, from January 1933 to June 1934, an NCTE Committee on Research studied classroom practices and concluded the following:

> The specific aims of written expression reveal what is, perhaps, an alarming emphasis upon mere technicalities of expression. Results of classroom observation throughout the country indicate a similar preoccupation with grammar and the drill pad, with correspondingly little opportunity for the actual expression of ideas. (719)

By 1947, Porter Perrin, the president of the NCTE, noted that "even though there is a growing body of data that points to the ineffectiveness of the workbook method in furthering actual communication, workbooks continue to be used at all levels, principally because they are easy for the teacher" (359).[1]

Nevertheless, despite a great deal of evidence that it was ineffective, drill in grammar and usage continued. It was the "appalling" lack of preparedness of the students themselves, some critics argued, that led to the obvious use of drill. As one commentator noted, "If there were any proof needed to support the theory that drill work is necessary to supplement the lack so apparent among students applying for admission to the English Composition classes of our colleges and universities, no-credit classes as found in these colleges would be all-sufficient evidence" (Conkling 50).

The survival powers of "drill-and-practice technologies" is a powerful theme in the history of composition and writing centers. But what accounts for this persistence? Why have drill and practice continually offered (and continue to offer) a "salvation" of sorts to beleaguered composition faculty? Mike Rose (1985) traces the origins of widespread drill and practice to the "efficiency movement" of the 1930s when scientific reasoning and measurement greatly influenced educational decision-making. Rose sees the drill-and-practice approach as powerfully important, not because of its effectiveness, but because of its symbolic power: "[Drill and practice] gives a method—a putatively objective one—to the strong desire of our society to maintain correct language use. It is very American in its seeming efficiency. And it offers a simple, understandable view of complex linguistic problems" (345).

Perhaps another answer to the persistence of these methods can be found in the tension between inclusiveness and exclusiveness that has characterized many institutions of higher education during times of increased enrollments by "nontraditional" students. According to Rose, drill and practice and "scientific solutions" are particularly attractive "in times of crisis: when budgets crunch and accountability looms or, particularly, when 'nontraditional' students flood our institutions" (1985, 345-46). Called upon to serve a democratic function (once a high-school education was not quite enough to ensure success in a competitive job market), higher education accepted this "openness" (sometimes reluctantly[2]) by accepting large numbers of students despite their preparation. However, these students stretched the boundaries of pedagogy and curriculum. In some ways they were under-prepared for college-level writing, but in other ways, they created scrutiny of college-writing practices, scrutiny not particularly well accepted by those in charge. While many of these practices have changed over the years, the intractable drill-and-practice work has remained because it performs two powerful functions: 1) By "individualizing" work in the laboratory, the burden of success and failure is clearly shifted onto students and away from the practices and institutions themselves. 2) With drill-and-practice exercises assigned in a laboratory, classroom teachers can clearly wipe their hands of the "dirty work" of teaching some things that are very difficult to teach and learn. It is much cleaner to turn such matters over to a laboratory (and later a computer), and this practice acts as a powerful sign that we've done something about the "problem."

Thus, remedial writing laboratories and later "clinics" proliferated nationwide, and in the 1940s accounts appeared from such varied institutions as Park College (Campbell, 1942), Iowa State College (Mallam, 1943), the University of North Carolina (Bailey, 1946), and Wayne University ("Composition Clinic at Wayne", 1950). By the 1950s, the large number of World War II veterans enrolled in our nation's colleges and universities simply reinforced prevailing notions that had taken hold in the 1920s and 1930s. As Robert Moore noted in *College English* in 1950: "Writing clinics and writing laboratories are becoming increasingly popular among American universities and colleges as remedial agencies for removing students' deficiencies in composition" (388). Moore made it quite clear that such measures were in the students' best interests, and it was up to students to make best use of them: "With the laboratory, as with the clinic and all other remedial devices, satisfactory results are most readily secured when the student, whatever the means of his coming, is personally convinced of the desirability of improving his writing skill" (392).

Occasionally, a commentator would display some indication that it wasn't merely the students' fault that writing was difficult to teach and learn. For instance, a 1951 Conference on College Composition and Communication workshop recommended that "the writing laboratory should be what the classroom often is not—natural, realistic, and friendly" (18). However, by the late 1950s and early 1960s, a new instructional movement found a perfect match between drill-and-practice grammar instruction, the "individualized" learning of a writing laboratory, and a post-Sputnik faith in high technology. Familiar arguments were brought forth, and many practitioners found yet another reason to perpetuate old—and often discredited—practices. In this era, salvation arrived in the form of "teaching machines," "programmed instruction," and behavioral approaches to learning to write, where good "habits" are essential, and these habits are internalized through repetition and reinforcement.

B. F. SKINNER AND THE HABITS OF GOOD WRITING: THE ASCENDANCY OF TEACHING MACHINES AND PROGRAMMED INSTRUCTION

Few other approaches in the history of writing instruction have had quite the scientific backing as the late 1950s and early 1960s efforts to apply the psychological theories of B. F. Skinner. At a time, once again, when enrollments began to increase and non-mainstream students began to put pressure upon the resources of higher education, a technological solution was found that would "individualize" instruction and, as had been true for earlier remedial efforts, shift responsibility from institutions to individuals. This technology came in various forms—teaching machines, programmed textbooks, and, later, computer-assisted instruction—but all were based on behaviorist principles and the reduction of learning to write to the formation of "correct" habits.

Underlying the behavioral approach are the ideas of stimulus, response, and reinforcement as the essential mechanisms of learning. Skinner applied his work with "lower organisms" to education and surmised that "by arranging appropriate 'contingencies of reinforcement,' specific forms of behavior can be set up and brought under the control of specific classes of stimuli" (Teaching Machines" 140). More specifically for teaching and learning, "a student is 'taught,' in the sense that he is induced to engage in new forms of behavior and in specific forms upon specific occasions" (Teaching Machines" 138). These behaviors are broken down into "small steps of graded difficulty, so that mastery of concepts, understanding, and skills are gradually built up" (Lumsdaine, 1960, 13-14).

Essential to this theory is that "rewards" must be present to reinforce the "acceptable" behaviors and provide motivation (Frye, 1964). Behaviorists saw the students' satisfaction upon choosing the correct answer as an important reward. As one proponent described,

> It is satisfying to the student to know that he has answered a question correctly, to know that he is understanding. We have also learned that the more frequent the rewards the better the student assimilates the material. Ideally, he should be rewarded for answering each question correctly, even each part of each question. Also, it has been proved that more learning takes place when errors are corrected *immediately*. Fortunately, a basic characteristic of teaching machines is immediate-knowledge-of-results." (Frye 23)

Designers of teaching machines and programmed instruction consistently refer to two key arguments to support their ideas: 1) These materials can make instruction more "efficient" by individualizing the curriculum. Fast learners won't be penalized by the slow, and the slow can repeat their tasks without hindering the fast (Skinner, "Teaching Machines" 139). This instruction is in contrast to "group instruction," in which "even under the best of circumstances . . . the rate of presentation may be too slow for the fast student and too fast for the slow student" (Frye 23). 2) In an argument that "naturally" extends such teaching to a writing center, these devices are akin to tutors or are "based fundamentally on Socratic question-and-answer or problem-and-solution methods of teaching" (Lumsdaine 13). In a sense, the argument goes, teaching machines will transcend class/economic limitations and allow *all* students to experience the "functions of a private tutor in recitation and practice, with immediate correction of errors and feedback to the student" (Lumsdaine 6), previously available to only a select few. In fact, for some supporters, programmed instruction represented a "revolutionary device," capable of "freeing" students from the bondage" that was conventional schooling. According to Wilbur Schramm (1964), teaching machines would finally transcend the following evils:

> the waste of human resources where there are no teachers or where people cannot go to school; the waste of time and talent where all students are locked into the same place, and all teachers into the same routine; the tyranny of tradition which permits the study of a certain topic to begin only at a certain age, and expects a student to accomplish only as much as a questionable test of his ability says he can do; and the inadequacy of outmoded and inadequate curricula. (114)

While efforts to construct teaching machines would perhaps not fully succeed until the development of the personal computer[3], behavioral approaches did find an immediate application in the "programmed textbook." These texts are based upon Skinner's notions that "the whole process of becoming competent in any field must be divided into a very large number of very small steps, and reinforcement must be contingent upon the accomplishment of each step" ("The Science of Learning" 108). Translated into book-form, this idea appears as a question requiring a response in a "panel" on one page and the answer in a "panel" in the same position on the next page (Homme and Glaser 103). Of course, the primary difference between machines and texts is the ability for students to "cheat" in the latter and simply look at the correct answer. However, Homme and Glaser (1959) dismiss such concerns because with a well-programmed textbook, if steps are broken down into small enough increments and reinforcement is adequate, students will be correct in their responses (and thus rewarded) and have no incentive to cheat (which is unrewarded).

Importantly, this approach to learning, in its attempts to "individualize" instruction, is firmly at odds with ideas of writing as a social activity. Not only do students proceed "at their own pace," but they learn, essentially, alone. In the behaviorist view, "the teacher manipulates the instructional environment in order to bring appropriate behavior under the guidance of subject-matter stimuli" (Taber et al.,1965, 17). These "stimuli" are found in the text itself, not through the interacting with others (which are stimuli of the bad sort). Lauren Resnick (1963) discusses this dilemma as applied to the elementary-grade classroom:

> In a classroom, . . . the teacher does not automatically control all reinforcers. Children can provide one another with powerful social reinforcement whose effects may conflict with those of the reinforcements provided by the teacher. Self-instruction represents, in part, an attempt to gain a greater degree of control over behavior. Competing sources of stimulation and reinforcement are to some extent eliminated. (445)

Early on, the promise of programmed learning as applied to writing instruction was most obvious in teaching grammar and usage. Drill and practice—essentially an "individual" and socially isolating practice—had yet another "scientific" basis for effectiveness. By using these materials, "the teacher is freed to handle the truly creative teaching, where 'thinking,' 'understanding,' and 'problem solving' are involved" (Resnick 439). The "dirty" but necessary task of assigning practice in fundamentals could now be assigned not just to an "awkward squad" (Noyes) or to a "clinic"; instead, needy students would work with the tutor-text and be fully responsible for their own learning (or lack thereof). While Rose describes behavioral theories as applied to the "drill pad" of the 1930s, his description is no less appropriate for programmed instruction of the 1960s:

> The theoretical underpinning was expressed in terms of "habit formation" and "habit strength," the behaviorist equivalent of learning—the resilience of an "acquired response" being dependent on the power and number of reinforcements.

The logic was neat: specify a desired linguistic behavior as precisely as possible . . . and construct opportunities to practice it. The more practice, the more the linguistic habit will take hold. (344)

One of the earliest applications of programmed learning to grammar-and-usage instruction was Joseph Blumenthal's series of textbooks, *English 2200, 2600,* and *3200* (the numbers representing the number of "frames" or steps students would work through), first published in 1960 and still in print. In his remarks "to the student" in *English 2600,* Blumenthal echoes the arguments of Skinner et al. to convince the student of the efficacy of his text: "Using a programmed textbook is like having a private teacher who watches you as you work and who sets you back on the track the moment you wander off" (iii). And, ultimately, it was up to the students themselves—it was their responsibility—to make best use of this text. Science had done its part; now it was up to the individual student:

> If you will use *English 2600* in the mature way in which it is designed to be used, you may discover that, working at your own pace, you have achieved a better command of the fundamentals of your language—and in a much shorter time. You may also find that you have developed your ability to think and concentrate in ways that will help you in your other studies. You will have profited from letting science help you with its most recent and exciting discoveries about how people learn. (v)

Blumenthal's and other programmed texts proliferated among composition classrooms in the 1960s as more and more non-mainstream students challenged institutions to accept and provide for them. A 1961 Conference on College Composition and Communication workshop on "Teaching Machines and Programmed Instruction" saw representatives of five major publishing companies in attendance. Additional workshops in 1965 ("Report of the Workshop on Administering the Freshman Course," "Report of the Workshop on New Approaches to Teaching Composition") and 1966 ("Report on the Workshop of Students Needing Remedial Help") suggested programmed instruction as a means of remediating under-prepared students. And a 1966 *College Composition and Communication* editorial suggested, "Students who need special help may be assigned to a 'catch-up' class, given a programmed textbook or some other self-instructional instrument" ("Teaching the Disadvantaged" 38). Other writers looked to programmed learning for dealing with the burgeoning population of ESL students (e.g., Spencer and Holtzman; Hall and Hall).

The language of behavioral psychology was particularly attractive to those English teachers who saw learning to write as the cultivation of "proper" habits. For some supporters, the promise extended beyond merely grammar and usage: "Because it aims at shaping behavior rather than conveying information, 'Programmed Learning' could be applied to the teaching of English composition, which is itself a complex mode of behavior, perhaps less desirable than generosity, but more easily mastered" (Huntley 1962, 7). For others, the challenge was to reconceive composition as a "set of habits," after which "we teachers of composition can propose a useful goal to our students with humility and promise some hope of achieving it" (Huntley 1965, 137). Supporters of "building-block" approaches struck a bonanza with programmed instruction as one devotee wrote in a 1962 *College English* article: "A machine with the strength to block the advancement of a student incapable of mastering, for example, parallelism could prove the greatest boon to teachers of composition since the invention of the red pencil" (Rothwell 245).

Programmed materials were, as Skinner had noted ("Teaching Machines" 143), akin to a private English tutor. As one writer noted in *PMLA*, "[the teaching machine] works individually with the student, can indeed come into the student's home, guides him in his work, corrects him when he is wrong, prevents him from skipping important points, works almost intimately with him" (Morton 4). Another writer, in discussing her experiences with using teaching machines with Korean veterans, found the "autotutorial" superior to actual tutors. After all, "a mechanical tutor did not embarrass [students] by correcting them in public" (Rowland 92).

And once again, the justification of relieving instructors of the "necessary" but unfortunate task of teaching mechanics was brought forth in defense of programmed learning for the composition classroom:

> Virtually all remedial English at the college level could be handled by automation, with the machine as an impartial judge of a student's ability to move ahead. Teachers, relieved of the executioner's role, could then become counselors rather than taskmasters. Their human talents, at a time when trained talent is scarce, could be salvaged for situations better suited to them than mere drill. (Rothwell 247)

Or, as another commentator wrote, "our students and their mechanical tutors will do their necessary drill work out of our sight—and hearing" (Morton 1960, 6).

Throughout these justifications is the assumption of the necessity for drill-and-practice work, despite decades of evidence of its failure. As enrollments burgeoned, arguments needed to be marshaled that would preserve some sense of the status quo. What had been successful in the past was to appeal to "individualization" and "student responsibility." If students were under-prepared, institutions would give them auto-tutorial methods—validated by "science" and truly "student-centered." If students continued to fail with such materials, well, then it was surely students' own fault if they—through "improper" socialization or inadequate schooling—haven't mastered the "right" language habits. Reducing writing to "a set of behaviors" or good and bad habits such as nail biting and politeness also makes it quite easy to then sort students—usually along socio-economic and ethnic lines—according to whatever linguistic behaviors seem "mastered" by the time they enroll in college. By using teaching machines and programmed texts, teachers could be assured that they had fulfilled their responsibility, and it was up to the students to overcome their past preparation. A grant-funded "experiment" with "automated" instruction at the University of Houston described this "problem":

Generally speaking the students in our remedial sections were deficient in verbal skill. Needless to say, there appeared to be an indifference toward, maybe little understanding of, ideas or cultural values commonly associated with higher education. It would be an understatement to say that teaching such raw recruits has been difficult. (Dorough and Shapiro 1964, 18)

Since programmed texts were designed for "success"—that is, the point was for students to answer the questions correctly, not to add up incorrect responses—institutions were off the hook. As one writer noted with regard to programmed texts, "Failure—in the usual sense—is by definition impossible. Failure to finish the program is alone possible, and this is entirely dependent on the time the student is willing to give to it. Certainly, it is the most 'democratic' form of teaching imaginable" (Morton 3). At last, higher education and English departments had found a way to be inclusive and exclusive at the same time.

As has been true with other technological "innovations" in education, programmed learning, after an initial euphoria, experienced what Larry Cuban (1986) identifies as the stages of, first, "scientific credibility" and then "disappointment" (5). In the former stage, several articles appeared that "tested" programmed learning approaches with traditional" instruction. For instance, Charles Simon found that composition sections using *English 2600* showed "no transfer of the book's instruction to application in writing. Moreover, insofar as the 'better learning' it purported to offer in comparison with the other texts, there was no evidence that it succeeded as well" (19). At the University of Houston, "a programmed course was developed" whose students were compared to those taught by "a traditional lecture method" (Dorough and Shapiro 5). Researchers found that "the lecture and program instruction methods employed were equally effective, on the average" (9) to teach mechanics of language. Unfortunately, when examining performance on actual writing tasks, the authors note that "no really acceptable or reliable means of scoring was ever established and the information will not be reported in this paper" (8).

As was true in Houston and as I will next present with regard to the Comp-Lab project, experimental results often showed no significant differences between groups taught by programmed instruction and those taught by "traditional" methods when it came to learning English fundamentals. Supporters of programmed instruction would declare this a victory, however, since their methods were less expensive and less "burdensome" to the teaching staff. Still, two particular aspects of these studies are troubling: 1) "Traditional" instruction is never quite defined. Certainly lectures on comma and pronoun usage are a waste of time for most students. Comparing any instruction to such techniques is bound to find some difference. 2) The underlying assumption that work on fundamentals is essential and separated from real writing tasks is never challenged. As in the two studies I described above, transfer of "skills" to actual writing is problematic (or impossible to research, so say those at the University of Houston).

By the time a 1966 Conference on College Composition and Communication workshop convened on "Teaching Machines and Programmed Instruction," some dissent could be heard after the initial euphoria. As the recorder concluded, "There was a discernible impression from the statements of several consultants and participants in the workshop that there are no current programmed texts which can be wholeheartedly endorsed for English" (193). It wasn't that participants were rejecting these materials on theoretical grounds; simply, the materials needed to be improved. Implicitly endorsed were the functions of individualization, the shifting of responsibility, the persistence of drill-and-practice methods, and the release of composition teachers from such dirty work. A rarer view was that expressed by a 1968 *College Composition and Communication* editorial on "The Status of Freshman Composition":

> If the approach is not effective, it is understandable that some colleges make such courses as inexpensive and easy as possible, herding large numbers of students into lecture halls or televised classrooms and marching them through the pages of *programmed textbooks* dealing with old-fashioned grammar to the neglect of the intellectual aspects of the composing process. (emphasis mine, 82)

Such voices never really dominated the debate, and by the late 1960s and early 1970s a "new" phenomenon arose as "the writing laboratory approach" recycled itself (after 70 years of reinvention) and proliferated nationwide. For many, writing labs were a "natural" home to programmed learning, truly apart from the classroom and ready to be "technologized" with whatever means available.

PROGRAMMED LEARNING IN THE WRITING CENTER: THE COMP-LAB APPROACH

By the early 1970s, reports on the use of programmed materials in the writing center began to appear in journals and at conferences. For example, the Community College of Baltimore "stocked the laboratory with a modest number of programmed texts, twenty-five separate titles" (Otterbein 1973, 296). This remedial writing lab, where instructors used referral slips to assign students having particular grammar/usage difficulties, performed important functions for both student and instructor, according to its director: "The student can obtain individualized help in his particular areas of weakness at a rate determined by himself" (Otterbein 298). The instructor, on the other hand, managed to maintain the "proper" level of cleanliness by assigning all vestiges of messy instruction to the writing lab with its programmed texts. As a result, the instructor is "relieved of the often onerous and frustrating task of teaching grammar and mechanics, and thus is freed to devote more time to those areas of composition instruction for which his training and experience have prepared him" (Otterbein 298).

The use of programmed materials in the writing lab was also the subject of primary research. In a study of comparing "auto-tutorial grammar materials" as a supplement to class instruction with four hours per week of class lecture, Tomlinson (1975) found no significant differences "in student writing proficiency." However, auto-tutorial students had a "more favorable attitude toward remedial composition instruction" (8). Though offered more as an indictment of the lecture mode to teach writing rather than a scrutiny of programmed texts, Tomlinson's study indicates some measure of acceptance of programmed materials for the writing center.

Still, some professionals were more skeptical of programmed learning. For example, Rudolph Almasy reported that programmed texts were rejected by students at the West Virginia University Writing Laboratory, and given the lack of alternative models of instruction, the lab became "a mere proofreading service for desperate students with papers in progress" (400). By 1978, Lil Brannon and Jeanette Harris would target programmed materials for particular scorn in their talk to the College Teachers of English of Texas:

> The material that the student plows through (albeit at his own rate) is neither appropriate to his particular needs nor, in many cases, pertinent to his writing problems. The various mechanized material and programmed texts that are available commercially tend to range from the insultingly elementary and asinine to the unimaginatively complex and repetitious. (2-3)

The authors were particularly incensed by the "anti-tutor" nature of such materials, implicitly contrasting the behaviorist "skills approach" to writing center work with an approach more attuned to helping students shape written discourse amid an array of complex influences. Brannon and Harris recognized the easy allure of programmed materials as writing centers proliferated but stressed that students' learning should be the primary concern. Students should be treated as "responsible adults who are motivated to learn rather than as children who must be enticed by clever, TV-like material or as automatons who can be plugged into a machine or a programmed text. If writing centers are to become a viable, permanent part of university life, academics rather than gimmicks must be our concern" (7).

While writing centers were quickly becoming viable and permanent, despite these cautions programmed learning materials were becoming similarly entrenched. By 1981, Muriel Harris would identify two models of "writing assistance": the "writing lab" and the "writing center." In the former (and Harris identifies the CUNY Comp-Lab approach as the prime example), the emphasis is on "products" and lab work is concerned with "word-form correctness" (2). To achieve this goal, materials used in writing labs include "self-instruction books, cassette tapes, [and] computer-assisted instruction" (2). Harris, while being broadly descriptive for an audience not familiar with such work, also issues a caution: "Amidst all the hardware, modules, progress charts, and sign-in sheets, the student can get lost in the shuffle" (3).

Thus, by the late 1970s and early 1980s, programmed materials seemed an inevitable feature of many writing centers. While they might not have been the sole means of instruction in some places, the tools of programmed learning constituted an important "technology" in the writing center toolbox. As indicated in "Priorities and Guidelines for the Development of Writing Centers," appearing in Gary Olson's influential *Writing Centers: Theory and Administration,* "The center should obtain a wide variety of equipment such as tape recorders, files, filmstrips, films, and *programmed materials*" (emphasis mine, Cox 83).

The development and relative acceptance of programmed learning led naturally to the question of whether such an approach could be more desirable than a writing center staffed by peer or professional tutors. One of the more visible and well-funded attempts to address this question was the Comp-Lab project of York College of the City University of New York. In a series of articles appearing in the late 1970s and early 1980s (Epes, Kirkpatrick, and Southwell; Kirkpatrick; Southwell), the creators of this project describe their "autotutorial writing laboratory, where students work on their own, not in a one-to-one relationship with a tutor" (Epes, Kirkpatrick, and Southwell 1979, 19). Designed to augment classroom instruction for basic writing students, Comp-Lab consists of weekly modules, focusing on "a single grammatical feature." In the original design, the modules were made up of audiotapes and an accompanying workbook (which are still being published; see Epes and Kirkpatrick; Epes and Southwell). In later versions, the authors took advantage of evolving technology and created computer-assisted modules (Southwell).

To justify their approach, the creators of Comp-Lab present arguments by now familiar. Most importantly, they see the bifurcation between "composition" and "grammar" as an important one to maintain for instructional purposes. For the creators of Comp-Lab, instruction in the classroom has a specific focus on "higher-order concerns," and self instruction in the laboratory is separate, skills-focused and remedial. Additionally, Comp-Lab's creators present their approach as a superior alternative to the tutor-staffed writing center, that ["Comp-Lab] can be more effective in instructional terms" (Kirkpatrick 1981, 15). However, is Kirkpatrick justified when she claims that "results of a formal evaluation of the Comp-Lab Project suggest that heavy emphasis on written correctness, along with extensive structured practice, not only improves students' error rates but also has an even greater impact on the overall quality of their writing" (21)? A close look at that evaluation reveals reasons to question her enthusiasm.

It is important to note that the goals of the class to which Comp-Lab was originally a supplement, English 100, consisted of primarily mechanical, sentence-level criteria. For instance, by the end of the course, students would need to demonstrate "the ability to write at least one paragraph which establishes one specific main idea and develops it" and also demonstrate "control of" a variety of mechanical aspects, including agreement, verb forms, tense consistency, plural and possessive forms, and sentence boundaries (Epes 1988, 22). In other words, the primary aims of the course, whether taught via Comp-Lab or without, were essentially the sentence-level aims of the Comp-Lab units. And how would the non-experimental or control sections accomplish these goals? We are only told that it was through "traditional methods" (Epes 1979 "Comp-Lab Project: Assessing the Effectiveness"). If we can assume that such methods included class-wide lectures on the particulars of language use, it is not difficult to imagine the results of a comparison.

At any rate, the results do indicate some interesting findings. While Comp-Lab's creators declare superiority over "traditional" approaches and even a tutor-staffed writing center, the comparison of the Comp-Lab students with a control group found that while both groups improved their error rates, the Comp-Lab students outperformed control-group students in "three out of six variables," not surprising considering the focus of their instruction. However, perhaps most important is to examine the transfer to students' actual writing. In the words of the evaluators: "The holistic evaluation, therefore, shows a noticeable gain for both the Experimental and Control Groups. Though the gains were slightly larger for the Experimental Group, the differences in the performance were not dramatic nor statistically significant" (Epes 1980, 92). In other words, differences between groups could have been due to the way scores would have been naturally distributed along a normal curve, not necessarily due to Comp-Lab.

The greatest improvement for Comp-Lab students as compared to control was for those students who *failed* English 100. While the directors see this as suggesting that Comp-Lab has "particular benefits for students whose writing level is low when they enter the course," another explanation might be found from a note contained in the outside evaluator's report: "Perhaps the larger amount of writing done by the Experimental [Comp-Lab] group (some 1,500 words per week as compared to about 300 for the Control group) helped to improve their writing skills" (Epes 1980, 94). In other words, those taught by "traditional methods" were learning to write by composing barely one full page per week, while the Comp-Lab group was writing three times as much. If anything, one wonders how the control students managed to keep pace with the Comp-Lab students, considering their instruction.

The "success" of Comp-Lab then is that it did no worse than traditional" methods, while costing less and using fewer human resources, an attractive option in the face of tight budgets and fiscal restraint. This success, though, would always be quite dependent upon not so much the teaching methods themselves but upon the students, we are told. After all, it is students' responsibility to be motivated and seek "independence." When the creators tested Comp-Lab in a variety of "non-college" settings, including two high schools, a labor union, a training program for temporary workers, and staff development in a psychiatric hospital, "success" was not quite as unequivocal as at CUNY-York. In fact, the variable of success had little to do with the learning materials themselves; instead, success was found at sites where "learners were more experienced in managing their own learning, where they had stronger and more tangible motives for improving their writing skills, and where institutional commitment and flexibility were more clearly present" (Epes 1983, 3). As seventy years of writing instruction has shown, the shift of responsibility from institutions to individuals (or from learning materials to individuals) is a tried-and-true method of managing under-prepared students. After all, the thinking goes, if they cannot learn with what we give them, then they simply don't belong.

Perhaps the most troubling aspect of Comp-Lab for writing center professionals is not so much claims of success as compared to "traditional" classroom methods or to one-to-one tutoring, but a decidedly anti-tutor attitude. For example, in the project's final evaluation, opinions were solicited from other institutions who were using Comp-Lab. One devotee at the Polytechnic Institute of New York gives the following commentary:

> [The Comp-Lab materials] meet a need that in many places is met by live tutors, but they do so far less expensively and far more reliably. . . . Let me mention some of the drawbacks that [tutors] represent: they need to be trained; they can be absent, or late; they can be wrong in what they tell students; they can become unethically involved in producing a piece of writing; they can become part of an endless variety of complex, and distracting, social relationships with their tutees. All of these problems, to name a few, Comp-Lab bypasses. (Epes 1980, 177)

As an example of isolated and decontextualized approaches to composing, Comp-Lab seems to have few peers. Whether or not it is successful is perhaps less important than what it represents: the responsibility for learning "fundamentals" is up to the students (after all, they've come to college under-prepared for reasons entirely of their own making). What better way to provide learning opportunities than to do it in ways that maintain a comfortable barrier between the pristine classroom teacher and the messy drill-and-practice lab. Even those "complex and distracting" problems of "live tutors" can be avoided at a fraction of the cost.

For the writing center field, Comp-Lab is the culmination of seventy years of development. When, in 1981, Muriel Harris bifurcated writing assistance into two approaches—"the writing lab" and "the writing center," with the former the primary home of programmed learning and drill-and-practice approaches—the question for many writing center professionals was whether the writing lab would die out like a Neanderthalic lineage to be later uncovered by educational anthropologists. However, the power of such approaches to address long-standing dilemmas of access and equity in higher education is far too tempting for many institutions as higher and higher forms of technology are developed.

LESSONS LEARNED?

Recently, a participant asked the readers of the internet discussion list WCenter for advice on "the purchase of remediation software." While the first wave of respondents castigated the writer for being "fifteen-years old" in her educational objectives, several others braved the turbulent waters and recommended some titles. Programmed materials, now found in computer or book form, continue to be produced. The arguments used to sell those products and the assumptions about learning and teaching imbedded in them are eerily familiar. For instance, one computer-based product, *AllWrite!* from McGraw-Hill, dangles a modifier before its potential users and conjures up a familiar appeal: "Covering basic grammar and usage (with additional tips for ESL students), punctuation, and spelling in context, students can practice at their own pace in a writing center or computer lab. Writing instructors can then use valuable class time to focus on other writing issues." Another program, *SkillsBank* from the SkillsBank Corp., finally makes clear in its promotional materials just what it is that classroom teachers will do with their time once they have turned the onerous task of teaching grammar over to a computer: "SkillsBank can go a long way toward giving your students the individual help they need, freeing you to emphasize other aspects of students' writing such as quality of thought and presentation" (SkillsBank Corp). Whether or not every writing center is stocked with these materials is not as important as the reductive assumptions about learning and teaching writing that such instructional approaches represent, assumptions that are easily allied with the latest in high-tech solutions.

My reading of the technological evolution in the writing center from drill pads to programmed texts to computer-assisted auto-tutorials leads to the following conclusion: until writing assistance is more substantial than symbolic, until responsibility is more equally shared among institutions, instructors, and students, and until inclusiveness commands the resources necessary, our technological future will merely reflect our technological history. MUDs, MOOs, and other innovations might flourish in their own right, offering exciting possibilities for improving writing instruction, but attitudes toward the place of under-prepared students in higher education are substantial forces. Writing centers have always been intertwined with such attitudes, and technology is often the vehicle through which these attitudes are realized. Whether in the form of drill pads, teaching machines, programmed texts, or drill-and-practice software, technology has played a powerful role in writing centers past, primary agents in casting writing centers as "clinics for correction" and "houses of remediation." The lure of technology is seductive for all of us. How else can one explain that in the same journal, one year apart, one writer can claim that at his institution, "the computer lab is being transformed into a writing center where students can work individually on specific programs to remedy their deficiencies and to develop their writing skills" (Stark 1986, 5), while another writer asserts that "self-instruction books, tapes, video and slide programs' too often do little more than give 'first-aid' and 'treat symptoms,' perpetuating the image of a 'lab's' work as remedial, trivial, and expendable" (Waldo 14)?

As the writing center field grows and matures, examining its practices through both systematic and informal research, perhaps such divisions will be mediated. In the meantime, publishers will send us flyers, advertising the latest technological solution to deal with those difficult problems of teaching "fundamentals" to under-prepared students. Administrators will approve budgets for computer systems and reject funds for hiring additional tutors or increasing tutor salaries. And while we might find ourselves responding to the seductive appeal of technology, instead we need to remind ourselves of what our goals are for student learning and how we believe that learning to be best enabled. Writing center professionals can be a skeptical lot, experienced in carefully reading texts and uncovering hidden agendas; when it comes to our future with technology, that skepticism is perhaps our greatest asset.

NOTES

1. Nearly 40 years later, George Hillocks would conclude the following from his meta-analysis of over 500 research studies:

    School boards, administrators, and teachers who impose the systematic study of traditional school grammar on their students over lengthy periods of time in the name of teaching writing do them a gross disservice that should not be tolerated by anyone concerned with the effective teaching of good writing. (160)

2. As an example of the ambivalence some educators held toward the "new" students coming to the nation's campuses in the 1930s, consider the following comment: "Most of the privately endowed institutions make use of their privilege of refusing poor students, many of them taking no more than a third of the applicants. The state-supported institutions are less fortunate" (Fountain 312).

3. Ironically, Skinner himself showed great skepticism of the computer as a "teaching device," calling them a "fad" in 1968: "A simple, programmed cheat-proof workbook would do what computers do at a fraction of the cost" ("Computers Called 'Fad'" 5).

CHAPTER NINE

Virtual High School Writing Centers
A Spectrum of Possibilities

Pamela B. Childers
Jeanette Jordan
James K. Upton

T HE THREE OF US HAVE BEEN INVOLVED IN SECONDARY SCHOOL WRITING CENTERS for longer than we like to admit. Although our ages, backgrounds, and schools differ, we agree that computers, when used in writing centers, are tools for teaching writing across disciplines. We believe that writers should not be forced to do all phases of their individual writing processes at a computer [1]. We also are aware of the new literacies (Heath 1990; Selfe 1989) necessary to use this tool and realize that our students are far more comfortable with them than we are. However, we have witnessed the tendency of teachers to use all the whistles and bells without considering whether writing and learning are improving because of them. We agree that word processors have improved our typing ability, but is that what writing with computers is about?

While we each teach writing and English in secondary schools and direct WAC-based writing centers, our situations differ in many ways: Jeannette's school is a large public one, nationally recognized for excellence and situated in an affluent, suburban community with education as a top priority; Jim's school, also public, is urban, with innovative teachers functioning under extreme financial constraints and with a diverse population and discipline problems; Pam's institution is a relatively small, affluent, private day/boarding school for boys, dedicating major financial commitments to technology and educational endowments. The following excerpt from one of Jim's letters exemplifies the dichotomy of our environments:

> Another bittersweet letter. I take pride in that you and others are interested in our writing center efforts, even though we are literally a center without walls . . .or floor . . . or ceiling . . . or chairs . . . or desks . . . or any other physical objects save filing cabinets or resource information in the English office. And, in this age of technology, we have no computer(s) let alone a lab designated for writing center use. I read about what other centers are doing in using technology to enhance their services

and visit other centers which are technology-oriented, and I become very frustrated and even angry that our language arts department and writing center have been virtually ignored in our district's technology utilization plans.

Jim is aware of what technology other secondary school writing centers have; however, Jeanette and Pam have the opposite concerns. They both have the technology but remain cautious about how it fits into their writing center goals. They do not want their writing centers to become computer labs (Graves and Haller 1994), and they do want to keep the important dialogues about writing alive (LeBlanc 1994) and foremost in their facilities. These tensions reveal a number of important questions: Do we as writing center directors adapt our philosophy and goals to the technology or do we adapt the technology to our writing center philosophy and goals? Do we allow the techies to tell us what we must do with the technology in our writing centers and WAC programs? Do we "re-vision" our philosophy and goals based on what we know will empower our students to be better writers in the twenty-first century?

In this chapter, we provide detailed histories of each coauthor's writing center, its mission, and the role(s) technology play(s) in each program. Each coauthor also provides an assessment of technology's advantages and disadvantages within secondary school writing center contexts. Following these presentations, we summarize current technology's advantages and disadvantages and make predictions about technology in twenty-first century secondary school writing centers.

GLENBROOK NORTH HIGH SCHOOL WRITING CENTER

Overview

Glenbrook North High School (GBN) is a public school with a primarily college-bound student body located in Northbrook, Illinois, a suburb about 20 miles north of Chicago. Stu Snow and Paula Williams created the writing center in 1988 when they cleaned out a storage closet and gave up their planning periods to work with students on writing. At about this same time, they collaborated with English teachers from other area high schools to form the North Shore Writing Center Consortium to bring together secondary teachers interested in developing writing centers and to support them as they planned and implemented their programs. Technology was a frequent topic of discussion: Were they going to include computers? If so, would that be the focus? Each school ultimately worked out its own system—some "heavy tech"; others "no tech"; the rest in between. GBN combined its tutorial services with technology as it became available.

In 1990, GBN's writing center, The Write Place, underwent a massive reconstruction. No longer was the writing center just a closet with teachers volunteering their time. The district purchased 30 Macintosh LC computers for the English Department and expanded the writing center facilities into two additional rooms. Unfortunately, the writing center was closed for the year as teachers waited for the computers to arrive and the rooms to be remodeled. Meanwhile, the superintendent mandated a writing advisory grade in English, social studies, science, math, health, and business and created the position of a writing specialist in each school.

The Write Place's expansion continues: the writing center has 35 Macs and 1 PC; the school literary magazine, newspaper, and yearbook staffs create all of their layouts in the desktop publishing area, which houses six PowerMacs, scanners, digital cameras, and a multimedia station for digitizing sound and video. Students use the writing center facilities to work on any writing assignment, and all staff may reserve the computers for their classes and consult with the writing center staff. In addition to the center's computers, teachers and students have access to three other Macintosh labs and two PC labs, networked and with a T1 line direct internet access. Twelve Macintosh and four PC laptops are available for staff checkout, and 30 portable word processors are available for student signout from the writing center. Additionally, all departments have access to portable multimedia presentation units.

Although The Write Place is affiliated with the English Department, it is actually a school-wide resource. The writing center is made up of three adjoining rooms: the conferencing area/WAC room, computer lab, and desktop publishing room. The conferencing area/WAC room is where most of the individual conferencing takes place and where we keep the writing resources for WAC. Writing center staff members usually work in this area, but venture into the adjoining computer lab to assist teachers when full classes utilize the center. The computer lab is a large room that can accommodate a class of 30 students and has a teacher station that projects images onto large screens for demonstration/presentation purposes. A smaller computer room, the desktop publishing area, is located off the main computer area. All areas are separated by walls that are glass from about waist high to the ceiling so that people can see into the various rooms. All of the rooms are connected by doors to allow free movement among the rooms.

Another massive renovation project will move the center away from the English area to the very front of the school along with the new library. This location will allow extended hours and easier access for students and community members. Currently, our writing center is open 15 minutes before school starts and 30 minutes after the last class ends.

Despite the physical and staffing changes, The Write Place's basic philosophy remains. The writing center is more a service than a location; it is the staff rather than the technology. It offers a nonthreatening atmosphere designed to help writers identify, understand, and refine their personal writing processes. As stated in The Write Place training manual, staff "offer questions in place of corrections, support instead of criticism, and understanding rather than evaluation."

GBN has made a substantial staffing commitment to the writing center. A computer technologist, writing coordinators, teachers from across the disciplines, and students all work together to keep the writing center a beneficial service to the school.

Technologist: A computer expert with excellent people skills, he staffs the lab throughout the day, assists students with their individual questions, works with teachers, and presents to full classes. He also assists the literary magazine, newspaper, and yearbook staffs, including late-night deadline sessions. Additionally, he services the computers, orders the software, and is entirely responsible for the operation of the computer lab.

Writing Coordinator: This is a 4/5 teaching position shared between Stu and me. Responsibilities include: supervising the writing center, running the writing across the curriculum program, training and supervising student tutors, developing outreach programs, coordinating staff development with regard to writing issues, proofing materials mailed from school, staying current with writing topics, communicating information to faculty, conferencing with students, coordinating all writing contests, maintaining the writing center website, working with faculty on professional writing, and developing workshops for faculty and students.

Cross-curricular staffing: Science, math, social studies, PE/health, and English each have a WAC teacher representative who works in the writing center. They work one period a day in the writing center, attend meetings, and function as liaisons between the writing center and their respective departments. Representatives were selected from these disciplines because teachers in these subjects are required to give "writing grades" on the students' report cards in addition to the regular subject grades.

Students: Approximately 50 students serve as Write Place staff members each year. Students apply as juniors and, if selected, are trained and work in the writing center for their junior and senior years. Students work 90 minutes each week in the center and sign up for their slots based on their free time. They receive .25 credit on a pass/fail basis for their work. In addition to working in the center, students attend monthly training meetings and participate in the center's outreach programs.

With several computer labs throughout the school, we have repeatedly emphasized that we are a writing center and not a computer lab. The premise that computers are merely tools for writers to use guides our choices regarding technology. Students come to the writing center to do their writing for all curricular areas because of the available technical and academic personal assistance. Consequently, we made the choice not to have internet access on the computers in the writing center even though the wiring for it was present. We did this because all other labs have access, and we wanted to keep our focus on writing. Students do their research in other labs, but still come to us when they're pulling it all together for their presentations and papers. The Write Place is, however, networked to the school's other labs so students and faculty may access files they've created and saved elsewhere.

Advantages of a Secondary School Online Networked Writing Center

Theoretically, students using online services can access the resources of the writing center and ask questions of the staff at any time from any location. Students can log in from their homes late at night and investigate questions that arise as they write. This sounds great because most students do their writing on their own computers at home. High school students have very little free time during the school day because their days are filled with classes and after-school activities such as sports or work. The only time they really have to write is when the writing center is closed. An online writing lab allows accessibility at any time if someone is there to respond. Additionally, the online writing center encourages independence and self-sufficiency. As we prepare adolescents for college, part of what we need to do is to allow them the chance to work on their own and learn what strategies work for them. Sometimes adolescents become dependent on their teachers, lose confidence in their own instincts as writers, and are unsure what to do if their teachers aren't available. Secondary teachers are usually easy to find, however, and students get their questions answered. They won't have that luxury when they go to college and find that their professors have specific office hours on certain days.

Actually, the primary advantages to the secondary online writing center are more for outreach than direct writing instruction with our own students. Accessibility to resources outside our school is a very useful aspect of being online. Additionally, with an online writing center, students can collaborate with and get feedback from other students whom they would never be able to work with under different circumstances. Another advantage is that schools with internet access but limited funding can attain the same resources as those which are more affluent. Online writing centers can remove or at least diminish some of the geographical and financial barriers that many schools face.

Disadvantages of a Secondary School Online Networked Writing Center

Even though I "jumped on the bandwagon" and followed the lead of university writing centers, I see problems with OWLs at the secondary level. That doesn't mean that they shouldn't exist or that I'll be pulling our site off the web. Instead, it means that we as high school teachers must step back and examine what our students really need as young writers. We can't just do things at the high school level because they work at the college level. Even though many high school writing centers are based on university models, high school faculty adapt their writing centers to fit the secondary setting. Even so-called "college prep" high schools such as ours are NOT colleges. Our students may come off as being mature, but they are still adolescents who present unique problems and opportunities.

As such, developmental issues are a main concern in considering online services and high school students. These writers are in the process of learning how to become better writers and need the personal interaction that happens in a face-to-face (f2f) conference. The most effective way to teach writing is through the one-to-one tutorial model used in writing center conferences. In the writing center, we work in conjunction with classroom teachers, who would like to be able to meet with all of their students but just don't have enough time given the high student load and hectic schedules. Our primary goal as writing center staff members is not to make the paper better but to help students become better writers. To do that, we guide students along, prompt them with questions, respond to their questions while we teach them what kind of questions to ask about their texts. Most questions generated at first by high school students deal with grammatical issues because they often don't recognize the "bigger" problems with their texts. Although the major concepts we work on in the writing center are focus, organization, and development, students don't normally come in with questions about those topics. It's more vague: "Look this over and tell me what you think" or "Check it over to make sure the grammar is right." Part of what we do at the high school level is teach them in the conferences to look at their whole piece and what they're trying to say. It is through this dialogue that students learn. We work with them so that they have a better understanding of themselves as writers and how to approach their texts. Through their visits to the high school writing center, students hopefully learn to ask the bigger questions about their texts and address those issues in their writing. I don't see how this personal interaction can be effectively duplicated online.

Their lack of maturity and confidence poses another problem with online feedback: students are very emotional about their writing and have fragile egos. Comments made online lack the nonverbal cues that help the writer and staff member understand each other.

Another problem with OWLs is the logistics in general. In order for students to access the OWL, they must sign on to the internet and go to the website. For our students, that means using the modem and dialing up their service. It's a time-consuming process that they're not likely to use. If they have a question, they'll ask somebody at home, wait and ask someone in the writing center in the morning, or just blow it off. Also, since many students are working on their papers the night before they're due, the turnaround time that happens with their online questions is just too slow. By the time one of us gets to the questions, the students are already at school and can just as easily ask us in person. Or, it's too late, and they've already handed in the paper.

BURLINGTON COMMUNITY HIGH SCHOOL WRITING CENTER
Overview

Burlington Community High School, located in the city of Burlington, an urban setting in Iowa, is a four-year high school of approximately 1600 students with an "Alternative School" of approximately 150 students at another campus.

The writing center is literally "the idea of a writing center." After investing $100,000+ to research and develop a writing center and after documenting its valuable services for students, staff, and the community (and winning an NCTE Center of Excellence Award), the district discontinued funding. We continued to operate the center with volunteers who worked during their prep time (which raises many ugly contractual issues and professional/personal conflicts)—currently four teachers. We do utilize student tutors for many of our services, but even these efforts are limited by lack of location.

Our center's mission statement involves providing four services: (1) drop-in or assigned remediation, reinforcement, or enrichment services to individual students or groups of students; (2) in-class presentations and interactions about writing-learning activities, i.e. research processes and products, prewriting graphic organizers, response techniques; (3) work with all staff on development of writing-to-learn and writing-to-show-learning techniques and strategies by also functioning as the clearinghouse for storage and sharing of such teacher-developed activities; (4) 'extra' writing and learning related activities beyond the school day such as our 'Study Skills Night' and our work with students and parents on college entrance and scholarship writings. These efforts have expanded to work with local business managers, secretaries, etc.

The staff is obviously a paradoxically diminishing increasing problem. While seven teachers volunteered to work with students or other classes during their planning periods, now four do. I work part-time as the district's 'Excellence' facilitator, so my time for center work has been lessened. Some volunteers became tired of harassment from other teachers about their choice of how to use their prep time and frustrated that the administration and board have never expressed any appreciation for their efforts and have made no indication that future funding is possible. I provide this background not to suggest those of us who continue to work are somehow heroic/idiotic, but the background of the center and how it is viewed by staff, administration, and the board will dramatically impact the teachers' attitudes in using any future technologies we may be able to designate for center use.

Clearly, our center operates on a most informal basis. The list of teachers willing to work with students either during their planning period or before/after school is posted outside the English office, and students who wish to meet with a teacher contact the teacher directly or leave a note in the teacher's mailbox. Most teachers who work as writing center tutors either stay in their rooms during their planning period or leave a note indicating their location.

The most 'public' of our work is the activities we sponsor after the school day; i.e. our 'Study Skills Night,' 'Read Around the Clock,' work with writing contest entries, work with college applications and scholarships. As I indicated above, we do work with local management and secretarial groups in improving communication skills.

Our use of technology in center work is clearly in the B.C. (Before Computer) age. Our computer availability in working with students is limited to a computer a teacher may have in his/her room or the computers available in the small computer lab in the library. Some writing teachers used to utilize the Mac lab in the business department to teach writing when the lab was free, but staff reduction has eliminated any free periods in the lab.

Despite our past of doing without, there have been some indications that we may move into technology-supported education. As part of our 'Excellence' program, all teachers have been afforded the opportunity to take computer courses through the district, and many have taken advantage of this opportunity. However, not all teachers have access to computers or to the software used in the classes.

Beginning in the 1997-98 school year, the State of Iowa is providing $325,000 a year for the next five years for our district to implement an approved technology plan. At BHS, all teachers will have a Mac 475 or Mac 575 computer installed by the fall of 1997, and the entire building will be networked to the office. Supposedly, each teacher will also have access to the internet. There has been little discussion of how many printers will be available or where these printers will be located. Many have asked about scanners, HyperText, HyperStudio, PowerPoint, and other sophisticated software, but no one has an answer as to what software will be included with the machines or will be available as options.

The language arts department made a most effective appeal/argument to use either the 'technology' or 'Instructional Support Levy' money to create a networked computer lab for the department, but we were told that there is no room available for such a lab."

Advantages of a Secondary School Online Networked Writing Center

Those of us who work in the 'idea of a writing center' can only speculate about the myriad of advantages of an online writing center to individual students and to our center's efforts. Clearly, such a center would enable a student to seek and provide a wider range of responses to works-in-progress, allow for greater information access through the Net and students in other schools, submit writings electronically, develop technologically supported relationships through email sharings, and a host of other benefits to the individual.

We see the networked lab as a more effective means to teach prewriting and revision skills, to practice effective proofreading/editing skills, to teach research via the Net, and other technological dreams.

Disadvantages of a Secondary School Online Networked Writing Center

We literally don't know of advantages or disadvantages of an online center . . . except we already work with students who see the computer and software (research paper software) as the end of the writing/learning process. They assume that work done on a computer is somehow superior ('good enough') simply because it was done on a computer. They fail to see that the computer is a tool just as a typewriter and paper and pen are tools to help people discover and share their perceptions of the world in which they live. We do sit with students at monitors and work with them on their writing and thinking skills, and we believe the interaction between the writer and the reader and the text, whether on paper or on screen, is the key to effective tutoring.

THE McCALLIE SCHOOL WRITING CENTER
Overview

The McCallie School, located on historic Missionary Ridge in the city of Chattanooga, Tennessee, has approximately 760 day/boarding students in grades 7-12. It is an all-male college preparatory school with an afternoon coordinate program with Girls Preparatory School, is active in the Tennessee Association of Independent Schools and the National Association of Independent Schools, and is accredited by the Southern Association of Colleges and Schools.

I started the Caldwell Writing Center (CWC) at The McCallie School in the fall of 1991 after a year of planning. Having previously created a writing center at Red Bank Regional High School in Little Silver, New Jersey, I was aware of the advantages and disadvantages of computers in a writing center. When I first visited McCallie, all offices contained computer terminals, all faculty had Mac Classics and printers, and students had access to Macintosh computers with dot matrix printers in the computer lab. Because these were the computers of choice at the school, I designed the CWC with all Mac Classics and HP DeskWriter printers. The computers were connected to a Mac SE30 fileserver, plus we had an LC and Apple LaserWriter at my station for faculty use. Over the next five years, faculty began purchasing computers for home use through a school no-interest payroll deduction program, and we added a Quadra 650 to the CWC. As software required more memory, we began adding to the memory of the Mac LC and Classics to make them last another year. In the meantime, a unilateral decision was made over the summer of 1995 to convert to an all-PC campus. Two new PCs with an HP DeskJet printer were added to the CWC, and I was given one of each at my station as well. The following year all Classics were replaced by PCs, and the three DeskWriters were replaced with one HP LaserWriter. Even though I had requested a Power Mac, I was told that there was not money for such "questionable technology." The LC and Quadra were put in a special area with the Apple LaserWriter. As more students needed access to Mac computers, another LC was moved into the CWC. Also, over those years we have added four Alpha Smart or Alpha Smart Pro portable word processors for students to sign out. These became very popular with students who did not own computers. Students would take them to class or home for the weekend, then they could come to the CWC and send their text directly into a Word file to print on either a Mac or PC. By the fall of 1997, there were over 250 computers available on campus, with internet access and email capability for the use of all students and staff.

The initial commitment to the CWC computers fell mainly in the hands of the Caldwell family who had created the endowed chair in composition and funded the computers in the CWC. By 1995, McCallie had taken on a major commitment to technology throughout the school. By the fall of 1995, all faculty had a PC and printer on their desks, courses in Windows, Word, Access, Excel, Netscape, and html were offered, and DTFs (Designated Technology Facilitators) were selected for each department. As a member of this group, I have remained involved in what is happening with technology, yet most of the decisions are made elsewhere in a technology committee that includes administrators and the director of technology. The commitment has included the addition of computer projectors in many classrooms and a technology room called the Sand Box where teachers may use scanners, digital cameras, editing equipment. Through funds provided by many alumni, McCallie has made a major financial commitment to technology.

The CWC's philosophy has not changed since we opened its doors in 1991. It is "a low-risk environment where there is a reverence for writing." Just as Jeanette's and Jim's facilities, we provide many services for students, faculty, staff, and parents. Our students may drop in, come with a class, or schedule individual conferences. Through workshops in the CWC or in classrooms, we are able to focus on particular aspects of writing from how to take a timed essay to how to determine authentic research on the internet. Our faculty and staff use us as a resource for creating writing assignments and assessment tools, designing writing-to-learn activities, helping with fund-raising letters, using online/phone grammar hotline, answering questions regarding use of technology, and serving as a resource for finding appropriate writing materials. Each year I offer workshops for new teachers and departments to meet their writing in the disciplines needs. Faculty come to the CWC to ask about writing contests, professional writing, grant proposals, and ways to work with other teachers to help their students learn. We also answer parents' questions and help them with projects, as well as serve as a resource for alumni.

Located in the middle of the hallway on the third floor of the Academic Building, the CWC has full windows towards the hallway and overlooking the city and mountains in the distance. The room contains a divider that can be closed to separate the computer side from the workshop side. The computer lab is located in an adjacent room and can be used for overflow during non-teaching periods. The staff includes a full-time director, part-time assistant director, and night writing assistants. All staff have been trained in responding to student writing as well as use of computers for writing. Just as in Jeanette's writing center, we focus on asking questions to help students become empowered to improve their own writing. As director, my job involves overseeing the daily functioning and staffing of the writing center, teaching the peer tutoring course, counseling faculty on writing assignments and assessments appropriate for meeting their goals, giving mini-lessons on writing in the disciplines to classes, assisting faculty with their own professional writing, acting as a liaison in pedagogical debates between classroom teachers and administrators, keeping all records of use of the CWC, offering faculty workshops, preparing materials for faculty and student use, and acting as a writing resource person for the school community. Steve Reno, my assistant, spends his mornings teaching composition at the University of Tennessee at Chattanooga, then works with our students in the CWC as well as teaching one tenth grade English class. Just as Jeanette has a male counterpart, I highly recommend teams of male and female writing center staff. Students, in our case boys, often prefer to work with Steve because of the outstanding rapport he establishes with them.

A peer tutoring elective course is offered; sometimes 3-4 students will sign up for the course taught by the director. The CWC is open weekdays from 8 a.m. - 4 p.m., Sundays from 7-9 p.m., and Monday through Thursday from 6:30 - 8:30 p.m. Students also have access to staff through email and phone during other hours.

Students primarily use the 15 PCs and 3 Macintosh computers for word processing, email and internet access. We have T1 lines, networked lines and servers that enable students to go directly to Eudora and Internet Explorer from the CWC. They may check their mail from home, dormitory room or anywhere on campus. They may also access their files anywhere, so that if they start a file on Word 97 in one location, they may save it to their own file on the T Drive and access it from any other location. Our standard software includes Office 97.

Unlike some writing centers that consider themselves computer facilities, we are a writing resource for students and for staff that uses computers to teach writing. CAI software is not part of our environment in the sense of "drill and kill"; rather, we use software programs as resources for particular writing, thinking and learning activities. For instance, we have NIV Bible Study, CollegeView, StudyWorks, and other CD programs installed on many of the computers for use in conjunction with discipline-specific writing assignments.

This year the school is providing an ordering service so that students may purchase Toshiba laptops that can be plugged into our own network. Although not currently required, the administration is studying the possibility of making McCallie an all-laptop school in the near future.

Advantages of a Secondary School Online Networked Writing Center

The greatest advantages of an online, networked writing center should be immediacy of access to information, but then that assumes that the system is working, that everyone knows to back up all files, and that students know how to locate credible research online. I especially like the speed at which one can ask and receive answers from colleagues, collaborators, experts, and students. Phone tag can take days, and one may still not get the information in a timely fashion; whereas, an article, a URL or other information may be shared within a single morning or afternoon. For instance, when I am helping a teacher design a writing activity he wants to use for his math classes when they visit the writing center, I can send him a draft of the assignments and assessment, he can revise and return them to be logged on all computers before the students arrive. We don't have to photocopy the directions; they are merely downloaded. Instead of hard copy for the students to print out, they email their writing to each other and/or to the teacher with copies to me. I set up new mailboxes for different projects so that we can keep records of all this work. Also, we conduct writing and thinking projects as part of collaboratives with college students. Without email and internet access, the students would not be able to discuss the readings on a website and email each other for writing and response. These are a few advantages as well as the more obvious ones of ease with collaboration and publication.

Also, having an online, networked writing center prepares our students for other college experiences with writing and technology. Former CWC peer tutor Tripp Grant emails from college: ". . . working with Eudora last year saved about thirty stress points for me this year. Learning the whole email and internet thing last year has helped me so much already this year. I have so many teachers who want homework emailed to them. All my new friends hate to use it because I think they are unfamiliar with it. I am very comfortable with the technology used here because I used it at McCallie" (9 Sept. 1997 email).

Disadvantages of a Secondary School Online Networked Writing Center

The biggest disadvantage of an online, networked writing center is the possibility of losing f2f time with students and dependency on computer technicians and programmers who may control what hardware and software you get without considering how you might use it. In many situations, I know that if I had the student read his draft aloud to me, he would have caught his own mistakes. However, when he merely sends a draft to me and I respond with comments in all caps, brackets or bold, there is no dialogue. Less responsibility for learning seems to fall on the student.

Just in the last week, our networked system was down periodically over four out of five days. Students who planned to have their work done early couldn't do their research anywhere on campus, work on their writing, print out drafts, or even get on the system. My fear with a school full of laptops is that the now more-frequent excuses of "the network was down" for not doing one's writing on time will increase even more.

Another problem with technology in writing centers is that writing gets pushed further from the physical space unless we stay on top of the situation. We have become more technologically trained people "policing" computer use in writing centers and trying, at the same time, to maintain some sense of atmosphere appropriate for writing.

Every year more students are coming to secondary schools computer literate; newer operating systems and versions of software become available, and we are focusing more on the subtle differences of software than on organization, content, structure, purpose, and audience for a piece of writing. I hear many of my secondary and college friends, too, talking about getting hardware and software changes with no manuals or consultation before the decision has been made. What then occurs is that writing center personnel, just as classroom teachers, spend more time worrying about the operation of the technology and less time responding to writing, thinking and learning. What I hear again and again is that the top priority has become technology rather than learning. Schools talk about budget crunches for salaries and decent learning facilities, while spending sometimes hundreds of thousands on technology. It's a tradeoff for sure.

CONCLUSION

Summarizing our thoughts about technology in secondary school writing centers is not easy. We certainly agree that we must prepare our students to use technology *before* they go to college or to work. We also agree that the technology should be used to support our WAC-based writing center philosophy and goals. That is, technology should be used to support and enhance writing, thinking and learning as well as to improve student attitudes toward writing. Finally, whether working at a monitor or with hard copy (paper), fact-to-face interaction is a vital part of what we do and why we do it. That part of our job involves much more than just writing, thinking and learning; it involves verbal exchange, negotiation, and socialization skills in a "low-risk environment," as Pam calls it. Jeanette makes the point that our secondary students "are in the process of learning how to become better writers and need the personal interaction that happens in f2f conference . . . I don't see how this personal interaction can be effectively duplicated online." Jim agrees, saying that the interaction among writer, reader and text, "whether on paper or on screen, is the key to effective tutoring." We see technology as merely something to support what we do but not to replace it.

Jeanette brings up an interesting question about email and internet use: Do we eliminate email and internet access in the writing center if it is available elsewhere on campus so that our facility focuses on writing? Pam's feelings are mixed. Although she hates "policing" internet and email abuse while students are in the writing center, she uses both for writing activities in classes across disciplines. The whole question of credible research on the Net is part of our work with writing of research papers, explaining about plagiarism, and teaching appropriate use of citations. She knows, too, that many colleges also use both as part of their everyday writing.

Don't get us wrong; we appreciate the ease of professional communication with colleagues through listservs and email, and of writing collaborative works such as this (If Jim had been able to email his drafts, they could have been cut and pasted into this piece rather than typed. Also, we would have been able to communicate more frequently to get feedback of drafts. Believe us, we would have preferred writing this chapter with everyone online). However, for secondary school students, how does an online writing center help them? It is easier and faster for them to pick up the phone and call us or wait until the next morning to catch us in person rather than to send a question or document and wait for a response in a timely fashion. Since many secondary school students still don't have access and/or don't write their papers until the wee hours of the night before they are due, how would an online writing center help them?

In his latest letter to Pam, Jim admitted that he has actually "received a new Mac with an email address. It is a Mac IIsi, and no one knows where it came from." Since he spends so much time on new learning and teaching innovations, we look forward to seeing how he will effectively use his limited technology. One thing is clear to all three of us; we will continue to learn and discover new ways to improve student writing and thinking with technology as a tool. Our heads are not in the sand; however, we will also not be brainwashed or "glitzed" into believing that any technology is more important than our interaction with students of all ages and ability levels to improve their writing, thinking and learning.

NOTES

1.   One irony of working collaboratively on this chapter is that two of us have access to email, while the third must resort to "snail mail."

CHAPTER TEN

The Community College Mission and the Electronic Writing Center

Ellen Mohr

I N 1984, WHEN MY SUPERVISOR INVITED ME INTO HIS OFFICE TO "TALK ABOUT" purchasing computers for the Johnson County Community College (JCCC) Writing Center (the Center), my only prior knowledge about computer technology came from a month's stint of working for Lee's Temporaries one summer between teaching terms. That computer was the size of a small closet and ate data cards that I fed it for two long weeks. I didn't know what the cards were for and I didn't want to know what the machine did with them. I just prayed I wouldn't create a melt down or some other catastrophe. So, my first reaction to my supervisor's proposal was apprehensive excitement. Since then, I have webbed, netted, and surfed, not to mention sundry tasks without metaphors, only euphemisms.

THE JCCC MISSION

Community colleges have one major universal mission: to serve the community with lifelong learning. Community colleges actively seek out community needs. JCCC prides itself on its institutional research department and its many surveys to gather and analyze information from the Johnson County community (Kansas' largest county), and from students. No new instructional programs are implemented without assessing needs with a survey. Community college students tend to be consumers demanding the best equipment, quality instruction, and ample resources. Community colleges respond to these demands—putting the "customer" first. In *Generation X Goes To College*, Peter Sacks (1994, 162) discusses the recent shift of instructor-centered education to student-centered learning. In the community college the focus has long been with the student/community/consumer. As early as 1986, community colleges viewed their role in technology as the means to computer literacy for the community.

To acknowledge its role in helping to keep the community abreast of the changing technology, JCCC revisited its mission statement several years ago. The new mission promotes JCCC as "a comprehensive college committed to serving the current and emerging needs of the residents of Johnson County for higher academic education, technical/vocational education and lifelong learning, incorporating instructional methods and current technology in the teaching and learning process." To emphasize the technological focus, the annually revised college objectives show a continued interest in providing current technology and training for JCCC's employees and students. A suburban community college such as JCCC includes adults hoping to learn skills to get better or different jobs, high school graduates hoping to get into a career or transfer to a university, and high school students earning college transfer credit. Clint Gardner (chapter six) profiles community college students, noting that their busy lives encourage online writing centers. Like Salt Lake City Community College (SLCCC), JCCC's students are busy, often working 40-hour-a-week jobs, carrying 15-18 credit hours, while attempting to balance those schedules with their families. They want to get through school fast, and as part of that consumer-educated mindset they expect the school to provide services where and when they need them. Consequently, like many community colleges, JCCC provides many services students need to succeed in the form of resource centers (writing center, math lab, learning center) along with a variety of developmental courses. Unlike SLCCC, JCCC, so far, does not provide these online resources—but, who knows what the future holds.

The JCCC Writing Center's mission is to "promote the college's mission of lifelong learning and service to the community by providing an environment for nurturing independent writing; valuing progress, not perfection; emphasizing process, not product." The recursiveness of the writing center services reinforces process writing by providing many resources (figure 1). Emphasizing writers, their skill levels, and assignment goals, tutors guide writers through the maze of choices.

The Center supports the college's mission by supporting the community through the Grammar Hotline and one-credit flexible, individualized modules which businesses and individuals can use easily. The Center also supports technology literacy by reinforcing strategies taught in the collaborative computer composition classrooms. We like to be innovators often foraging the way for others, and since our financial base is one of the country's most affluent counties, we can afford technical innovation. JCCC has kept up with the rapidly changing technology, at least with equipment. Within its ranks and trenches, however, the movement has not always been smooth.

In the early years of computers, the Center helped students learn word processing. Then as students came by with more computer competency, staff concentrated on providing programs to help improve the students' writing skills. The Center now provides internet instruction as more students come online. At the 1997 National Writing Center Association conference in Park City, Utah, I was amazed at how many writing center directors were their colleges' technology trainer about the internet, web design, and email instruction.

Figure 1
Recursive Writing Center Process

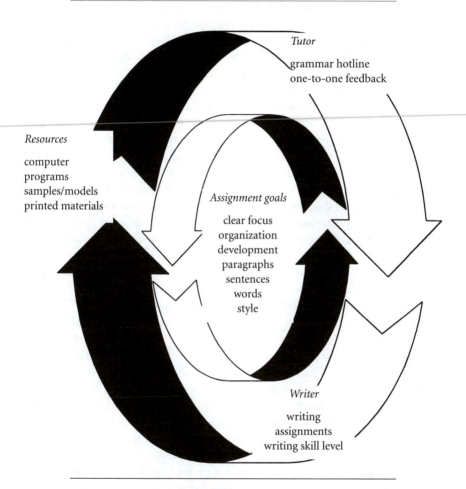

Tutor

grammar hotline
one-to-one feedback

Resources

computer
programs
samples/models
printed materials

Assignment goals

clear focus
organization
development
paragraphs
sentences
words
style

Writer

writing
assignments
writing skill level

EARLY TECHNOLOGICAL EXPERIMENTS

From the advent of its technology, JCCC has provided the support needed to train staff and instructors. Thus, my first step was to arm myself with knowledge. I took a computer literacy course where I learned something important: first I must decide what I want computers to do for us in our center; then I choose software and hardware to fit those needs. I wanted a management system because our client numbers were climbing, and we were required to keep records and produce monthly reports. I also wanted first-hand knowledge of word processing for our staff and students. These two tasks did not seem too overwhelming or ambitious at the time.

We initially purchased two TRS-80s, one for the management system and reports and letters, the other for word processing. My computer literacy course instructor wrote the record-keeping program we still use. Superscript, the word processing program on the other TRS-80, and Smart, the next program used, were easily replaced by WordPerfect. They were, however, a good training ground for our computer literacy needs. Our tutors and students using the Center always knew the most about the programs' capabilities and experimented and wrote various mini-programs. It was a simple time.

In 1989 the English Department developed a collaborative computer classroom for teaching composition with a mission to connect computer literacy and writing. Twelve computers (PCs) were provided for twenty-four students with the intention that students would collaborate to learn strategies to improve their writing process. Because many early programs used in the classroom were first tried in the Center, the task of supporting computer instruction also fell to the Center as students and instructors came to practice newly learned strategies and to invent new applications. The Center continues to support students and instructors in the collaborative computer classrooms (now there are two) as they tackle sophisticated applications and computer-assisted writing tasks.

Four Apple IIe's and more software followed. I would scan vendor catalogs reading the colorful descriptions for software which promised to "improve writing and communication skills" in ten or fewer exciting lessons. Some were good; some were terrible, unfriendly, and often worthless. Even though more programs were available, they were rarely designed for adult learners or were riddled with programming problems, mechanical errors, even wrong information. Others were so difficult to use that they gather dust on a shelf. We could have written our own software, and I even took a course, bought authoring software, and attempted a simple program. I discovered I had better things to do with my time.

Also, in those early years software vendors didn't allow preview time. You bought, you kept, and many of us ended up with a graveyard of unused programs. In the late 1980s and early '90s, Project Synergy, spearheaded by Miami Dade in partnership with IBM, was launched to help remedy software evaluation problems. Synergy was sponsored by the League for Innovation in the Community College, an organization founded in the middle 1980s and made up of over twenty of the most prestigious community college districts in the country. From its beginning, this organization has been at the forefront of technology, holding conferences to showcase the latest in classroom innovations. For Project Synergy, representatives from all of the League colleges reviewed and evaluated existing software in three areas: writing, math, and reading—I represented JCCC in the writing review. At least three representatives reviewed over 100 composition software programs, and the results were published and a program written so instructors could give the criteria they wanted in a program; in turn, they would receive a list of software titles which met or partially met the criteria.

Several observations can be made from this project. First, as educators we came together to talk about new technology and how it could be used to teach writing. Second, software vendors and publishers began to listen to and even seek the advice of higher education instructors. The project received so much national attention that the software publishers had to pay attention to what instructors wanted, and they had to allow 30-day trial periods. Third, I realized that using technology to teach writing skills wasn't going to be a passing phase. Philosophically, I had to come to terms with what place computers had in our JCCC Center.

Other community colleges have not been so lucky. Some have had writing centers evolve out of computer labs, making the computer, not the tutoring, the focus. Also the position of writing center director is highly marginalized in many community colleges, either a part-time or a low paying staff position. Sadly, the turn-over of community college writing center directors locally has been overwhelming, and I am one of the few full-time permanently employed community college writing center directors. Sometimes the writing center consists of one person, several computers, and a corner in a library or learning center. In other words, the college support is just not there, making any technological innovation difficult or downright impossible.

LESSONS LEARNED

Thus, I come to my evolving philosophy that has been borne out of my and my community college counterparts' experiences.

Writing Centers Should Not Be Computer Labs.

Students use the computers to improve their knowledge of writing rules but work with tutors to incorporate and apply the rules to their actual writing. MicroLab, for example, works especially well to connect writing, computer assisted instruction, and tutoring, and over half of the Composition 121 instructors now tie their students' work to this program by either having all of their students take the assessment or by pointing out frequent errors for students to review in the program. Our English Department has as one of its composition program objectives that students will write standard edited English. Since most instructors do not want to spend much class time reviewing grammar, usage, and mechanics, and since most students are reluctant to use a handbook, the Center provides this instruction. Yet the writing center policy clearly states "No Proofreading," a rule strictly upheld. Students still (after almost 20 years of marketing our services) expect us to proofread their papers. Computers help us teach and reinforce rules as they apply to the individual writer by using the students' graded papers to apply computer module exercises to specific errors. Students do not work in isolation on computer programs that may have no bearing on their actual writing.

Students Do Not Use Our Writing Center Computers to Type Their Papers.

Students bring drafts for review and use the computers to revise. Like many colleges, JCCC provides open computer labs for word processing and if students used our lab for all of their word processing needs, we would become a computer lab. We encourage students to bring disks and hard copies, and at a table or on the computer they work with a tutor on ways to revise.

Style Checkers can be used, but with caution.

Too many students don't understand style checkers' limitations. Again, tutors help writers understand their revision choices. Most style checkers, as their title indicates, look for ambiguities, colloquialisms, and nuances. Developmental writers grasp for sound structure—organization and development—and style checkers confuse and side-track them.

Computers Will Never Replace Tutors.

The student-tutor interaction is the most important writing center strategy. Computers are only an enhancement to student learning. If a program is used in isolation (from the tutoring), often it has no value. Several years after computers became a real part of our writing center instruction, I noticed that our tutors and instructors put students new to the English language and students with learning disabilities at computers rather than dealing with the students' problems one-on-one. Day after day these "difficult" students worked in isolation at the computers. They didn't complain because they believed practicing grammar exercises was a means to learning "correct English." When I addressed this problem with the staff, they began looking at alternative strategies to work with this student population. Now even when students work at the computers, the Center's tutors and instructors maintain contact. Students are not allowed to work at length at a computer before actually writing.

Constant Review and Evaluation of Computer Programs is Vital to Quality Instruction.

We have learned that the more interactive the program the better for the student. Monitoring student use and noting improvement in the student's writing is essential. We have also noted errors in programs, not only programming problems but actual errors in usage or grammar. Not all software is written by educators. I maintain a notebook that describes the various programs and suggests ways to use the software, and I update the book frequently as we see better program applications. One program we didn't use much when we first purchased it was *Blue Pencil*, an editing and revision program. An instructor in the center began using the program with one of our module students and discovered its value in teaching editing skills. A grammar program we purchased was pure text with little interaction so we shelved it as we could see no viable application for it.

How and When to Use software is Important to Tutor Training.

Software will go unused if not taught to staff—not only how to use but when and with whom. Several years ago we bought *Guides*, a program for developmental writers which has tutorials on organization and development of paragraphs, sentence structure, and fundamental writing rules. I then was on leave from the center for a year interning in our staff development program, and when I returned, I discovered that no one used the program. Last year when we purchased *6th Floor Media*, I asked tutors and instructors to review the software and consider its applications. Several gave the three-part program cursory consideration; most did not even look at it. This year I have planned several training sessions around the software.

MORE TECHNOLOGY = MORE PRESSURE

We now have eighteen computers available for students, the management system computer on the secretary's desk, and her own PC for word processing, email, etc. Seven are networked and online, while the others are old and inadequate for anything but supporting software programs incompatible with Windows 95. We have CD players on the Gateways and Power Macintoshes, and one machine has audio and recording hardware to support a program called *Ellis*, an ESL program that works on written and spoken language skills. Throwing in four Power Macintoshes and one MacIIci reveals that the Center houses a full technology range—obsolete to state-of-the-art.

In the early 1990s the college made a decision to standardize hardware (IBM compatible or p.c.'s) and some software (Word Perfect, Power Point, Microsoft programs). This decision pushed uniformity across campus and made networking easier. By the end of 1995, all full-time faculty at JCCC had computers on their desks and were linked to the college's networked system. By the end of 1996, all were linked to the world and the writing center's seven PCs were online soon after.

Although every instructor has a computer on his/her desk, not every computer can handle the information the instructor would like to have delivered. The college works to change this fact—replacing computers every three to five years. However, changes are rapid and many times requested computers, having moved through layers of signatures and paperwork, are obsolete by the time they are approved and delivered. Over five years ago, I asked to link the Center's computers to the composition computer classroom via a server so that Center programs could be shared with the instructors in the classrooms and so that when the classroom was in use, students and instructors could use the writing center computers to access information found only in the classroom. We are just now being provided that access. In 1995, my office computer was updated to a Gateway 2000 P5-60, and for me it was state-of-the-art. Now my hard drive is full, my memory short, and my frustration growing because I cannot load the *6th Floor Media* program, and I often lockup when "surfing the net" for usable websites. I am not due for replacement hardware until the year 2000. However, I am well aware that I am ahead of my counterparts in many other colleges. I am online and working.

Once we were all online and networked, pressure increased. It wasn't enough that we had to learn the ups and downs of computers and educational software in a writing center, we now faced college-wide networking, getting online to the internet, and designing web pages. Taking advantage of our staff development training program, in a two-year period, I took workshops and courses in *Windows 95*, *Word Perfect*, *Power Point* (two generations), *Excel*, the World-Wide Web, *Netscape* and *Netscape Gold*, library data-bases, *Pine*, *Microsoft Exchange*, *Microsoft Scheduler*, and Web Wizard to learn how to design a home page and html coding. Some information I retained because I used it immediately and have continued to do so. Other programs I use less frequently and have to relearn each time, which is, to say the least, frustrating.

Programs bought for the Center require my training myself and then training our tutors and instructors. Our tutor training program, certified by the College Reading and Learning Association, includes numerous sessions on computers and writing and their place in a writing center. In the notebook I keep that categorizes the various software programs and describes and suggests ideas for using the software, I have grouped the programs as follows:

- grammar checks and editors, such as Editor, Grammatik, and Correct Grammar
- English as a Second Language, such as Ellis, Toefl, and Tutor Tapes
- drill and practice (which includes not only grammar and mechanics but also sentence structure and paragraph organization and development), such as Learning Plus and Guides
- grammar and mechanics assessments, such as Que Intellectual and MicroLab
- editing and proofreading, such as Blue Pencil, Que Intellectual, Compris, Perfect Copy, and Elements of Style
- documentation styles, such as online handbooks and Citation

Many newer programs are highly developed and require more learning time because they coordinate sound, video, and interactive activities in a networked writing environment. Also, numerous websites are constantly being created with access to grammar and mechanics rules and drills and a variety of writing instruction. What we used to have to either develop ourselves or buy is now available for free. What impact these sites will have on existing software and software being developed is hard to predict, but change is inevitable. We try to provide links to websites or home pages that are especially helpful not only to our students but also our instructors, but the sites change and require constant surveillance. Keeping current is a growing challenge.

We also add email and listservs to the list of growing responsibilities. I feel compelled to be on several campus-wide listservs, our variety of composition courses listservs, a local writing across the curriculum organization listserv, the

National Writing Center Association listserv, and then because I am on several executive boards, those listservs. I turned on my computer one morning after attending a three-day conference to discover I had over a thousand messages. To sort through those messages and answer or note the more demanding ones took most of my day, and I probably deleted two-thirds of them with cursory or no reading. It is not uncommon for me to have one hundred messages per day. I would love to be an active member of the interesting discussions taking place on these listservs, but most of the time I merely interlope, siphon the best of the discourse, print and file it in a thick folder for later reference.

The center's online grammar hotline must be checked daily. We do not receive many questions because most of our community clients still use the telephone hotline; however, we have received requests to read manuscripts from remote areas like Denmark. This fall, several of our writing instructors have asked their students to email a question to the hotline, an assignment that has begun to fill our mailbox. As the online hotline requests increase, we must monitor the line more frequently, and assigning this task to different tutors each day helps to keep the service active and less burdensome. We still encourage students to bring long manuscripts into the Center rather than our trying to answer complicated questions via the phone or computer. Our view has always been that students should seek their own answers with our guidance. A major part of the tutor training is teaching strategies, such as probing questions and understanding available resources. I would also like our tutors to become part of the writing center tutor listserv, but so far I have found that they just don't have time to become active in those discussions when we serve so many students.

Our home page—designed, created, and maintained by me—is simple, could provide more information by adding links, and could be more attractive. I have rewritten one of our credit modules—a basic paragraph writing course—and a college programmers is putting it into html code. With the course online, students will be able to work at home or on other computers available at the college or their work, making our course accessible to students who live in remote areas of Johnson County or who are unable to come to the campus for various reasons. They can email drafts and/or questions to us. In turn, we will then need to check those messages daily and respond appropriately. With development and management time, seven other center modules could eventually be online. However, these distance learning classes raise new concerns: Do students have the needed hardware and software available at home? How do we manage the contact time with these students and maintain the courses' integrity? How do we know who takes the course? How do we deal with state "seat time" requirements? What about copyright laws? How do we manage the work load? Certainly, one fact is for sure; these courses will redefine the instructor's role in the writing center.

As internet access became available for students on our campus, we discovered more students were coming in at the research stage of writing papers. Even though the librarians will provide internet and database research instruction in any class, many instructors choose not to use that service. Consequently, students come to us for help, and even though we advise going to the library, we usually walk them though the process at one of our computers. The Center also has become the authority on documenting electronic resources in various styles. We updated our handouts, and internet research and documentation became a part of our tutor training. Furthermore, we developed a handout on how to evaluate resources and distributed it to instructors and students. We have a one-credit module on research skills which we are revising and hope to have online soon.

What does all of this technology mean to the community college writing center? In 1983, *Time* magazine surveyed its readers and concluded that microcomputers would improve the quality of student writing. After almost fifteen years, can we verify that the quality of student writing has increased? Based on the mountains of articles being written and published addressing this and similar questions, I would surmise that many instructors, researchers, and students want some answers and proof that computers do help students to write better. Most of us can point to strong anecdotal evidence of real progression: Computers reinforce the nonlinear, process approach to teaching writing. Writers become better readers of their own work and more willing to critique other writers' work. Revision has become a reality because students are more willing to change, add, and delete when they don't have to retype their whole paper. Computers individualize instruction reaching all levels and styles of learners. They can help us handle our growing number of students with learning disabilities. They provide us with another strategy to help us reach students, not by replacing the personal one-on-one instruction but by reinforcing and enhancing it. Computers make more information accessible and provide collaboration networks.

However, the downside is that more information does not necessarily mean more knowledge or higher quality education. Information doesn't mean anything unless it is synthesized into some real meaning, an act which requires critical thinking or (in Bloom's Taxonomy language) application, association, and evaluation. The computer, armed with the most sophisticated software, cannot picture the person behind the words. It cannot empathize or read body language. The human connection generated by student-tutor interaction is irreplaceable and no machine can duplicate it. Still as writing instructors and writing center directors, we must know what is available. Then we have to sift it to see what to keep and how to used it in our centers, because each has its own culture. We must continue to share our experiences, good and bad, online and at conferences, with our writing center counterparts and connect with our campus colleagues to stay attuned to the rapidly changing workplace and classroom. We must continue to discuss, debate, and/or question any and all changes which technology brings to education, because the nature of the rapidly moving industry triggers an over-reaction pulling us into a cyclone of hyperactivity before ever asking *why*.

CHANGING ROLES FOR THE CENTER

In a community college, where one of our major concerns is developing work-place skills, we recognize the importance of teaching critical thinking and vital communication skills. Helping students to evaluate the vast information on the internet has become a new Center objective. Center assistance now reaches beyond its physical boundaries and is accessible to anyone who has a computer and a modem. Many instructors use email and listservs to conference with their students outside of the classroom, and students are becoming comfortable with the internet and online instruction. Technology in the classroom is helping to change the old paradigm of teacher- and subject-centered to student/learner-centered, and that shift is long over-due. Writing centers have always been learner-centered, and, as directors, we know the power of students taking control of their own learning. To that end, we attempt to stay true to our philosophy that personalized instruction is best, and we prefer not to review drafts online. We continue to encourage students to bring their papers into the Center, to ask questions, and to keep control of their own writing. If students want to enroll in our online composition course, we will then encourage emailing papers. The fact that we are trying to provide a variety of services and meet all of the needs of the community supports the college's and the writing center's mission.

CHANGING ROLES FOR THE DIRECTOR

Our role as writing center directors is changing, too. Back in 1984 before computers, I spent most of my time working with students, designing hand-outs, and helping tutors devise various strategies for working with our clients. Now, I tutor students rarely because my time is spent evaluating and learning programs to teach my staff, revising our courses to include new software or internet sites, answering email and browsing the listservs, staying familiar with internet research, contacting technicians to repair or correct problems caused by software or student errors, along with the usual tutor training and report writing. I am fascinated by the use of technology—the extent to which it is applied—such as the virtual writing center as Clint Gardner describes (see chapter six), and I wonder how different the online messages are to the person-to-person dialogs taking place in "real" centers. I think about how here on our JCCC listserv messages are consistently being misconstrued. A careless or thoughtless phrase, a sensitive reader, and a general disregard for the diversity and extent of the audience can cause all sorts of problems, such as hurt feelings, angry and hateful rebuttals, and new barriers to open communication. Nevertheless, I like the idea of an online website with resources for instructors who assign writing in their classes and with resources for students who are assigned a variety of rhetorical opportunities.

Recently, as I look at upgrades and new programs, I observe that once again computer software publishers are failing to produce software compatible with the equipment we are now using, i.e., *Windows 95*. Technical problems are a constant aggravation even though we do have a technical service representative who is easily paged to provide quick assistance. (Although we are constantly fearful that he will find a better paying job off campus.) The Academic Achievement Center, which is in a different program with a different supervisor, has acquired a half-time technical assistant but right now we do not have that option. Still, I try to hold true to my 1984 promise—"Computers will never be the focus of the writing center."

WHAT NEXT?

Thinking about what the future will bring, I cannot imagine what further impact technology will have on education and specifically on writing centers. I believe being cautious, even skeptical, is in our best interest as are our continued open discussions. Regardless of whether or not a writing center has computer access, technology will touch it. The future probably includes more demands on the writing center to be current with the internet and its many resources, to provide personalized instruction for the distance learning classes, to investigate new software tools for writers, develop online student/faculty surveys, and to serve a growing population in a variety of writing tasks and computer-assisted writing tasks. We cannot deny the general population view that the computer is the common tool of writers, workers, teachers and students.

Writing center directors and writing instructors must address issues surrounding computerized instruction and writing. As a community college writing center director, I know the computer can enhance the writing process, and I know that employers value employees who can write well and who are comfortable with rapidly changing technology. We have an opportunity to reinforce our philosophy that writing is a skill that can be learned, that the role of the writing center is to help writers gain confidence and control over their work yet be aware of the value of having their papers peer critiqued. Then as an enhancement to those services, the Center can teach writers strategies for using their computers as a tool to better writing.

So, what do I conclude from my early experiences with computers? I must continue to spend some quantity (and quality) time with our computers. And then, when my neck starts cramping, sending dull pains down my arms, my eyes glaze, causing me to squint, and my left leg turns to stone out of pure boredom, I should forget about answering all that email, quit fussing with my home pages, and realize I can't possibly find all of the internet sites on *vegetarianism* or *whatever* nor read the 8000 plus ready-to-use compositions available to JCCC students. That's when I should turn off the monitor, stretch, and get out in the sun for a nice long walk. Real beats virtual any day—always has, always will.

CHAPTER ELEVEN

Random Memories of the Wired Writing Center
The Modes-to-Nodes Problem

Ray Wallace

INTRODUCTION: THE WAY IT USED TO BE

WITH THE RAPIDLY INCREASING APPLICATION OF EDUCATIONAL TECHNOLOGIES in many aspects of college curricula, this seasoned writing center director, with more than sixteen years in the front lines of one-to-one instruction, can only blush when remembering the heated, serious, debates over whether to buy a new 512k computer (even with dual disk drives and the latest version of MS-DOS) over staying the course with a CPM-run Kaypro metal box. It only seems a few years ago. He remembers quite clearly, too, as if it were only yesterday, the debates over Wordstar versus Leading Edge Writer, WordPerfect over Word, Mac versus DOS, Windows versus Mac, and now Netscape versus Explorer. Sure, our technology has increased in its touted capabilities, its availability, and its cost—but have we in the writing center world improved on our basic mission of helping various writers increasing their writing abilities. Frankly, the jury is still out on this question!

In the most recent history of technological application to education, writing centers acted as the proving grounds for such application in the teaching of writing for two important, yet practical, reasons. First, writing center directors generally kept current on technological innovation in their field. They read the main pedagogic journals and, more than others perhaps, read the ancillary journals related to educational technology to see how others were using this technology to improve education in their respective fields. Hence, when a particular technological innovation came to the fore, the use of the personal computer to teach writing for example, writing center directors were usually already more aware of what had been tried and what were the possibilities for future growth, than, say, their colleagues in more traditional literary fields. Second, writing centers themselves were generally small spaces requiring relatively little economic investment in order to ensure effective pedagogy. Therefore, when a department or division got a request for a increased technology in the writing center, it was usually a small, yet manageable request; the writing center never asked for a great deal of equipment for its actual space—a few computers and a printer were a much less expensive experiment than a request for an entire computer lab, and so such writing center requests were generally agreed to by higher administrators eager to show they could make "cutting edge" decisions.

THE CURRENT SITUATION

However, now, we have moved a great deal further along the learning curve than deciding whether to purchase a few Macintosh computers for the corner of the writing center in the basement of the English department building. One very important advancement is simply that writing centers now have a much wider audience on campuses, and the former "insular-ness" we felt as minions of the English department has now been replaced by a much more centralized motif at the center of university's missions to improve undergraduate education, writing across the curriculum, and to show accountability.

Writing centers have outgrown their armor: protection previously used to do battle with English departments as to their worth. They have already shown they are vitally needed within English departments, but much more importantly, writing centers have already proved their worth and necessity to upper administrators across campus. Therefore, today more and more writing centers are in fact university centers for learning assistance, not remedial labs for freshman composition programs. One result of this increased importance across campus is that writing center staff have assumed more decision-making responsibilities in terms of the application of a cohesive plan for educational technology across campus. In conclusion, the days of this staff worrying about the three computers in the basement writing center are now being supplanted by this same writing center staff now being asked to make sure that writing centers (satellite centers across campus), electronic writing classrooms, word processing labs, and faculty desktop computers, are not only compatible, but compatibly used.

While perhaps not yet the case at every college/university writing center to date, these changes are occurring at a remarkable pace. More and more writing center directors and staff are now expected to add computer expertise to their bag of tricks. The image of writing center as calm, safe, place for students to escape the rigors of a complex academic environment to explore rhetorical/grammatical/stylistic options in their writing is rapidly changing. Of course, the central mission of the writing center remains the same: tutor writers to write better. However, the writing center itself is now seen as a major player in the university-wide effort to improve writing skills, and, as university administrators are wont to do, they feel that technology thrown at the problem will resolve the problem, and that technology thrown to faculty had better be used on students. Therefore, more and more writing centers are being placed in the limelight—administrators are giving us computers without us even asking for them, and in return they want to see these computers in use. This expectation of increased use of technological applications can lead to two very different scenarios.

SCENARIO ONE: *THE WRITING CENTER AS TECHNOLOGICAL CENTER*

The Writing Center, located in the University Union, physically opens its doors at 8:00 a.m. each day. However, of course, since the computer network never shuts down, the writing center has never really shut down either, and the first job the director has is to download all the questions from the online writing center database that students posed to it after closing time at 8:00 p.m. the night before. Whole papers, paragraphs, and more simple questions have been e-mailed to the virtual tutor—and most of these need answers within twenty-four hours! The staff begin to enter the center and log-on the network, check e-mail, and answer some of these overnight queries the director has forwarded to their individual e-mail mailboxes. On the agenda this morning before 9:00 a.m. (when students physically can enter the center) are two classroom visits across campus—tutors have been asked to talk to history and biology classes about conducting research on the internet, a professor of sociology wants to discuss improving students' writing in an online discussion group she has set up for her sophomore class, and an English professor needs to put together a homepage for her graduate Shakespeare course.

From 9:00 a.m. to noon, a steady stream of students enter the Center, are assigned computers, and tutoring proceeds at a hectic pace. At noon, all computers are off-limits for ten minutes until a virus-scan and clean is conducted. At 1:00 p.m. the director must present a workshop for new faculty on network privileges, WWW page construction, the writing center's role in assignments, and scheduling a writing tutor's visit to a class. Faculty from across campus arrive at the center at 2:00 p.m. to explore compressed video as a possible method of one-to-one conferencing, and two tutors demonstrate this tool from opposite ends of campus. At 3:00 p.m. another virus-scan and clean and by 3:30 p.m. the network software tells the director that every terminal on her network is in use; ninety percent of users using word processing software, composing software, or approved pedagogical homepages, the other ten percent of users are opening email and surfing (and are asked to give up their terminals for those students waiting for tutoring). From 4:00 p.m. to close at 8:00 p.m., the number of undergraduate tutoring sessions diminishes, while graduate student visits increase—a small-group writing assignment for a graduate physical education course requires four networked computers and a tutor's terminal be assigned, and another business writing seminar for the community has been scheduled for the small computer seminar room located next to the writing center. Here, the director will demonstrate a new integrated office software package, as well as discuss memo etiquette on the net. At 8:00 p.m. the Writing Center closes, the online writing center comes online, and tutors finish logging tutoring sessions on their laptops to be downloaded to the central record keeping files on the network. The director checks her email, the network, looks around the writing center, and leaves for the night.

OR

SCENARIO TWO: *THE WRITING CENTER AS TECHNOLOGICAL DISASTER AREA*

The Writing Center, located in the bottom floor of the English Building opens at 8:00 a.m.. The director enters to find that the network mysteriously shut down last night at 9:00 p.m. When the network shut down, since all are interconnected, all electronic writing classrooms in the English department are now inoperable, as are the computer-activated answering machines on secretarial, faculty, and staff desks. A quick call to the computer center arranges a 10:30 a.m. (at the earliest) visit from an overworked, edgy, technician. Tutors wander in (late) and English faculty rush in to see what they should do in class if the computers don't work (the director of writing does not come in till around 11)! At 9:00 a.m. tutoring sessions are slow—students can't print until the network is up again, and so really have nothing to bring to the session. By 10:45 a.m., the network is up and running again, faculty and tutors are getting e-mail again, and classes are running smoothly once more. At 11:45 a.m., the network crashes, sending three papers into the ether somewhere, producing groans and not a few tears, and more faculty winging it in the electronic classrooms.

The director fires up four laptops for tutoring sessions, but they don't have the latest software versions and too many students' files are incompatible. By 1:00 p.m., the "old" grammar hotline rings—students want to use this medium instead of the on-line writing center since they have received no replies to their questions posed last night. This quickly become unwieldy. By 2:00 p.m., the network is up and running again, although none of the satellite centers have computer access yet—a problem since the writing center in the college of business is supposedly presenting a tutoring workshop in ten minutes.

At 3:00 p.m., a virus is reported on all computers in two electronic labs and the writing center computers—a virus the scan failed to detect, and all students who used these computers must be contacted to tell them not to use any other computers, but instead to return to the center to be de-bugged. By 5:00 p.m., three other labs across campus are infected by students who did not get the message in time. The computer center director calls; she is not happy with us!

Director closes the center at 5:15 p.m. in disgust.

THE REALITY OF "IMPROVED" TECHNOLOGY

As the co-author of a successful 1.7 million dollar Title III federal grant for implementing technological innovations as a means of improving writing skills among developmental students, let me assure you that both scenarios can and will become reality very quickly without some very careful advance planning. Adding lots of new technology into a writing center because someone gives you the money to do so is without a doubt the biggest mistake a writing center director can make!

First, let me clarify this statement by noting that here I am not talking about adding less than a dozen computers into the writing center. The addition of this number of computers into a writing center is not considered very technologically advanced by the Ed. Tech. gurus—in technological terms this writing center is simply catching up with the mainstream—and this is an important misreading of our mission in the writing center world. What the introduction of technological innovation into the writing center environment generally refers to is network-able terminals linked to a central computer, with access to other electronic writing classrooms, compressed video, email, internet connections, perhaps even an online writing center, and current, supported, hardware and software.

The key problem with this move, from modes to nodes if you will, is that it is not writing center driven. Instead, educational technologists and higher ranking administrators are making too many of the decisions in the implementation of new and improved technology in the writing center. If writing center personnel are not included in these important planning discussions to implement more technology into their environment, and their comments and evaluations are given no more than simple lip-service, then, if you will pardon the war-metaphor, those outside the trenches will be making the decisions as to what types of weapons the troops really need to win the war. Hence, the key problem with a technologically-advanced writing center that has been planned by the generals instead of those on the ground is that often it ceases to be a writing center, and, instead turns into a glorified computer lab.

We in the writing center world have worked diligently to explain to our colleagues what it is we do and what it is we do not do in the writing center. We offer students an audience to bounce their writing ideas off, we tutor students in the areas they have problems in, and we do not evaluate their work in the same way in which an instructor evaluates their writing. We are different. We are not a classroom, we are not teachers, we are not red-pen wielding enemies. We are stand-alone professionals in our academic endeavor; a status we have worked very hard to attain. We are the good guys in a system full of bad guys for first time college students. However, when technology begins to be institutionalized throughout the university, and it arrives in the writing center, then the writing center and the perception of the writing center changes very quickly.

When writing centers take on too many computers, they become computer labs. If the primary role of the tutors changes from tutoring to assuring that computers are working and that students can use this technology, are they really writing tutors anymore? The answer is, of course, no! They have become computer technicians, and soon faculty and students alike will expect them to act primarily in this capacity.

Also, the writing center director can soon change roles under this new system. If the writing center changes into a glorified computer lab, then the former writing center director stands a good chance of now being seen as the current director of electronic writing classroom. What this means in terms of day-to-day duties might be quite a drastic change for this key professional. Instead of working on improving writing across the department or university, this person may instead end up ensuring that computers are running, faculty are trained on these computers, and that software is up to date. Who is going to prepare this director for this change in roles? Who is going to mentor this director in making these technological decisions? Who is going to help insure that this director remains current?

Finally, the space the writing center itself once located is in danger of changing also. Administrators hate to see computers sitting unused and a writing center with computers not in use in many deans' eyes is a classroom not in use! The idea of a room with thirty computers not being used as a classroom is very hard to overcome for many administrators. Indeed, for many students who have to line up for an available computer in a lab, the idea of passing a writing center full of computers that they cannot use unless they are being tutored is also a bitter pill to swallow. Writing centers can disappear almost overnight.

In addition, a closer examination of the development of online writing centers is important here. While, of course, an innovative and important method of reaching non-traditional and commuting students, many of these OWLs have already grown into, or have the potential to become, something completely different. While a closer examination of these on-line centers is already covered in this collection, it is important to realize the passive nature of these web creations. In many cases, it is as if writing center directors have simply digitized their old grammar handouts to be placed on the web. Now, we in the writing center world already know that a handout on fragments is not very useful unless there is a tutor there to judge the tutee's reaction to it, and so a digitized handout, even with its very own URL address, suffers the same fate.

We must not forget that the very selling point that made writing centers so vital in the past, our human touch, might be what is lost here with an over-reliance on technological application.

THE COMPROMISE SOLUTION

However, moderate increases in technological advances and their implementation into our curricula are not going away, and it is unreasonable for writing center directors opposed to these increases to expect any such decrease. As writing teachers we have prospered with the advent of computers. More students are attracted to writing because of computers than in spite of them. We know writing is more fun on a computer, we know writing, or at least rewriting, is easier on a computer, and we know our students appreciate the ease of the spell checker and thesaurus. In addition, we also know that our students love surfing the net; we have many students who would never think of opening a book for enjoyment, but think nothing of spending two-three hours a night reading a wide variety of homepages.

Simply stated, for writing centers to survive, grow, and prosper in the next wave of technological advances, we must reinvent ourselves. However, in this process of re-invention, we must not allow ourselves to be redefined by someone else, we must not allow our important pedagogical task to be subsumed by technological babysitting roles, and we must not allow technology to supplant students as our primary responsibility.

RE-INVENTING THE WRITING CENTER FOR THE TWENTY-FIRST CENTURY

In an effort to reinvent the writing center, we must look at how we became so successful in the first place. We were successful against many odds because we offered a service that people needed—we put a human face on a complex skills, we offered a helping hand when others refused to reach out, and we offered a relaxed atmosphere to those who needed reassurance that they could indeed learn to write well.

Despite all the technological advances mentioned in this chapter, students still need human interaction to help them write more effectively. Computers, hardware and software, T1 cable, interactive video conferencing, homepages, online writing centers, modems, networks, and the like, all offer technological ease of processing and producing text. Only a human voice, a reader, and, in the context of a tutoring session, a face across the table can give contextual feedback to the writer in real-time—when it is most important. An email message can provide a certain degree of encouragement; a smiling tutor simply provides more!

We must regain the leadership role we once had in the evaluation of educational technology. We must be seen on campus as leaders in his area and not followers. As leaders, we can help appropriately integrate technology into both classroom and writing center, without making either area totally dependent on this technology. As writing specialists, we must recognize the importance much of this new technology has brought to our students' views on writing. Surely, we can all agree that if it were not for email, many of our students would not be writing outside their academic requirements; we cannot say that these same students were busy writing letters to each other and to friends all over the world in the pre-email days. So this technology has more students writing more often and we should be happy about this.

In terms of the writing center itself, yes, we should give our students opportunity to compose on computers, to interact with other writers about their writing on computers, either through networks, chat-rooms, or email, and yes, we should understand how to teach/tutor using these various technological innovations. But, we should also not lose sight of the fact that we need to get students off the machines also to talk about ways to improve their writing. We need to do what we do best, tutor writing face to face. We need to make sure that our writing centers do not close down or turn into computer labs. Instead we must re-advertise within these computer labs that we are available to help writers improve even more. Students understand that computers are not the panacea for their writing problems; they are enjoying writing on computers more than when they wrote with pens, but they also know that a tutor will help them improve even more.

CONCLUSION: JUMPING OFF THE VIRTUAL FENCE

In reviewing this essay, it becomes clear that there are both advantages and disadvantages to a more fully "wired" writing center. However, this debate needs closure and fence-sitting eventually leads to splinters in not so comfortable places. Yes, technological applications are going to improve the services writing centers can offer, but only if we do not allow technology to assume the primary responsibility for the transmission of the knowledge we have to share. We must use technology more effectively to retain our human side, our naturalness, and our ability to gauge human perception of information. To this end then, our goals as writing center personnel for the forthcoming century should be as follows:

1. to understand technological innovations and the potential applications to the tutoring environment;
2. to promote the writing center as the human-side to writing improvement;
3. to continue offering increased writing tutorial services across campus;
4. to conduct more research into how various technological innovations can improve writing skills;
5. to serve as a consultative group before other wide-ranging technological applications are implemented by administrators and others unaware of the pedagogical impact of such decisions

Writing centers can and must work hand-in-hand with those who design and promote education technology. We must not however, allow technology to drive pedagogy. As such then, writing centers should remain open, friendly, non-classroom-like environments, with great tutors and limited but readily available access to needed writing technology; they should serve primarily as a valued, individualized, pedagogical resource, and only secondarily as a possible additional technological resource center.

We need our web pages, our online writing centers, our writing assistance software packages, our networked computers, and our ever-increasing hardware innovations. However, we need students to be attracted to us as people who can help them through a one-to-one arrangement, over a cup of coffee, with a paper (or a part of a paper) in an environment that screams "time out!" We need to keep selling ourselves as the "Time Out" space—time out from teachers, computers, spell checkers, grades, online questions, and the pressures inherent in writing in this technological age. We need instead to be what we have always been, the "Play Ball" space—the place for people to take risks, discuss options, read to each other, and work like writers around a table. Once we get the students into the writing center to talk about their writing, to really discuss their writing with a real person, then we can return them to the technological utopia someone else has created for them. In the long run, my bet is there will still be a place for us in (and in spite of) all this technological innovation. Frankly, my sneaking conviction is that as technology continues to change the face of writing instruction and writing centers in general, more and more students will welcome the opportunity to talk with a caring tutor at some point in their writing process.

CHAPTER TWELVE

Computers in
the Writing Center
A Cautionary History

Peter Carino

I N RECENT YEARS HISTORICAL INQUIRY HAS FOUND A NICHE IN WRITING CENTER scholarship. Most of this history has addressed macro issues—such as the professionalization of writing centers (Riley 1994), global notions of center theory or practice (several in *Landmark Essays* 1995), the development of writing center organizations (Kinkead 1995), the nature of early centers (Carino 1995 "Early"), and models for historicizing the center (Healy "Temple," Carino 1996). Micro issues such as tutor training, one-to-one techniques, or computers in writing centers have received less attention as the scholarship has first tried to trace a broader historical arc. Yet these smaller matters certainly underpin macro-histories. Computers in particular present a challenge for center historians because from the early workbook-on-screen programs such as the Comp-Lab modules, to the cumbersome heuristics of early CAI programs such as WANDAH, to today's OWLs, MOOs, and MUDs, computer applications in writing centers have been so varied that it is difficult to draw historical generalizations.

Further complicating this project are the entanglements of center history with larger institutional contexts. While centers can usually reach at least uneasy consensus on matters such as tutor-training, attitudes toward students, and the like, computer use in the center is more closely tied to local funding, technological expertise, and politics—matters further outside the control of directors and tutors than, say, one-to-one pedagogy. For example, at one university a center, without asking, receives twenty networked computers because the administration must spend a large technological grant or state allocation. The center then must craft a pedagogy to include the technology, though lacking the expertise to do so. On a campus less flush the center may have to make do with hand-me-down hardware despite its expertise. These are extremes, but various scenarios in between have governed the acquisition and implementation of technology in writing centers. While many have often risen to the occasion, the technology has at least partly determined the direction of many more.

And technology can be a determining force in more ways than one. As Neil Postman (1992, 8-9) writes, "technology imperiously commandeers our most important terminology. It redefines 'freedom,' 'truth,' 'intelligence,' 'fact,' 'wisdom,' 'memory,' 'history'—all the words we live by. And it does not pause to tell us. And we do not pause to ask." While Postman speaks here of the larger culture, the same effect obtains in technological applications in writing centers, as computers have contributed to defining center pedagogy and the notion of the center itself. Indeed, at many institutions in the 1980s newly-created computer classrooms were designated as "writing labs," appropriating a term that had been long filled by face-to-face (f2f) centers. In the grip of such forces, centers have not always "paus[ed] to ask," happily implementing technology to satisfy larger campus entities such as a writing program or central administration. This response is somewhat understandable given the romance of technology—its promises of efficiency and ease, its promises of status in terms of funding and a recognized place on the cutting edge, whether on campus or in the profession. Other times, centers have "paused to ask," indeed have paused to scream with Luddite recalcitrance, taking the humanist high ground to fend off perceived threats of obsolescence.

This tension between technological endorsement and technological resistance marks writing center discourse on computers since the early 1980s, providing several sets of polarities from which a historical view of computers in the writing center might be drawn, a historical view that, like many other histories, reveals only conflict as its thesis. Though this thesis may seem obvious, unpacking it allows for investigation of several less obvious issues regarding centers and computers. Thus, it is within conflict that I want to situate this history of computers in writing centers.

Viewing the techno-history of centers as conflict necessarily excludes other possible constructions, such as ameliorative notions of progress—and there has been progress—or Marxist critiques of economics, politics, and technological determination. Though these structures, like others, could easily drive this history, foregrounding progress would ignore some of its costs and capitulate to the global capitalism which computers help support, while a Marxist perspective would engender too easy a chic radicalism that condemns the system in which center professionals willingly participate and from which they benefit. Likewise, I could place pedagogy at the center of this history, tracing and demonstrating the ways in which centers have struggled, usually creatively, to implement technology to help student writers. Though not centered, issues of progress, economics, politics, and pedagogy will necessarily arise in various combinations as polarities or intersections from the broader thesis of conflict.

This is not to say that centering conflict renders a master narrative delivering The Truth, and certainly I recognize my own situatedness as a writing center director conflicted by technology. That is, I am not among the more zealous who imagine computers can enable centers to do everything on campus but take over the athletic program, nor as I oversee a beginning OWL in my own center am I a romantic technophobe, though I like to proceed more slowly than some, as the cautionary title and tone of this history indicate. From this position, I choose conflict as the organizing principle of this brief history, for I believe it allows the largest number of voices to speak. I am not saying these voices, a sample of roughly fifteen years of scholarship on writing centers and computers, will not be inflected by my own; nevertheless, I believe that, set in conflict, they can provide a richer sense of computers in the writing center than other histories I might construct. But before turning to writing centers, it is necessary to outline briefly the broader context of computers and composition against and within which center history unfolds, for composition history demonstrates some of the same technological conflicts centers encounter while simultaneously standing as another point of opposition and commiseration against which to trace the writing center's individual history.

COMPUTERS AND COMPOSITION

Computers and the Teaching of Writing in American Higher Education, 1979-1994: A History, by Gail Hawisher, Paul Le Blanc, Charles Moran, and Cynthia Selfe (1996) provides a detailed history of computers in composition, and, as I hope will be evident, adumbrates some of the same issues relevant to writing centers. This work contextualizes a sixteen-year pedagogical history in the technological developments that made electronic writing instruction possible: early experiments on mainframe computers, the personal computer, LANs, hypertext, WANs, email, the pentium chip, and computer mediated communication systems such as real-time chat, MOOs, and MUDs. Situated in these technologies, computers and writing instruction are historically examined, perhaps a little too incrementally but nevertheless effectively, in five periods beginning from 1979 through 1982 and in three-year segments through 1994:

1. 1979-1982: The Profession's Early Experience with Modern Technology. Here Hawisher et. al. identify a struggle between current-traditional and process pedagogy, with grammar-drill programs and style checkers existing side by side with such early CAI developments in process software as Hugh Burns's Topoi, Selfe's and Billie Wahlstrom's Wordsworth, William Wresch's Writer's Helper, and Lisa Gerrard's SEEN, among others. The key development technologically in these years is the availability of the micro-computer (as opposed to main frame instructional systems such as Brigham Young's TICCIT and the University of Illinois's PLATO) which made it possible to view the computer not only as a data processor "but as a writing instrument." (46)

2. 1983-1985: Growth and Enthusiasm. In these years, computers and composition professionals grew in number and visibility with a special interest group at CCCC (dubbed "the fifth C") in 1983 and the Assembly for Computers in English (ACE) recognized by NCTE in 1985. Additionally, journals (most notably *Computers and Composition*) and newsletters were founded, the first Computers and Writing conference was established, instructor developed CAI software began to be distributed commercially, and NCTE published *Computers in the English Classroom: A Primer for Teachers* (1983) and an edited collection of essays, *The Computer in Composition Instruction: A Writer's Tool* (1984). Pedagogically, as new and easy word-processing software began to appear, word processing, with its composing and revision potential, began to challenge CAI for dominance in classrooms. Technologically, the first LANs began to appear in classrooms, and the first hypertext program for microcomputers was released.

3. 1986-1988: Research, Theory, and Professionalism. As the chapter title indicates, these years are celebrated as a time of further growth, with increased visibility within composition (9% of the sessions at the 1987 CCCC), the growth of professional organizations and journals, the increasing publication of books on computers and writing, and the dovetailing of LAN technology and early email use with post-process collaborative learning and constructionist pedagogies. At the same time, research anxieties began to appear over the fact that "Most studies failed to discover important differences between students writing on- and off line" (147).

4. 1989-1991: Coming of Age—The Rise of Cross Disciplinary Perspectives. This chapter might just as well have been called "growing pains," for while the authors report rapid advances in hypertext, LAN, and WAN technologies, they also report the lagging behind of classroom practices due to a lack of knowledge and/or funding. There is, nevertheless, a "coming of age," as scholars in the field began to politicize and theorize their work on computers and writing, in keeping with the shift from the individual writer of process pedagogy to the politicizing and contextualizing of all acts of composing in social pedagogies. In doing so, scholars and teachers began to confront the unsettling possibility that, imbricated in the larger culture, "electronic writing classes . . . supported only a limited potential for change." (201)

5. 1992-1994: Looking Forward. While the authors here speculate on technological developments in computer mediated communication (CMC), next generation processors, multimedia, and the internet, among others, they also lament the beginnings of a fragmentation in the field and the increasing division between privileged researchers and the underclass of graduate and adjunct teachers who actually teach beginning writers. In terms of pedagogy they speculate on how computers fit in with composition's increased interest in the cultural politics of literacy, which has sometimes fostered feminist and cultural studies analyses that question the notion that new computer technologies provide "the egalitarian social spaces promised in the research literature." (250)

This snapshot of Hawisher et al.'s history is necessarily reductive and can in no way do justice to the book's depth and texture. While the incremental organization of the book may seem lockstep (and my summary definitely does), the authors are also aware of the synchrony of history, recognizing that some of the grammar drilling and style checking programs they locate in current-traditional beginnings persist today or that the macro history they construct in narrating a sixteen-year period may at times recur in a local setting in a compressed time frame. At whatever point in time, Hawisher and her colleagues also discuss numerous issues affecting those involved in using computers to teach writing and in researching this practice: among others, community formation, struggles for respect in English departments, battles to have computer work valued in tenure and promotion decisions, fights with administrators for funding, attempts to educate colleagues, the commitment to improving student writing, fear and enthusiasm toward technology, and feelings of marginalization both on campus and in the profession. Such issues writing center professionals know all too well, yet despite these shared concerns, Hawisher et. al. barely mention writing centers. "Writing Laboratories" are listed only once in the index, and they discuss labs only in the context of conference teaching, erroneously reporting them as facing the prospect of being transformed into computer classrooms:

> The writing rooms described by Garrison and Murray, and the conference-centered or tutorial based pedagogy, whose literature was assembled by Muriel Harris in *Tutoring Writing: A Sourcebook for Writing Labs*, foregrounded the student writer's writing and the teacher/editor's intervention. With the advent of the microcomputer in the 1980s, the already established writing labs and writing workshops became computer-writing labs and classrooms, with teacher editors conferring, one-to-one, with student writers. (29)

While some blurring of boundaries likely occurred as many computer classrooms were designated as "writing labs," I think the thousands of peer tutors working f2f during the years discussed would be surprised to learn that they had been replaced by teacher/editors working on computers. Thus though Hawisher, LeBlanc, Moran, and Selfe offer a finely detailed and historigraphically sophisticated document on the entrance and continued presence of computers in composition, though they provide a socio-techno-cultural context for thinking about writing instruction and computers, it is necessary to look elsewhere to attempt to document the impact of computers on writing centers, a task to which I will now turn.

It would be tempting to adopt the same chronological sequence for writing centers that Hawisher and her colleagues construct for composition, but though much of their chronology applies to writing centers, the trajectory of center history differs as centers likely began implementing the technology after composition programs (an assumption based on the scholarship as well as on institutional funding hierarchies). Furthermore, as a different pedagogical space, centers had as many different as similar problems and successes. Because of these differences and due to limitations of space, I will create a somewhat different chronology, but though proceeding chronologically I will attempt to address the recurring issues that demonstrate that history is also synchronic.

FEARS AND HOPES: THE EARLY YEARS, 1982-1986

It is difficult to pinpoint the first public expression, either in print or at a conference, about computers in writing centers. In the first four years (1979-82) that Hawisher et. al. designate for historical treatment, no articles in the *Writing Lab Newsletter* discuss computer tutorials. Similarly in the first book on centers, Muriel Harris's 1982 collection of essays *Tutoring Writing*, only one article treats computers: Don Norton's and Kristine Hansen's "The Potential for Computer-Assisted Instruction in Writing Labs." As its title indicates, the piece is optimistically speculative, but it evidences many of the same tensions that will continue to define the writing center community's future discourse on computers. On the one hand, Norton and Hansen conclude that "CAI may yet make it possible that across the nation learning will occur more effectively at computer terminals than in more traditional settings" (161). On the other, the authors lament the costs of terminals and fees to plug into the instructional programs of the TICCIT and PLATO mainframes, the difficulty of creating software (a concern shared in composition circles), and the limitations of computers at that time to teach more than discrete skills.

Since it seems likely that microcomputers and word processing, both then commercially available, would have been big news in those days, the lack of articles in *The Writing Lab Newsletter* before 1982 and the limited coverage of the Norton and Hansen piece suggest that centers had not yet received the technology in significant proportion. But a spurt of discourse on computers in writing centers only a year later bears out the cliche that technology moves fast. The *1984 Writing Lab Directory* (compiled in 1983) lists 88 of 184 centers as having at least one computer, and center professionals began to make their voices heard, with three articles directly treating computers and two discussing them within broader topics in the *Proceedings of the Writing Center Association Fifth Annual Conference* (1983) and at least one paper delivered at the First Midwest Writing Centers Association Conference the same year.

These six articles outline the same conflict between CAI and word processing application found in composition circles. Evidently early CAI programs for prewriting, such as Hugh Burns's Topoi or Lisa Gerrard's WANDAH, had not reached writing centers, for to writing centers at this time CAI usually meant current-traditional grammar drills or at most style checkers. Countering these were word processing programs, hailed as a powerful tool for process writing. At the Writing Centers Association (now ECWCA) Conference, Mary Croft extolled the use of word processing to "diminish the concern over the physical act of writing and the worry over neatness and correctness," arguing that computers allow for "thorough revision not merely surface revision" and "encourage students to be both abandoned experimenters and disciplined self editors" (58-59). Croft denounces a CCCC presentation she saw the previous year on a CAI program used to flag grammatical errors, claiming it turned the computer into "just a big, expensive red pencil" (59). She also cautions against grammar software, saying "I haven't seen any I really believe our students can't live without" (60). Like Croft, Beatrice Johnson, in the same proceedings, celebrates the potential of word processing: "From free writing through final proof reading, writers find the Apple an efficient tool" (105). Finally, Janice Neuleib in an article on center research challenges directors to forego "merely putting on a computer exercises that do not work in books" and to implement instead the "valuable tool" of word processing (215-216).

In contrast, at the same conference, two articles promote grammar instruction via CAI. Frances Key, of Ball State, arguing the benefits of multi-media autotutorial programs, claims that flagging surface errors on computer forces the student into "precision in thinking" (137)—though never really explaining how. He also values the privacy of autotutorials, computer assisted and otherwise. Don Payne, of Iowa State, offers "a comprehensive sequence of lessons dealing with spelling, proofreading, vocabulary, and error" (239), though concluding his piece with hopes for developing pre-writing heuristic programs. Payne's accommodation of the technology is clearly the most current-traditional of the six. But while endorsing his pedagogy, he also apologizes for it, opening the essay with a discussion of an "administrative arrangement [that] means we have a narrower focus than many writing centers, that we concern ourselves more with mechanics than with general compositional skills" (239).

Considering the range of positions here, one wonders how these presenters may have reacted to one another had they attended one another's sessions. On the one hand, this diversity testifies to the writing center community's tendency (still healthily in place) to tolerate a variety of opinion. Indeed, well before this conference center professionals were implementing instruction beyond grammar and identifying themselves with the by then entrenched process pedagogies, yet Payne's and Key's papers were welcome. On the other hand, while demonstrating the community's capacity for accommodation, these articles also, and more importantly, indicate its situatedness in the same pedagogical debates going on in computers and composition and in larger cultural debates regarding technology. Recall the plight of Don Payne at Iowa State. In an institution with a large engineering program, his lab was technologically rich in terms of the software development resources he reports coming out of the university's Computation Center. These riches, however, result in graduate students in computer science assigned to program for his writing center. Though working with the programmers, he has difficulty maintaining control: "For instructors accustomed to more autonomy in developing instructional materials, this mixture of managerial and consultative roles may convince them that indeed they are the ones being integrated into some other system" (242). Payne's lament echoes the early caveats by scholars in computers and composition that teachers, not programmers, must control software development (Hawisher et. al., see also Wresch). In larger cultural terms, Payne warns that though the title of his essay speaks of integrating computers in the center, "one of the first things you discover when you begin working with CAI is that in many ways you are fitting into another discipline, not just incorporating technology" (241). Here Payne echoes Neil Postman's contention that when a new technology enters a culture, the result is more than additive; that is, what results is not the old culture with something new added but a new culture.

The anxieties of these early discussions are laid bare by Dennis Moore in a paper presented at the 1983 Midwest Writing Centers Association Conference with the provocative title, "What Should Computers Do in the Writing Center?" To this question, Moore flatly answers that we don't yet know and then forcefully derides what he sees as the techno-evangelism of the voices in the 1983 issue of *College Composition and Communication* dedicated to computers. For instance, when Collette Daiute (in an article deemed "seminal" in the editor's note to the issue) claims that the cursor "reminds the writer that the program is waiting to receive more input, which encourages the writer to say more and to consider whether what is written makes sense," Moore rightly asks how a mere blinking light can accomplish all that for a beginning writer. In addition, in response to Richard Lanham's early style-checking program, Homer, Moore notes, as many others have, that style checkers merely count words and flag particular grammatical and stylistic elements (-tion words, to be verbs etc.) without any regard for context or rhetorical purpose: "There seems little point in telling a basic writing student that she has written 205 words in 17 sentences with an average of 12.05 words per sentence—a typical Homer item" (8). To be fair to Lanham, he himself recognized the program's limitations in print. Nevertheless, Moore's near jeremiad asks the writing center community "to take a critical attitude toward educational computing: to learn all you can about it and to keep asking questions" (2).

It would be easy to dismiss Moore as a Luddite or to argue that the conflicts I cite are more pedagogical than technological in that they pit grammar-drill-on-screen against word processing, current-traditionalism versus notions of process writing at the time. However, one wonders how the technology affected the persistence and implementation of both pedagogies. Take, for example, the Comp-Lab modules, a self-paced workbook series with audiotapes that had enjoyed some popularity in writing centers before computers (see Epes 1979; Epes, Kirkpatrick, and Southwell 1983; Baker and Whealler). One would think that contemporary with Maxine Hairston's process clarion, "The Winds of Change: Thomas Kuhn and the Revolution in the Teaching of Writing" (1982), such materials would die a rapid death, but two years later Comp-Lab's software version was featured in an essay by Michael Southwell in Willam Wresch's NCTE collection, *The Computer in Composition Instruction: A Writer's Tool* (1984). Southwell touts computerized autotutorials as transferring "responsibility for learning to the learner" (93), a nice alliterative phrase but one that collides with the collaborative pedagogy and tutor talk being championed in the same year by such revered writing center scholars as Steven North and Kenneth Bruffee. Nevertheless, despite its current-traditional moorings, Southwell's article enjoyed status alongside numerous others by some of the most notable scholars, then and now, in computers and composition, most of whom, in contrast, were looking to adapt process pedagogy electronically. Granted that Comp-Lab may have been one of the better autotutorials of its time, I do not think it cynical to say that had it not gone electronic, it would have withered on the shelves of most writing centers by 1984 and would never have seen print in an NCTE publication, least of all in one hailed as "a breakthrough" (Hawisher et. al. 84).

As in composition studies, computers continued to engage writing center scholars following the earliest work. This it not to say there is a large body of work following the initial pieces, but certainly interest was growing. Jim Bell (1989) reports that between 1984 and 1988 *The Writing Lab Newsletter* published thirteen articles and nine software reviews, making computers the second most popular topic, and essays continued regularly in regional conference proceedings. While these essays express some of the same tension as the early work, they begin to take on a less conflicted tone, demonstrating more confidence and resulting in a genre I will call "the success story." Essays in this genre begin by raising concerns about technology, usually to ease humanist anxieties, and then move to an ameliorative narrative of successful pedagogical implementation. For example, Richard Marshall's "Word Processing and More: The Joys and Chores of a Writing Lab Computer" (1985) rehashes all the problems of implementing computers—technological fear, software needs, possibilities of losing documents, maintaining the equipment—but concludes confidently with several solutions and a plea: "Please Santa, send us a few more computers" (181). In a similar "success story," Robert Royar (1986) discredits studies that were claiming word-processing does not change the revision habits of inexperienced writers, arguing that instruction in revision and the right software will do the trick. Charles E. Beck and John A. Stibrany (1985) corroborate Royar's claim in a study of graduate students at the Air Force Institute of Technology.

It would be redundant to recount the many essays in the "success story" genre. Suffice it to say that they tend to illustrate what Stuart Blythe (1997) has called "a logistical view" of technology: the assumption that technologies are neutral tools whose benefit or bane depends on those implementing them. This view, Blythe argues, ignores the possibility that technology transforms culture, an argument that had long been advanced by noted technological critics such as Postman, Joseph Weizenbaum, and Hubert Dreyfus. Postman's position has already been cited, but Weizenbaum (1976), an early developer of artificial intelligence (AI),[1] warns that technology transforms the very way we think of ourselves in our surroundings. He notes that AI, for example, tends to cast computers in human metaphors (witness also the cute anthropomorphic names often assigned to composition programs: Wandah, Homer, Wordsworth, or more specific to writing centers, OWL). Weizenbaum argues that this attitude reciprocally causes us to think of humans as machines, in terms of a Cartesian rationality long considered limited in philosophical tradition. Weizenbaum's positions are bolstered by Dreyfus in his seminal challenge to AI, *What Computers Can't Do* (1971, 1979) and his revised edition, *What Computers Still Can't Do* (1992).

It would be unfair to charge early center professionals working in computers with technological naivete in confidently ignoring such questions in their "success stories" (in fact some of their trepidations show they were not ignoring them completely), for they were using computers to help students write and to solidify the institutional place of their centers. Given institutional constraints, the lack of time to reflect on technology, and the need to create more effective pedagogies, it is not surprising that success stories, as a genre, continue in subsequent years side by side with more restless discourse.

NEW TECHNOLOGIES, NEW PEDAGOGIES, NEW QUESTIONS: 1987-1991

As LAN and hypertext applications began to make their way on to campus, the number of articles in the *Writing Lab Newsletter*, as well as in conference proceedings of the time, indicates a continual but not significantly increasing stream of commentary. The notable exception is the special issue of *The Writing Center Journal* entitled "Computers, Computers, Computers," and its appearance governs my choice of 1987 as the point of demarcation for a new historical segment. Closing this period, Jeanne Simpson's and Ray Wallace's 1991 collection of essays, *The Writing Center: New Directions*, despite its forward looking title, contains only one article on computers, and after its dedicated issue *The Journal* surprisingly published only one more article in these years (in the 1991 Tenth Anniversary Issue) and not another until 1997. This lack of a marked increase in publication on computers in writing centers may be attributable to the increase of LAN and hypertext technology. Not only was this technology likely beyond the budget of most centers, LANs also lent themselves more readily to creating user groups in classrooms than to tutoring one to one. Thus it is not surprising that many articles on computers and writing centers (see, for example, Berta 1990 or Brown 1990) duplicated the logistical success stories previously discussed, concentrating on microcomputer applications for various purposes, usually with the typical anxieties of previous years ameliorated by claims of student success and without much technological or cultural reflection.

The special issue of *WCJ*, however, demonstrates that center professionals, though still seeking instructional applications, were returning to the critical perspectives prevalent in the initial work but glossed over in the success stories. Fred Kemp's lead article, "Getting Smart with Computers: Computer-Aided Heuristics for Student Writers," challenges binary thinking that would see computers as threat or panacea, arguing that "computers can do marvelous things for us in our classrooms and learning labs, but only if we are imaginative enough to forsake the anthropomorphic prejudices of robotry and develop truly innovative instruction based upon characteristically computer abilities" (9). With this stance, Kemp aligns himself with artificial intelligence researchers such as Weizenbaum to argue that the difference between human intelligence and artificial intelligence is "so vast, especially in terms of Natural Language Processing, the similarities are theoretical, not practical" (9). Though observing the benefits of computers, Kemp advises writing center professionals to "to employ a very sophisticated, and possibly new, understanding of the writing process" (9).

Kemp's admonition parallels what Hawisher and her colleagues trace in the composition community at large: that by the mid- to late eighties, more social and politicized notions of context were beginning to create a post-process, culturally-interpellated, constructivist model of composing that questioned the simplicity of the student-centered, often stage-model notions of the process movement. That post-process models rendered composing far more complex an activity than CAI programs then could represent or address begins to surface in Jeanne Luchte's bibliographic essay on process software available in 1987. Luchte organizes her essay in terms of pre-writing, organizing, drafting, revision, and editing—the steps of the process model—and then evaluates the degree to which computers might facilitate each step. Yet as she concludes her essay she is not fully confident in this model: "Though I am delineating the five processes to examine how using the computer can help teach them, I should stress that the most viable computer applications will be those that address the process integratively and cohesively" (18). With this statement Luchte recognizes that composing is recursive—one of the earliest arguments challenging step-models of process—and implies that CAI software had yet to account for recursiveness. Luchte's reservations emerge more prominently in the issue's paired reviews, by David Partenheimer and Bill Emmett, of WANDAH, which by this time combined CAI features and word processing and was entering the commercial market as HBJ Writer. Partenheimer essentially trashes WANDAH, arguing that its heuristic, editing, and revision features are intrusive and cumbersome and (echoing Kemp) that the program "encompasses only a fraction of the skills involved in effective writing" (53). Even Emmett, taking the pro position, lukewarmly contends that WANDAH/HBJ Writer gives beginners "one more tool" but concedes that the program soon "will be outdated" (58).

While neither Kemp, Luchte, Partenheimer, nor Emmett directly allude to social notions of writing, they implicitly and explicitly doubt that the software fits what was known about composing. This stance separates them from early objectors to computers and writing, who couched their fears more in terms of traditionally humanist objections to machinery. Conversely, these later commentators base their objections on informed experience with the technology. Situated thus, they repeat not only the disappointments of composition studies (Hawisher et. al. chapters five and six) but also those of AI researchers, who were beginning to realize the difficulties, if not impossibility, of programming computers to account for all the social subtleties encoded in language and the "consensus knowledge" humans employ in making decisions in complex acts such as writing (Dreyfus 1992, xvi). Faced with this problem, the U.S. Department of Defense had discontinued funding for all AI research except neural-network modelling by the late 1980s, and the Japanese government had discontinued funding AI research altogether.

Because post-process pedagogies such as social construction, feminism, and cultural studies rhetoric deflated some of the early promise of computers, writing center scholars sometimes turned from pure pedagogy to begin investigating ways in which computers affected social situations related to composing. The beginnings of this line of inquiry are illustrated in Pamela Farrell's "Writer, Peer Tutor, and the Computer: A Unique Relationship" in the special *WCJ* issue. Farrell reiterates the same pedagogical claims for the computer as writing tool as earlier advocates had, but adds that the computer promotes collaboration among students of "varying social, educational, and ethnic backgrounds" (29). This happens, according to Farrell, because tutors and tutees, often hampered by social difference (which would be quite powerful in Farrell's high-school setting), direct themselves toward the computer, an interest they share, and away from the writing deficiencies of the tutee or the social positions of either party. Farrell's essay, given the complexities of social difference that subsequent scholarship has revealed, is, in retrospect, a bit too much the happy tale, the success story. However, in 1987 her introduction of the social element into discourse on computers in the writing center implies that she was starting to reflect upon the technology in ways beyond its obvious application as a tool for teaching process writing.

This focus on social dynamics also occupies Maurice Scharton two years later in his "The Third Person: The Role of Computers in the Writing Center" (1989). Scharton presents four case studies that demonstrate how various aspects of computer writing helped four different students with four different writing processes. One student learned to ask for help (no small accomplishment); another discovered possibilities of macrostructural changes, working with a tutor who encouraged her to play with the block-and-move function like a video game; a third overcame his obsession with grammatical correctness; and a fourth realized that document design and appearance are often part of the social contract between author and audience. In each case, students surmounted their problems because the computer, Scharton implies, defused some of their previously inhibiting behaviors. Like Farrell, but with less obvious enthusiasm, Scharton argues that "the computer supplies a social basis for that relationship [tutor-tutee] because it represents a common interest and a new language with which to discuss that interest" (40). While one might argue that Farrell and Scharton barely scratch the surface of social theories of composing, their work signals an increasing awareness of new questions and a more sophisticated stance toward technology.

In addition to concerns grounded in newly developing social pedagogies, writing center scholars, though not in large numbers, were beginning to examine uses of technologies other than word processing and CAI—but again not without conflict. Joyce Kinkead's "The Electronic Writing Tutor" (1988), in *The Writing Lab Newsletter*, is likely the first work that considers email tutoring. Kinkead endorses email as a means of reaching commuting students off-campus or students in distance education courses. Simultaneously she raises issues that show an awareness of the social complexities of writing and the politics of institutional culture. On the former, she argues that though email "combats the problems of time and distance," it does not equal the "value of dialogue in a f2f conference" and is no "replacement for the immediate questioning and discussion of tutorials" (5). Kinkead not only demonstrates an allegiance to the collaborative dialogue underpinned by social theories of composing but also warns against administrators who, lacking theoretical sophistication, might view email tutoring as a more efficient and cheaper method of delivering tutorials. A pioneering anachronism, Kinkead's essay, in its concern with distance learning and electronic tutoring, foreshadows themes and conflicts that become increasingly important for writing centers of the 1990s.

Irene Clark's "The Writing Center and the Research Paper: Computers and Collaboration" (1991) is another work that turns its attention to the possible effects of then new technologies. In possibly the first writing center article to discuss hypertext applications, Clark describes "Project Jefferson," a program in which students working with tutors access a pre-programmed bank of texts online to research and write a documented essay. She stresses the collaborative nature of the tutor's role in helping to find, evaluate, and use information, citing, like Farrell and Scharton, the computer as a social intermediary. Though sometimes representing research writing in the "steps" of early process pedagogy, Clark recognizes that tutors must explore with students "different models of the research process" rather than a right way (212). What is significant here in terms of future applications is Clark's emphasis on "evaluating the quality and relevance of the articles" accessed to discern "the relative merit of one source over another" (213), a function that will become crucial with the availability of unregulated internet sources of information such as news groups, listservs, and, of course, the world wide web. Clark expands on this concern in a 1995 essay (to be discussed below) on teaching "information literacy," but her position is already outlined in this 1991 piece.

Before turning to the years both Kinkead's and Clark's work implicitly predicts, I would like to close this section by examining Janice Neuleib's and Maurice Scharton's essay, "Tutors and Computers, An Easy Alliance" (1990). Published in the prestigious tenth-anniversary issue of *The Writing Center Journal* issue, looking back on the eighties and forward to the nineties, describing a center with a variety of state-of-the-art hardware and software, and demarcating the year with which I end this period, this essay expresses numerous hopes and reveals numerous anxieties as centers were moving from one decade to the next and from a pedagogy largely dependent on free-standing microcomputers to more widespread network applications.

In many senses, Neuleib's and Scharton's essay reads as if they do not want to utter an unkind word about computers, and perhaps in the tenth-anniversary issue of *WCJ*, they don't, preferring rather to argue that the writing center community had confidently and effectively accommodated technology. And to a degree they show it had, if their center represents others. Indeed, they touch on nearly all relevant issues of the 1980s: the aggressiveness needed to secure funding, the efficacy of word processing in the face of the limits of CAI, the effect of computers on the social aspects of writing, the use of computers as a public relations device, the need for directors to educate themselves in new hardware and software, the differences in resources among institutions. However, though Scharton's and Neuleib's is an informed and savvy essay, beneath its varnished seamlessness lurk several tensions worth noting. To begin, the essay is at times disconcertingly enthusiastic, as these outcroppings attest:

> The six years [since the introduction of computers in the center] have reflected the national revolution in computer use. (49)
>
> Tutors' assumption that everyone writes or ought to write on computers suggests to us that a revolution in our tutors' thinking has indeed occurred. (52)
>
> [Writing] becomes more like singing. In the computer world, we can all have a voice like Pavarotti's. In comparison, with text produced on a color monitor, print on paper is a pale and lifeless imitation of writing. (54)
>
> We explain to our visitors [administrators and "a steady stream of dignitaries" (56)] that the computers are there to close the personal distance between writer and tutor. So far electricity has warmed our tutoring atmosphere; we hope to keep it that way. (56).

This enthusiasm masks several unreconciled conflicts. Neuleib and Scharton speak of modelling writing behaviors by refusing to write themselves, "short of grocery lists and postcards," without a computer and take pride in the fact that several of their tutors feel the same way. "Thus a powerful force," they claim, "is operating in the tutoring situation to socialize writers to the new medium of transmission of knowledge" (53). They compare those who resist this "powerful force" to poor readers remembered from their childhoods: "The few who still do not like to use the machine are all too sadly familiar as the non-readers who struggled and eventually fell by the wayside unable to understand the symbols that would give them access to the world of text. We can still see their faces" (55).

To some degree, this subtle coercion and open condescension can be attributed to the satisfaction Neuleib and Scharton must have deservedly felt in securing equipment and implementing technological pedagogy. But one wonders that if all were so electronically well at their center, why three-quarters of their tutors, in answer to a survey, preferred discussing papers with tutees in hard copy, that "pale and lifeless imitation of writing." Neuleib and Scharton chalk this preference up to the tutors' desire to resist the temptation, promoted by the malleability of text on screen, to appropriate the tutees' texts and revise for them, a writing center taboo. But rather than leave it at that, they further support their tutors' resistance, saying it accords with their "strong feeling, voiced in conversation with our new president, that the computer has as much potential for impairing as for improving communication" (55). However, earlier in the essay they report making this argument to quell the new president's desire for grammar drill software, not to validate hard text revision. On the plus side, they also note that they want students to "consider text, as a human not a mechanical issue" (55)—good point and one I believe they believe—but curiously they never return to how computers might impair communication, or how the computer interfered with one-to-one revision, a fundamental element of center pedagogy, choosing rather to pile on excuses for the tutors's preference for hard copy.

Despite the essay's glossy veneer, the conflicts show through like scratches too deep to be sanded smooth and in hindsight (always 20-20 I know) raise the possibility that the community had not fully understood the implications of the technology with the same success as it had implemented it. These shortcomings can be largely attributed to the authors deserved pride in their lab's successes and the essay's occasion. The tenth-anniversary issue of *The Writing Center Journal* would not have been a likely venue to address the fear Hawisher et. al. cite in the composition community that "electronic writing classes . . . supported only a limited potential for change" at a time when almost 80% of the centers in the 1991-92 *National Directory of Writing Centers* reported using computers. This fear and new expectations, however, would continue to be contested in the 1990s as new technologies began to enter the writing center on a wider scale.

OWLS, LANS, MOOS AND WEBS: 1992-PRESENT

I choose 1992 as the opening of this last period in this history because it marks the year WCENTER, the writing center listserv, began and the establishment of Eric Crump's regular column, "Voices from the Net," which recounts selected WCENTER discussions in *The Writing Lab Newsletter*. I will not examine WCENTER, for it could be the subject of another essay, nor is it a direct delivery system for tutoring students. Rather I see it as the symbolic entrance of computer mediated communication (CPC) into the community on an increasingly wider scale. In addition, I would argue that the success of WCENTER positively contributed to the community's confidence in implementing new technology, serving as both

an example of technological potential and a source for hashing out new technological issues.

While most center scholars began to assess new technologies and new concerns, others once again demonstrated the synchronicity of history with some
articles focussing on concerns of the previous decade (see, for example, Vasile and
Ghizzone 1992 and Simons 1995). I will not treat work that goes over old ground
but only that which confronts and attempts to negotiate the potential conflicts
and possible changes wrought by new technologies. Much of this work appears in
1995 in the special number of *Computers and Composition* dedicated to writing
centers. Needless to say the articles here often touch upon conflicts previously discussed: funding, the relationship of pedagogical and technological expertise,
social issues in writing, and the like, but these issues are raised in relation to the
implementation of new online systems. And although some of the authors, like
their predecessors, ensnare themselves in their own enthusiasm, the majority
speak in a more evenhanded tone and demonstrate a critical sophistication sometimes missing in earlier work. Yet even the more sophisticated pieces are not
always able to resolve the problems they raise—not because these authors are
obtuse but because the problems are complex and in flux.

Muriel Harris's and Michael Pemberton's "Online Writing Labs (OWLs): A
Taxonomy of Options and Issues" surveys various technological applications available, from online storehouses of handouts accessible from a home page to synchronous chat systems. They also advise directors to consider local contexts in
implementing anything, noting that computerized centers vary greatly depending
on their purposes, funding, and available technological expertise. Although
Harris's and Pemberton's essay is primarily informational, their concerns surface
to show the power (positive and negative) of the technology to transform center
pedagogy and the way we think about it. Most obviously, in response to synchronous chat tutorials, Harris and Pemberton warn of "the losses in this faceless disembodied world as the lack of the personal contact may seem to dehumanize a
setting that writing centers have traditionally viewed as personal and warm" (156).
However, recouping this loss, they pose the possibility that chat systems create "a
world where gender, ethnicity, and race are not immediately evident" and where
the shy might be more inclined to speak. There may be some truth to this claim,
but it had been challenged in earlier work in the wider field of computers and
composition. For example, in a study of discourse on Megabyte University, a listserv on writing and computers, Cynthia Selfe and Paul Meyer in 1991 found online
talk to be dominated by "men and higher status members of the academic community" (read tutors for writing center chat) and to be much more adversarial
than the egalitarian space initially imagined (qtd. in Hawisher et al 209).

Though hashing out the ups and downs of sychronous chat, Harris and
Pemberton sound surprisingly neutral in their treatment of automatic file retrieval,
by which clients access handouts stored on a website. Often these handouts offer the

same type of grammatical instruction and information centers have distributed from file cabinets for years. This use of the technology evokes the storehouse metaphor of the writing center constructed by Andrea Lunsford in 1989 to denounce current-traditional center practice based on correctness and grammar drill. Much previous and subsequent center scholarship joined Lunsford in using this metaphor to repudiate the practice it represents. But Harris and Pemberton remain silent on the issue. To be fair, their essay, as its title professes, is more an informational taxonomy than a polemic. Furthermore, I believe Lunsford's metaphors gained an undeserved currency.[2] After all, people use handbooks for reference, and placing a corollary online can only provide good will for a center. Rather I raise this question to demonstrate how the technology can reshape our views of a pedagogy. Other than convenience, there is no evidence that handouts accessed online are any better than handouts pulled from a file cabinet. File cabinet or computer, each is a storehouse, a point I doubt Harris and Pemberton would contest. Yet redecorated by technology, the storehouse, generally regarded as a disreputable image of the writing center, is now redeemable, which may be good or bad, depending on the way we feel about storehouses. But however we feel, we need to recognize the pressures technology exerts on our feelings.

Ultimately, Harris's and Pemberton's work provides a useful compendium of the possibilities of technology, and though I would like to hear more from them about the issue of storehouse centers, essentially they avoid the seductions of technology that sometimes plague others. Also in the same issue, David Coogan's "Email Tutoring, A New Way to Do Old Work," though enthusiastic about the method, demonstrates that center scholars, in many cases, have become more guarded, more reflective. Though Coogan finally endorses email as an alternative, he recognizes many of the problems Kinkead had pointed out back in 1988, admits that he is not unreservedly "ready to recommend email to writing centers" (179), and concludes modestly that "Email gives [tutors and tutees] a chance to write and a chance to explore the meaning of writing" (180), a claim one could just as easily make for live tutoring. This same caution is evident in the article by Cindy Johanek and Rebecca Rickly, who in describing a survey of responses to a series of synchronous LAN interchanges among tutor trainees, temper their overall enthusiasm, pointing out that this application is "not intended to replace f2f discussion" and that "Negative responses should be attended to to help implement [the practice] more productively not only for the majority but for all tutors" (245).

In contrast, Virginia Chappell's discussion of a similar tutor-training effort, using asynchronous email discussions she calls "Party Line," illustrates that the unqualified "success story" is not a dead genre. Chappell does show, through quotations from her students' dialogues, the wonderful potentials of the medium as students collaboratively make knowledge about their tutorial experiences. However, with her assertion that "Email discussions allow students to write about, read, and respond to a broader spectrum of experience than do private journals, with all the vividness inherent in an electronic medium" (231), she lapses into the blinding assumption that the electronic way is always the better way. First, it is suspect to suppose that students will feel free to say the same thing (though they might say different things) in a group discussion, online or otherwise, that they would say in a "private journal." (Not surprisingly, privacy is often a casualty of electronic enthusiasm). Furthermore, Chappell's claims about "the vividness inherent in an electronic medium" recall McLuhan's cautions to a world where "the medium is the message." To be fair, Chappell demonstrates significant learning going in the "Party Line" group, but her essay lacks the temperance of Johanek and Rickly.

This temperance, as well as an innovative use of the technology, also informs Jennifer Jordan-Henley's and Barry Maid's "Tutoring in Cyberspace: Student Impact and College/University Collaboration," but their concomitant enthusiasm shows how technology can take us unawares. Maid and Jordan-Henley present an impressive method of sychronously connecting graduate-student tutors at Maid's four-year institution with tutees at Jordan-Henley's community college via MOO technology. The result is cyberspace tutorials as the miles between Arkansas and Tennessee disappear through the fiber-optic looking glass. Negotiating the difference between f2f and online tutoring, Maid and Jordan-Henley weigh the advantages and disadvantages of both—like Harris and Pemberton, the negative loss of personal cues in f2f tutorials but the positive loss of social pressure—and caution that "Solid writing center theory applies in cyberspace as it does in the traditional center" (212). All in all, this is impressive stuff, and Maid and Jordan-Henley are to be commended for their imaginative application of one of the newest technologies.

However, their essay contains a rather disturbing subtext. On the surface, it is evident that Maid and Jordan-Henley proceed carefully, but a closer look at their rhetoric indicates that center scholars, in their enthusiasm, are not always fully aware of the transformations technology can bring about without their knowing it. First, Maid and Jordan-Henley too easily fall into casting the non-electronic writing center as the "traditional center," a term used throughout. Were America a culture that valued tradition, this would be one thing, but in a nation cultishly dedicated to "the new," the f2f writing center—which has long celebrated itself as a space for anything but traditional pedagogy—is subordinated in a binary hierarchy with cybertutoring as the privileged term. Second, Maid and Jordan-Henley confess that they were "disappointed" (215) with students resistant to the technology. While their disappointment is understandable given their efforts, less understandable is their subsequent reference to these students as "dropouts" (215), a stigmatizing term associated with academic failure and reminiscent of Neuleib's and Scharton's casting of the less technologically enthusiastic as "slow readers." One wonders how the "dropouts" fared when Maid had to assign them grades in the tutor-training seminar in which this work was done, or how Jordan-Henley assessed the work of those who did not warm to the cyber tutors. While certainly introducing students to new and enabling technologies can be valuable, demeaning those who prefer other means of work violates the democratic principles "traditional" centers have long cherished. I doubt Maid and Jordan-Henley chose these terms—"traditional" and "dropout"—consciously, but that is exactly the point: technology can think in us if we are not careful. Thus one begins to worry when they conclude their essay with an enthusiastic flourish, suggesting the obsolescence of live centers: "Perhaps cybertutor Joel English was overstating the case when he said, 'I believe that virtual reality will continue to revolutionize writing instruction and education as a whole,' but then again, perhaps he was not" (218).

Indeed "perhaps he was not" if we can believe Dawn Rodrigues's and Kathleen Kiefer's 1993 essay in *Writing Centers in Context*. This book, as many writing center professionals know, contains descriptions of model writing centers at various types of institutions, from Harvard to community colleges. Rodrigues and Kiefer, of Colorado State, start out describing a marginalized center moved all over campus, lacking peer tutors, and dedicated to basic writing courses. Though this center makes some strides, the primary thrust of the essay (given a privileged space as the last in the book) details plans for CSU's Electronic Writing Center, a facility dedicated to a WAC initiative, to exist parallel with the old center. The new center will include cross-disciplinary efforts for developing software for writing in the disciplines, a large capacity for online tutoring, and access to electronic handouts as well as to the internet. Though this electronic center was largely in the planning stages at the time of the essay, one wonders how long the old center lasted, given its checkered history and the institutional commitment to the new one. In fact, a cluster diagram of the new center's place on campus accentuates its centrality with several campus entities, including the old center, as satellites. I am not questioning the wisdom or the efficacy of such a center at Colorado State. On a campus emphasizing "the sciences and engineering" (216), it is likely appropriate to its context. My fear rather is that such a center will become the benchmark for judging others and the desired norm in contexts where it may not be as appropriate. This possibility becomes evident when Rodrigues and Kiefer disclose that "some cynics began to suspect that the university as a whole valued computers over personal instruction" (216). This is a valid concern, but once again *ad hominem* is deployed to contain the more technologically cautious.

Computers will not go away, and we would be fools to want them to, but we would also be fools to ignore the wisdom Dave Healy shows when he writes, "Online writing centers represent a window of opportunity. Our challenge is to be reflective and self-critical while the opportunities before us are still fresh" (192). Healy's "From Place to Space: Perceptual and Administrative Issues in the Online Writing Center" (1995), as its title suggests, approaches technology in terms of its effects on the autonomy of the center as place, as opposed to (cyber)space, and on human relations such as the director's relationship to tutors as employees. On this latter point, Healy wonders how tutors might feel knowing every response they make to a client could be monitored electronically by the director. He also worries about the possible loss of "work-place community" and the knowledge transfer that occurs when tutors hear other tutors at work. Drawing on Geoffrey Chase's claim that "the ways in which our centers are designed—physically and socially—imply an ideology" (qtd. in Healy 191), Healy poses several questions directors would be wise to heed: "What is the ontological status of a virtual writing center, and what kind of relationship will clients develop with it? How will it be perceived by the rest of the academy? What possibilities and what threats are opened up by going online?" (191).

Like Healy, Stuart Blythe in his "Networked Computers + Writing Centers = ?" recommends caution, as he calls for a critical theory of computers in the center. Blythe reiterates several of the questions raised by Healy and also points out how center scholars have either looked at technology through "instrumental theories" that view it as a neutral tool or "substantive theories" that view it as a strong deter-mining cultural factor. He finds both views inadequate, the first because it is naive (my term, not his); the second, because it leads people to believe they lack power to manipulate the technology. Both theories, for Blythe, "place technology beyond the need or ability of human beings to intervene" (102). Blythe recommends that cen-ter professionals begin to ask questions, to intervene, to attempt to come up with theory that enables us to proceed "without feeling that we are trapped into a choice between accepting whatever comes our way or remaining adamantly anti-techno-logical" (102). Rather than this "take-it-or-leave-it" view, Blythe calls for theory that "prompts us to consider how we have implemented current technologies and who has been involved in that process" (105). Despite their cautions, neither Blythe nor Healy can be called a Luddite. Both recognize several possible benefits of computers. Furthermore, Healy, a few years back, managed a listserv for peer tutors, and Blythe coordinated Purdue's OWL and wrote a dissertation on tech-nologies in writing centers. But for each, enthusiasm is balanced with a measured thoughtfulness too often missing in writing center discourse on computers.

Content to move more rapidly is Cynthia Haynes-Burton in her "Intellectual (Proper)ty in Writing Centers: Retro Texts and Positive Plagiarism" (1995). Masterfully written in a frenetic style possibly meant to mimic in print the rapid-ity of hypertext, Haynes-Burton's essay moves with the speed of a Pentium II chip to challenge accepted definitions and prohibitions of plagiarism—long a thorny issue for writing centers. She metaphorically constructs current prohibitions as "a fortress" protecting capitalist principles of private property and implicating writ-ing centers in a "punitive system that brings students in line with a particular morality and a dominant economy" (88-9). Arguments about plagiarism have regularly entered writing center discourse with the emergence of social-construc-tionist pedagogy. Haynes-Burton adds to this debate by contending, as others have, that free access to electronic knowledge on the net (or "Infobahn" as she prefers to call it) challenges "our current system of accountability, academic scholarship" (89). She locates a model for an alternative to academic scholarship in postmodern art forms that pastiche together, allude to, and parody traditional artworks, as well as in the work of "Designers Republic," a design firm that appropriates and reshapes recognizable corporate logos to say something new. To the question of how these efforts might play out in writing—that is, what form "positive plagiarism may take" as an alternative to current forms of scholarship, she turns to the *MONDO 2,000 Users Guide to the New Edge*, suggesting that "a hypertext user can create a whole basket of links and 'publish' this as a kind of sampler, anthology, or work of criticism" (92).

There are some problems here. First, Haynes-Burton bases much of her justification for these alternative texts on contemporary challenges to the idea of authorship. In literary theory, these challenges certainly have been valuable in debunking naive notions of individual genius and have shown how culture contributes to textual production, yet theory has yet to account for why particular individuals in a culture—James Joyce or Toni Morrison, for example—become the ones who construct exceptional texts from their situatedness while others do not. In composition and writing center theory, critiques of individual authorship have been inscribed (and reified) in pejorative representations of expressionist rhetoric and "garret" centers, against which to portray the culturally situated writer of social construction. These representations of the individual author, however, have often relied on overstatement, constructing her as an isolated figure, when even a cursory historical glance indicates such an autonomous view of authorship never existed. Even formalist critics recognized that historically known authors often enjoyed cross-fertilizing relationships. We know that Melville talked to Hawthorne, that Emerson brought Whitman "to a boil," that the Bronte sisters read their works to one another, that Pound helped Eliot revise "The Wasteland," and that authoritative texts of Shakespeare's plays are difficult to establish because the plays were often revised by stage managers and even actors. One could catalogue more of these great moments in peer tutoring. In short, neither literary critics of earlier times nor expressionist theorists in composition have ever thought of individual authors as enjoying the degree of autonomy that Haynes-Burton and others posit to deconstruct. As for authors of scholarly works, though their names may be on a title page, their "collaborators" are recognized in the text and bibliography. And it is not for nothing that we call these references "citations," a word which not only signifies honorific recognition of others but which also shares Latin roots with *city* and *citizen*, evoking community rather than individualism. Second, Haynes-Burton's comparison of "positive plagiarism" to postmodern art and avantgarde design ignores the fact that the works appropriated in such pieces are so well known that they are self-citing or they could not elicit their intended effect. And finally Haynes-Burton does not recognize (at least not overtly) that the kind of writing she proposes would require a high-degree of literacy to discern the value of one text from another, something many student writers lack. Certainly every hot dog stand on Haynes-Burton's Infobahn does not serve the same grade of meat.

Though I have been rough on Haynes-Burton's essay, it is not one to dismiss, for it enters into new textual spaces that beckon writing centers to blaze some trails. Haynes-Burton attempts such trailblazing, boldly going where no one has gone before, but rather than scrap what she calls an "outdated notion of scholarship that is at odds with the digiototalitarian state in which we now live" (86), I think writing centers would do better to reject anything we can call "totalitarian," digio- or otherwise, and listen to Blythe to interrogate the substantive view of technology in which Haynes-Burton's essay eagerly participates. Irene Clark's "Information Literacy in the Writing Center" (1995) tenders a pedagogy for this effort. Clark defines information literacy as "the ability to access, retrieve, evaluate, and integrate information from a variety of electronically generated resources" (203). She goes on to describe a program in which writing center tutors work with novice writers to produce research papers from electronic and print sources. I give Clark's essay the final word in this discussion of new developments in the 1990s, for I believe it offers exactly the kind of advice writing centers need as they move into the next century. In short, Clark knows that anyone can operate a computer but only the literate can use it, and her emphasis on evaluating rather than merely accessing information makes her pedagogy the sort of driver's ed. course students will need to navigate future textual spaces, cyber or otherwise.

CONCLUSIONS AND FUTURES

If we have not already noticed, distance education is one of the hottest topics in administrative and legislative forums. It is cheap, it serves a broad clientele, and it can be tailored to individual student needs. Indeed it may not be long before universities begin pooling resources to offer courses by distance that could count toward degrees in any of the allied institutions. Such an arrangement is already in the works with the newly formed Western Governors University, whose campus, it is projected, will be totally in cyberspace. We in writing centers will need to be versed in technology if we are to be part of these efforts. At the same time we will need to assert what we know about live pedagogy to prevent the mere placing of services online simply because they can be, rather than because they should be.

As the world wide web expands with digital speed, chances are that it will continue to replicate our culture with cyber shopping malls, infotainment, virtual spaces for socializing, and the like, more than it will provide scholarly information. Yes, libraries are and will continue to be on the web, but libraries are on campuses and street corners too, competing, usually unsuccessfully, with designer boutiques, movie theaters, Super WalMarts, sports bars, video arcades, strip clubs, and amusement parks to shape the American consciousness. I suspect the proportions differ and will differ little, if at all, on the internet. Just as students have to learn to negotiate material culture, they will need to do the same in cyber culture.

This is not to say technology will not generate change, but as it does and as we develop pedagogy to respond, we should remember with Joseph Weizenbaum that "rejection of direct experience was to become one of the principal characteristics of modern science" (25). Granted direct experience is not always welcome—living in a house, a product of many technologies, is as sensible as it is comfortable. Likewise accessing a writing center tutor via computer to avoid walking across a dark campus at night is an intelligent decision. Nevertheless, we should maintain, as Michael Spooner does, that "flesh and blood is richer stuff than fiber optics" (8). If OWLS are going to carry us into flight rather than eat us like rodents, if MOOs are going to produce more milk than dung, if we are going to cruise the information superhighway without becoming roadkill, we will need to remain vigilant against the intoxication of our enthusiasm.

NOTES

1. Weizenbaum, an MIT computer scientist, created one of the first interactive programs, ELIZA. ELIZA mimicked Rogerian therapy, asking such questions as "How do you feel?" and then after the user responded, "Why do you feel that way?" Weizenbaum wrote the program as an experiment and initially was amused that people would engage with it but was horrified when professional therapists thought it could be effective in real therapy.

2. My position here is corroborated by Angela Petit in a 1997 article in *The Writing Center Journal*. Petit argues that such metaphoric definitions often divide writing centers into "rigid ideological categories" turning them into "purified spaces" (a term borrowed from Min-zhan Liu) that do not account for the fluidity of diverse student needs.

PART III

Resources for Wired Writing Centers

CHAPTER THIRTEEN

UnfURLed
Twenty Writing Center Sites to Visit on the Information Superhighway

Bruce Pegg

BACKGROUND: THE NWCA LIST OF ONLINE WRITING CENTERS

WHEN THE FIRST VERSION OF THE NATIONAL WRITING CENTERS ASSOCIATION page (http://departments.colgate.edu/diw/NWCA.html) appeared in January 1996, it included about five or six links to other writing center websites. Due to a lengthy web-crawler search and an exploration of sites indexed through the University of Maine's then excellent site of online writing centers, the NWCA list grew so quickly that at some point in the Spring of 1996 the list of writing centers online had to be moved to its own page (http://departments.colgate.edu/diw/NWCAOWLS.html) to ease downloading. Since then, through a combination of searching and suggestions from colleagues, sites have been added at the rate of a little over three a month, with major list revisions in March and October of 1997 deleting obsolete sites and adding still more. As of February 1998, 213 sites were included, and it was from this list that the sites reviewed here were chosen.

SITE SELECTION

Two major selection criteria were used: either the site offered a substantial resource of value to writers or the writing center community, reflected mastery of the HTML medium, or both. Thus, a site like the University of Richmond, though it employs a design, is included for its Writers Web section, while Michigan State's fairly simple site was included for its innovation and technical ability. For easy reference, the sites are also reviewed using the following system of icons:

The international symbol for information is used for sites who have information about their writing center, such as hours, location, and contact addresses, on their pages.

The chain icon is used for sites that contain links to other writing or writing center related sites.

This, and the next four icons, are for sites that feature handouts or related material original to that particular site. This first symbol, with a solid block of text, is for a site that has 10 or fewer handouts.

These icons, of handouts with 2 columns, are for sites that have 11-30 handouts. The letters A and Z indicate that the handouts are indexed.

These icons, of handouts with 3 columns, are for sites that have more than 31 handouts. Again, the A and Z indicate that the handouts are indexed.

These computer icons are for sites that have electronic tutoring via e-mail or multi-user domains. The first indicates that the site has tutoring exclusively for members of its own institution; the second is for a site that features electronic tutoring for anyone on the net.

The palette and brush icon is for a site that makes good use of graphics, such as image maps or frames, or that is exceptionally well organized.

This writing icon is used to indicate that the site features tutor training materials, such as tutor manuals or practicum syllabi, or material of interest to composition teachers. Like the handouts, this material must be original to the site.

The 'new' icon, used on many web pages to indicate new material, is here used to show that the site has been revised within the last three months.

BEMIDJI STATE UNIVERSITY

http://cal.bemidji.msus.edu/WRC/WRChome.html

This site's index page strikes a fine balance between humor and seriousness. The page features a red header logo on a plain white background; below is a menu in a borderless frame on the left of the screen with links and descriptions of the site's main areas. In the center of the screen, cartoon-like icons in an image map also function as links to these areas (see Figure 1).

Figure 1
Index Page: Bemidji State University Writing Resource Center

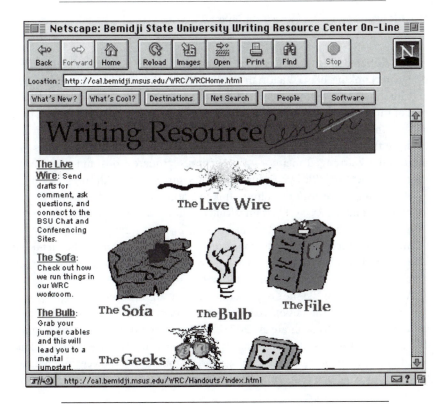

Clicking on The Bulb, for example, leads to a page of annotated links designed to stimulate writers, particularly those working on literature papers. Similarly, clicking on The Sofa leads to a page of information on Bemidji's real writing center, including a procedures manual and papers written for ENGL 312, Bemidji's Writing Consultancy course.

A third menu, of plain links, appears below the image map on the index page; items here could, perhaps, have been incorporated into existing sections or made into new ones. However, the site also features online tutoring, open to students and outsiders, and an indexed page of numerous linked and original handouts, making it complete and easily navigable.

BRIGHAM YOUNG UNIVERSITY – HAWAII CAMPUS

http://lc.byuh.edu/R_WCTR/welcome. html

The cluttered index page is perhaps a good indication of how oddly this site is designed. Looking like a Victorian book, with lovely clickable watercolor pen-and-ink images on a brown textured background, this page is a haphazard mixture of internal and external links (which are duplicated on the Surf the Net page and are, therefore, redundant here). Perhaps a better option for visitors wishing to navigate the site is to select the Reading/Writing Center image, which links to a more orderly arranged menu — a collection of square icons and their corresponding links (http://lc.byuh.edu/R_WCTR/sample/welcom2.html).

Here, though, the visitor can find a link to a bordered frames version of the site (http://lc.byuh.edu/R_WCTR/frames/gallery.html) which employs the same icons in a menu bar on the left of the screen. This site employs a completely different design concept, using a notebook image for the main frame. The menu-bar icons are unlabeled; placing the cursor over them leads to a description of their function appearing at the bottom of the screen.

As problematic as the site's organization may be, the Surf the Net page is worth the visit. Although the design concept for this page is different again, it makes good use of forms to facilitate an easy search of several different search engines. The Meet the Tutors section also makes excellent use of an image map (clicking on a tutor's picture leads to a brief biography of that tutor). A nicely indexed collection of original handouts complements the site, which certainly could use unifying in its next revision.

CALIFORNIA STATE UNIVERSITY–LOS ANGELES

http://web.calstatela.edu/centers/write_cn/index.htm

This site, which is offered in both frames and non-frames versions, is a good example of how a simple frames set-up can facilitate easy site navigation. Though the instructions provided for its online tutoring service are perhaps a little complex, and there is a lot of information that is of local interest only (such as how to pass California State's Writing Proficiency Exam), the Resources and Faculty Services sections yield some high-quality material. The former section, divided into two categories (Writing Tips and Grammar and Punctuation Tips) is a small collection of handouts, including really useful ones on Using the Words of Others and on Breath, Grammar, and Punctuation (which looks at punctuation from an historical perspective and which ultimately challenges the traditional grammatical way of looking at punctuation). The Faculty Services section contains articles about teaching writing, including ones on Good Assignments, What is an 'A' Paper, and a concise historical survey of rhetorical education called Ancient Rhetoric and Modern Literacy. Sections on helping ESL students and on Writing In The Disciplines round out this small but significant section nicely.

CALIFORNIA UNIVERSITY OF PENNSYLVANIA

http://www.english.cup.edu/wcenter/wcenter.html

Another frames site, with a bordered menu bar on the left hand side of the screen and a larger frame on the right hand side of the screen. When the screen loads for the first time, information about California University of Pennsylvania's real writing center appears in the large frame; due to a coding problem, when a link from the menu frame is clicked, this information stays in the larger frame, and new information, rather than replacing the original, appears in a new web browser. However, a nice user-friendly forms-based page for online paper submissions, and a useful series of links shows that the site has promise, especially as it has been recently updated.

CLAREMONT GRADUATE UNIVERSITY WRITING CENTER

http://www.cgts.edu/resources/wrtctr.html

Again, another very simple site, featuring only one very basic graphic which appears on most of the site's pages. Like California State Los Angeles, it also has pretty elaborate instructions for users of its online tutoring service (which is for students only). This site features an nice array of handouts presented in an easy-to-view table; sections on General Writing Tips, Working With Sources and on writing Specific Kinds of Papers (such as literature reviews and summaries) are complemented by an unusual offering of handouts for writers presenting at professional conferences. This section takes the visitor through the whole process of deciding what format the conference presentation should take, how to submit a proposal and abstract, how to deliver the paper, how to deal with responses and questions, and how conference presentations differ in the Humanities and Social Sciences. This, coupled with a useful online handbook on writing issues for faculty which includes sections on how to respond to writing and how to work with ESL students, and a small yet well-annotated list of useful internet sites, gives this site some real substance.

COLORADO STATE UNIVERSITY WRITING CENTER

http://www.colostate.edu/Depts/English/wcenter/wcenter.htm

For web page managers looking for different ways to organize an abundance of information clearly and logically, this site is one to bookmark. The entry page to this site is very simple, featuring two audio samples (the only writing center site to do so) and information about Colorado State's real writing center. Like several other sites, this page then has a link to an online center (http://www.colostate.edu/Depts/WritingCenter/index.html), leading to an index page which provides several choices as to how to browse the site. Users can opt to use the straightforward index of links on the main page, which is divided into six main categories. With the exception of the Tutorials and Send A Paper categories, clicking on each of these categories leads to a sub-index; clicking on an item here leads to a screen which adopts a three frame format. The left frame contains a menu bar, while the middle frame contains items which can be expanded out on the right frame (see Figure 2).

Figure 2
Three-Frame Format: Colorado State University Writing Center

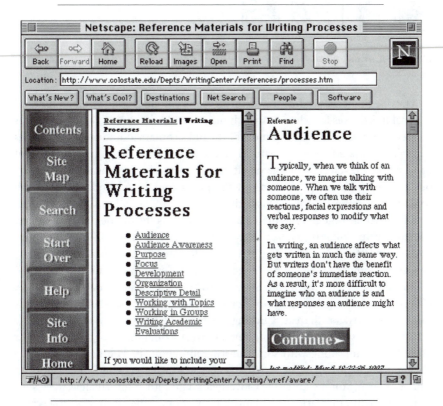

The other method of navigation is the menu bar, which is a borderless frame appearing on the left hand site of every screen in the site, and which provides various navigation options for visitors. With the exception of the confusingly-named Start Over button (which actually functions in the same way as a Back button on a browser) this method works well.

All the navigation systems on the web cannot help a site if it has nothing to offer; this site, however, delivers in several ways. The Assignments sections contains much useful information and syllabi for teachers of Composition, English, and Engineering courses with a writing component; the Reference Materials section also contains a wealth of handouts, all logically indexed. Sadly, the Tutorial section, which promises interactive tutorials for writers and readers" has yet to be completed, though the Send A Paper section provides easy-to-follow instructions for cutting, pasting, and sending a paper via a well laid-out page.

MICHIGAN STATE UNIVERSITY WRITING CENTER

http://pilot.msu.edu/user/writing/

The opening page to this site, featuring some simple graphics and an index of internal links, gives few clues to the whimsical world that lies inside. The index is divided into five headings, and most of the links contained under these headings will take the visitor to pages featuring a borderless table menu bar on the right hand side of the screen, a simple yet effective logo graphic for a header, and generous photographic images. Several of the pages contain sub-indexes; nearly all contain information of mostly local interest.

Of particular note among these pages, however, is the online publication *Peer Review* (http://pilot.msu.edu/user/writing/Peer_Review/prpg1.html), an in-house newsletter that could serve as a model for other writing centers wishing to engage in a similar project. A promised WAC Newsletter has yet to materialize.

But the jewel in Michigan State's crown is the elaborate HTML house, Cloverfield Manor, listed on the index page under the Resources for Writers heading as The Writers' Retreat. Clicking on the link takes the visitor to a page (http://pilot.msu.edu/user/writing/retreat.html) containing a graphic of the Manor's exterior along with some information about it. The Retreat is a truly imaginative attempt to create a virtual reality writing center which the visitor can enter by clicking on the Enter the Cloverfield Manor link. Immediately, the visitor is transported to the Parlor, the Manor's front room, which is, in reality, a screen divided into three frames (see Figure 3).

In the top left frame is an image map of the Manor's floor plan; to move around the house, all the visitor has to do is to is to click on a room and the screen for that room downloads in the right-hand frame. This, too, is an image map, and clicking on an item in the room (such as the calendar on the parlor wall) leads to a page of links (in this case, a list of Michigan State writing center workshops). For the less adventurous and more literal-minded, scrolling down the bottom frame reveals a written description of the room, as well as a handy link to a list of all the clickable items in it.

Sadly, the Manor, like the stately home of some bankrupt British baron, is in need of some serious repair. The items within the rooms are all links to outside

Figure 3
Cloverfield Manor Parlor: Michigan State University Writing Center

sites, and one could only wish that the same energy put into designing the retreat could have also been put into designing some original resources. And four out of the nine projected rooms have, in the words of the site's author, yet to be remodeled; since the site was last revised in May of 1997, one can only speculate that the construction crew have gone on a rather lengthy coffee break.

PURDUE UNIVERSITY'S OWL

http://owl.english.purdue.edu

The index page to the oldest and most comprehensive online writing center in existence is simple and uncluttered, with a logo of a computer disk appearing above a borderless table. The table is divided into seven self-explanatory sections and visitors can either choose to click on a color coded category heading to go to an introductory page for each category (which features the section's sub-index, sometimes in table form), dive straight in to one of the several links provided under each category heading, use the handy search engine for the site, or take a more leisurely paced self-guided tour (beginning at http://owl.english. purdue.edu/owls/tour/introduction.html).

And what an immense amount of information there is! There are over 200 connected pages of information here, though for most visitors, the highlight is the 130 downloadable handouts. As significant as the handouts are, however, a wonderful section of links for ESL students and teachers, and an excellent annotated bibliography of scholarly work on online writing labs (http://owl.english.purdue.edu/owls/owl-bib.html) should not be overlooked. Many of the links throughout the site are annotated and, in the Sites of Interest to Writing Teachers section, reviewed.

Organizing and maintaining a site of this magnitude is a formidable task, and inevitably leads to some, albeit minor, problems. The index page contains a number of redundant links (with the exception of the Resources for Writers and Purdue Resources category headings on the opening index page, all the images are links which are confusingly duplicated by other links placed immediately below them); the page summarizing the handouts categories is not especially helpful (the categories are clear enough in themselves); the section on Internet Searching could be refined (discipline specific search engines and indexes could appear together, for example); and older pages need to be revised to include the helpful menu bar that appears at the bottom of most of the pages on the site to make the site uniform. But in the face of such a resource, such criticisms seem petty; the countless number of other websites that have linked to the Purdue OWL, and the 8,700 hits a day that the site received during the 1997 Fall Semester, are proof positive of the site's stature in the online writing center community.

ROANE STATE COMMUNITY COLLEGE OWL

http://www2.rscc.cc.tn.us/~jordan_jj/OWL/owl.html

For anyone interested in exploring the possibilities of online pedagogy, this is certainly a site to bookmark. Another very simply designed site, the index page features an attractive logo of a great-horned owl; underneath it, a bordered table contains links that are both anchored to the index page or that lead elsewhere in the site. Highlights of the site include 35 original handouts, including a number of sample student essays, syllabi for a writing center practicum and several online writing courses, a useful index of handouts at other online writing centers, and articles on writing, writing centers and online writing labs by the site's author, Jennifer Jordan-Henley. One of them, MOOving Across the Information Superhighway (http://www2.rscc.cc.tn.us/~jordan_jj/OWL/MOOving.html) details the Cyberspace Writing Center Consultation Project, where graduate students in rhetoric and writing at The University of Arkansas–Little Rock (http://www.ualr.edu/~owl/index.html) offer online tutoring to students enrolled in composition, literature and technical writing courses at Roane State via an email paper exchange and a virtual conference in a multi-user domain.

SALT LAKE COMMUNITY COLLEGE

http://www.slcc.edu/wc/welcome.htm

The only online writing center boasting a writing center cam, this is another frames site, this time with the menu bar situated on the right-hand side of the screen. Unfortunately, this can be easily confused with the menu bar that appears at the foot of the main frame pages, which is intended for the main Salt Lake Community College site, and not for the writing center. However, the menu bar provides a link to an alphabetical Detailed Index, which provides an easy-to-use overview of the site in a bordered frame. Other areas of the site include Teachers' Writing: A Clearinghouse of Pedagogy (which currently contains a survey of Salt Lake Community College Writing Center users and a piece on email tutoring); an indexed list of links to writing and research resources on the net; links to syllabi for several online and traditional writing courses; *Cere*, an e-zine of creative writing for the Salt Lake Community College and neighboring Utah community; and online tutoring, where visitors can submit writing or writing-related questions in a number of ways (A MOO, a bulletin board, and a virtual tutor that takes papers or questions via a form or email).

UNIVERSITY OF GEORGIA

http://parallel.park.uga.edu/~sigalas/wchome.html

The opening page offers a choice of frame or no-frames version, the frames version featuring a menu bar of links on the left side of the screen, while the no-frames version has the same menu in a bordered table. The whole site employs simple pages with a uniform, gray textured background and contains much of local interest, including information on the University of Georgia Regents Testing Program. It is the Writer's Resources section, which includes a number of original and linked handouts, which is the part of this site to head for, however; the prize here is the huge section on comma usage, called "Commas: They're Not Just For English Majors Anymore." Though the accompanying exercise section, which uses forms to allow the viewer to click on a box and immediately check the answer, can be seen as a high-tech skill-and-drill exercise, the main page is a genuine attempt to demonstrate how to apply punctuation knowledge during the drafting and proofreading stages of the writing process; the jargon-free approach to the section and humorous examples also give this a fresh approach to the issue of comma usage.

UNIVERSITY OF ILLINOIS AT URBANA-CHAMPAIGN WRITERS' WORKSHOP

http://www.english.uiuc.edu/cws/wworkshop/writer.html

Another very comprehensive site with much to offer. The opening page employs a bordered frames menu bar on the left hand side of the screen; the index page, confusingly, duplicates the links and icons on the menu bar but employs different names for the sections, though it does provide a good representation of the site and its layout. (Interestingly, whether intentional or not, clicking on the Home link below the Writers Workshop logo on the menu bar will lead to a no-frames version of the site). Pages after the index page employ a uniform white background and logos, rather than the green textured index page which could have been distracting if over-used, though the header logos vary from page to page, making the site appear a little disorderly.

The main features of this site are the comprehensive Online Writing Guide and the really useful Best Websites For Writers section. The Online Writing Guide is divided into three sections: The Grammar, Writing Techniques, and Bibliography Handbooks. Each section is nicely indexed and tremendously helpful. Of special note is the Grammar Handbook, which ends each entry with a handy teaching tip for teachers using the material in class. I have some minor criticisms about the other two sections, however; the Bibliography handbook, which currently features sections on APA, MLA, and old MLA style, could be updated to include citations for online sources, while the Writing Techniques section could be better organized (the section on genre specific advice includes a link on using commas, and the advice given could also a little more responsive to writers across the disciplines).

Arguably, the most impressive section of the site is the section on the Best Websites for Writers, which provides really helpful annotations of a vast number of websites. Five categories are considered here; of them, the Writing Teachers Resource page and the Help for Students and Teachers of English as a Second Language page incorporate large amounts of information. Both pages utilize indexes at the top of each respective page and take a few seconds to download, but the wait is definitely worth it.

The site is made complete by links from the index page to pages of local information as well as links to two other smaller sections, on Reference Texts and Directories and on WWW Searching Tools; of these, the first could use some expanding. On the whole, though, this is a valuable site, and one can only hope that they continue to expand along the lines they have already established.

UNIVERSTIY OF MINNESOTA

http://www.Agricola.umn.edu/owc/

A site long on graphic ambition but short on technical prowess, this site could have potential if maintained properly. The index page to the site features images of a window and three doors marked Tutoring, Skill Center, and Staff (see Figure 4).

Despite being labeled, these images' functions are not readily apparent: the window, for example, is an external link to Minnesota weather, while clicking on the Staff door leads to a dialog box asking for a name and a password to enter a server whose function is not explained. Clicking on the tutoring door proves to be more inviting, however; the viewer is soon greeted by images of a blackboard, a clipboard, and an in and out tray. Clicking on the blackboard, on which is written "How to Use the Tutor," reveals that this page is for online tutoring; a long but clear list of instructions explains how to submit a paper. Going back and clicking on the in-tray provides an easy-to-use form for that purpose, and finished papers are then placed in the out-tray to be picked up by their authors. The clipboard, with the words "Leave a Message" written on it, functions, as one would expect, as a mail-to link.

The Skills Center also makes similar clever use of images, containing books on top of a file cabinet, a picture, a crystal ball, and two more doors, each labeled conveniently with their function. But it is here that the concept starts to break down. The page begins promisingly enough—clicking on the Books (labeled

Figure 4
Index Page: University of Minnesota Online Writing Center

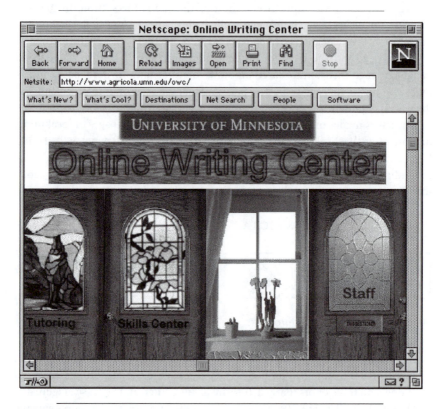

"WWW resources for Writers") leads to a page with a number of annotated links. However, clicking on the file cabinet marked Handouts leads to a dull, gopher-style index from which the handouts can be accessed (an open file drawer or something similar would have been more appropriate). Likewise, the crystal ball failed to live up to its promise. The Oracle, as it is named, promises to be a database of grammar information and a place where answers to email grammar questions will be revealed. However, an attempt to enter the database is met with an error message, as does any attempt to "open" the Classroom door, which looks to be some sort of chatroom. Clicking on the picture labeled Upcoming Online Workshops yielded no results at all.

With no information on the index page about the page's last update, it is impossible to determine whether this page will live up to its lavish, graphic promise; as at Cloverfield Manor, one can only hope that the contractors will finish their break soon.

UNIVERSITY OF MISSOURI

http://www.missouri.edu/~lcwww/wlhome.html

A busy index page features a number of moving images (visitors are greeted by an invisible hand writing the word "welcome" on a chalk board) on a gaudy yellow background; a bordered table in the center of the page contains the site's index. This contains mostly items of local interest, though a link to the University of Missouri's Writing Lab internship course (http://dewey.lc.missouri.edu/H120/intern.html) is of wider interest; while there, a visit to the course's newsletter is also worth the trip. Several links here are problematic, however: a link to a handout on APA documentation works fine, though the corresponding link to the handout on MLA documentation is inoperative, while links labeled Writing Workshop and Writers' Block Newsletter actually go to the University of Missouri's Learning Center .

But it is the link to Eric Crump's Online Writery (http://www.missouri.edu/~writery/) that most visitors to the site will be interested in. Here, in addition to a number of links to resources on the Net, Eric has put together the largest number of spaces for writing and writing related issues available through one site. Not only can visitors submit writing or writing-related questions to cybertutors via an easy-to-use form, but they can also subscribe to the Writers' Cafe, a listserv dedicated to writing issues, join ZooMoo, a real time virtual environment for writers," or even join one of several HyperNews forums (fiction, poetry and HTML help) to submit and/or discuss writing. The header frame at this site claims that you have entered a conversation coffeehouse for writers; judging by the number of different ways one can talk about writing here, the noise around the site must be deafening!

L'UNIVERSITÉ D'OTTAWA

http://www.uottawa.ca/academic/arts/writcent/

Though the simple layout and stark white background of the index page suggest that this site has little to offer, its Hypergrammar is well worth the visit. Called an Online Textbook and Workbook for English Grammar, it is perhaps more accurately described as an interactive, self-guided grammar tutorial.

Initially, it may seem a little awkward to use (reading the instructions is highly recommended) but anyone that has any facility with the old Hypercard-type programs should have no problem navigating this ingenious site.

UNIVERSITY OF RICHMOND

http://www.urich.edu/~writing

Like the University of Ottawa site, this simple set of pages contains a hidden gem: the Writers Web. A simple bordered table contains the index to over 50 original handouts, organized by the stages of the writing process; of note here are handouts on reading strategies in the Prewriting section, a cautionary handout on the warning signs of a rushed paper, a section on using sources, and a peer editing guide. The WAC focus of a number of handouts in this section is also a welcome addition

This site is also a part of the Epiphany Project, a project designed to integrate technology into the writing classroom. Though the main site is housed at George Mason University (http://mason.gmu.edu/~epiphany), the Richmond writing center houses an interesting survey on the problems of implementing electronic pedagogy and of using computers in WAC classes.

UNIVERSITY OF TEXAS AT AUSTIN

http:/uwc-server.fac.utexas.edu/

This is another neglected site which needs to perform a thorough revision of all its pages. A simple index page featuring a logo and a textured gray background lists links to several items, including a huge list of links for communication scholars, many of which are annotated; teachers of composition will also find some useful items here, including handouts on designing writing assignments, commenting on student papers, peer critiquing and approaches to teaching grammar and punctuation. Finally, this is another site with a newsletter for tutors or clients of the University's real writing center; sadly, though, the last (and only) issue posted is December 1995.

UNIVERSITY OF WISCONSIN

http://www.wisc.edu/writing

This site has recently been updated as a bordered frames site, and stands as a perfect illustration of the inherent problems with the frames concept; though the header and main frame fit nicely on the screen, the left-hand frame is too small for the menu bar contained inside it, making it difficult to use. Though it dispenses with the attractive photo images and splashy graphics of the frames version, the no-frames option (http://www.wisc.edu/writing/noframes.html) is, at least at this point in time, preferable. Here, the menu is presented as a bar on the left hand side of a bordered table, with new items appearing at the bottom of a bigger cell. To complete the design, a nav-bar and logo appear as an attractive header to the index page; here, a search option is incorporated to ease navigation.

Of note at this site is the Online Writers' Handbook, featuring a number of easy-to-find handouts on writing topics; many of these handouts provide lengthy yet clear illustrations of the topic under discussion. This is augmented by a small FAQ page featuring sections on grammar and documentation, and several pages of internet resources, with helpful annotations accompanying each link. Local information of interest to the wider writing center community includes information on the University of Wisconsin-Madison's Writing Fellows Program and a simple yet comprehensive and easy-to-use form for online tutoring.

WASHINGTON STATE UNIVERSITY

http://owl.wsu.edu/

A new site that already holds out tremendous promise, this is perhaps a glimpse into the future of OWLs, as it uses multi-media techniques to provide its services to writers. The opening page, a simple affair employing a header graphic and an image of an owl on a white background, leads to a number of internal links; these pages have the same uniform white background with an image map menu bar (a series of shelves with icons and labels to guide visitors to other sections of the site) on the right of the screen.

Resources of note here include the OWL Writers' Exchange, which is a wonderful twist on online tutoring. Registered visitors can post their papers in a bulletin board format, enabling online tutors and other visitors to comment on them and produce a thread of responses. The registration process itself is fairly straightforward, requiring a few minutes to fill out a self-explanatory form; visitors finding this confusing, however, can download several QuickTime movies (courtesy of Hooey the Helpful Owl) designed to guide them through the process. Judging by the number of submissions to the Exchange, this service looks like it could become one of the more widely used online tutoring efforts in the writing center community.

Unfortunately, the rest of the site is, as yet, not as well developed. The Resources section is small, featuring only a handful of links to other sites, but the links are annotated and a handy form enables visitors to provide annotations and ratings for recommended sites, making this a truly interactive site. In addition, a small list of other OWLs is also provided; unfortunately, this is not annotated, and is unhelpfully organized by geographic area. But this is a site to bookmark and revisit if it continues to be revised.

WILKES UNIVERSITY

http://wilkes1.wilkes.edu/~writing/

A bordered frame introduction page (with a menu in the left hand frame) employing no graphics provides several internal links, including one to a tutor's handbook. Though it contains a number of sections of local interest (such as filling out report forms), the handbook has several sections, particularly The Initial Interview, Discovering Patterns of Error, and on Responding to Clients Requests, that could be useful to tutors everywhere. Two other sections, on Generative Questions and Practice Situations, are equally useful but not linked from the Handbook menu, and can only be found by following the sequential links that appear at the bottom of each page.

This site's other valuable resource is a number of writing guides, containing sections on Writing Research Papers, Editing/Revising, and Grammar, Mechanic and Usage. Additionally, seven worksheets are included in this section; rather than providing exercises to test for comprehension of the above areas, they are mostly analytical in nature, providing a tool for writers and readers to evaluate workshops or conferences. As such, they seem out of place in this section, and would seem more at home in the Tutor's Handbook or in a section of their own. Of the two remaining sections, the Technology page seems to be most useful, making good use of screen captures to help people use different email programs. The other section, the Resources page, consists mostly of links to literature sites.

CONCLUSION

Choosing twenty sites out of the 213 writing centers on the NWCA list was not easy. Even sites that have only local information still have something to offer the wider writing center community, either by providing contact information, mission statements, or administrative information that can be of use to other centers, or by providing web page design ideas for those searching for new ways to present information on the net. Not everyone has, or needs to have, an owl, and though this review is biased toward sites that carry the most information, it is not meant to slight the other 193 sites whose presence on the net reflects their desire to make only limited use of it.

From the sites selected, however, certain conclusions can be drawn about the way that writing centers have embraced the new technology. Nearly all the sites have adopted design aesthetics that reflect the writing center's place in the academy: conservative enough to be taken seriously, yet adventurous (and in some cases, playful enough) to reflect the non-traditional role that we occupy in the curriculum. But whether by choice or by ignorance of the medium's potential, only a fraction of writing centers on the net have embraced the multi-media possibilities that are now prevalent among the commercial sites. Certainly, as the medium progresses, and advances in audio and video continue, we would all do well to consider how these areas will help us achieve our goals on the web.

The other problem that is all too evident in this list, as it is on the web as a whole, is the difficulty in maintaining a site. At least eight sites out of the twenty have not updated their sites in the last three months (fully a quarter of the sites on the NWCA list fit into this category); several more have revised or added individual pages without paying attention to other areas of the site that are rapidly falling into disrepair. As I have learned in maintaining the NWCA site, time devoted to keeping it up to date increases exponentially with the amount of material on it, a fact that anyone considering starting up a site, or with lofty ambitions for an existing one, would do well to consider.

But this list indicates an encouraging trend, one that I hope will continue as more sites spring up or expand. While all of our sites cater well to our clientele, either through our handouts, by providing electronic tutoring, or by providing links to other writing-related sites, it is good to note that we are also beginning to cater to our own profession. Nearly half of the sites in this review (and twenty-three in the entire NWCA list) have information concerning tutoring or teaching writing, a small yet significant percentage of the total number of writing centers online. It is encouraging to see the numbers of tutoring manuals and training course syllabi that are appearing on the web; soon, hopefully, our professional material will become as widely available as our handouts. Add to this the growing number of sites here that are beginning to imaginatively use the medium's possibilities, and it is easy to become excited by the wired writing center's potential.

CHAPTER FOURTEEN

Computers and Writing Centers
A Selected Bibliography

Steve Sherwood

*T*HOSE WHO HAVE WORKED IN WRITING CENTERS FOR MANY YEARS MAY REMEM-
ber when their centers received a handful of Apple IIes or IBM PCs with a pair
of 5¹/₂-inch floppy disk drives, no hard drive, and an impressive (at the time) 256
kilobytes of random access memory. As the scholarship that chronicles the marriage
of computers and writing centers illustrates, many writing center directors did not at
first know what to make of computers—or how to use them. Often, directors used
the machines to keep records of student traffic, to give computer-assisted instruction
in the form of grammar and syntax drills or, at best, to introduce student writers to
word processing. The articles and essays from this time—the late 1970s to the mid-
1980s—are pragmatic, consisting of hardware and software reviews, advice on how
to set up a user-friendly computer lab, or sometimes hostile backlashes against the
new technology as counterproductive to the writing center mission. In his 1979
Writing Lab Newsletter article Richard C. Veit compares and contrasts human and
machine-assisted instruction (i.e., auto-tutorial programs) and comes down on the
side of "humanistic labs." Of human tutors, Veit says, "even without training, they
have more to offer students than the programs and machines" (2). In a 1987 *Writing
Center Journal* issue dedicated to computers, Fred Kemp likewise challenges the
notion that computers can or should replace the human tutor.

Even as writing center practitioners grew comfortable with computer technology, maintaining the human element in writing center interactions continued to
be a central concern. By the late 1980s few scholars were advocating computer-
assisted skill and drill programs. Instead, most sought to understand how computers impacted student writers' composition processes and how best to facilitate
the writers' efforts. In a 1987 *Writing Center Journal* edition dedicated to computers, Pamela B. Farrell portrays the computer as neutral ground on which student
and peer tutor negotiate a more fruitful collaboration. In the same issue of the
journal, Jeanne Luchte examines the computer's role in student writers' prewriting, organizing, and drafting processes.

As free-standing computers with limited memories gave way to networks, the relationship between writing centers and computers continued to evolve. A few writing centers, including Joyce Kinkead's at Utah State University, began experimenting with the interactive possibilities that electronic mail offered. In a 1987 *College Composition and Communication* article, Kinkead notes the benefits of this approach to tutoring, including convenient, 24-hour-a-day access to assistance for nontraditional, shy, or fearful students who find it difficult to visit the writing center during operating hours. Since then, such innovations in computer technology as the World Wide Web have brought corresponding innovations in writing center design and practice. The most noteworthy, perhaps, was the creation of the online writing lab at Purdue in the early 1990s. Other OWLs soon followed, providing assistance ranging from online handbooks to consultations with cyberspace tutors. These consultations which began as asynchronous conversations (e.g., with the student submitting a text or question at 2 a.m. and the tutor replying at a more civilized hour) have in some cases become synchronous (or real-time) conversations in a virtual writing center located in a Multiple-User Dimension (MUD) or MUD-Object Oriented (MOO). As Muriel Harris says in a 1995 interview published in *Composition Studies,* "Writing centers have been incredibly inventive about reaching out. They're student-centered environments, and the *Writing Lab Newsletter* is filled with articles describing various writing centers that have inaugurated innovative activities" (Mullin 39).

As in the days when computers and writing centers first intersected, the introduction of OWLs, MUDs, and MOOs to writing center operations in the 1990s has brought an abundance of scholarship that ranges from enthusiastic acceptance of these new tutoring venues (and advice on how to set them up) to pieces that caution about pedagogical and ethical perils that cyberspace tutoring can pose (including the blatant editing of student papers). As before, one of the principal concerns of writing center specialists has been how to maintain in cyberspace the human element that so enriches face-to-face tutorials—in short, how cybertutors can overcome the lack of facial and verbal cues from student writers. In a 1994 *Writing Lab Newsletter* article, Jeffrey S. Baker questions the ethics of online tutoring because electronic dialogue does not permit the "conceptual indeterminacy" and potential creativity of verbal conversations (6). In a 1995 *Computers and Composition* article, David Coogan reflects that email tutorials collapse "the self into text where it becomes a rhetorical construct, not a social given" (171). For the most part, though, Coogan supports email tutoring because it closely reflects today's social constructivist views about the collaborative production of knowledge.

To make the best use of virtual writing centers, Diana George contends, writing center specialists will need to construct new theories on electronic discourse that inform the teaching of writing. In her 1995 article in *Computers and Composition,* George says, "We cannot simply add computers to a writing center any more than we can simply add tutoring to a computer" (334). A number of writing center professionals also point to the need for theory to inform tutoring in virtual environments, and in a 1997 *WCJ* article, Stuart Blythe attempts to delineate such a theory by examining the implications of three existing theories of technology—instrumental, substantive, and critical. As Blythe explains, instrumental theories "see technology as neutral" (95) while substantive theories see technology as the product of "a unique cultural system" and the shaper of "social structure and human endeavors" (95-96). In the end, he espouses the critical theory—which avoids important pitfalls of the other theories—as democratic and empowering, and therefore most relevant to the mission of the writing center. Since the critical theory is based, in part, on the notion that need drives technological development, Blythe argues that writing center professionals will have to get more involved in the design of computer software (either directly by learning to write programs or indirectly by having programmers write programs aimed at facilitating collaborative learning).

As Blythe acknowledges, his article "leaves many questions unanswered" (105). One could say the same about the directions the writing center-computer relationship will take in the future. However, as the body of scholarship represented in this bibliography makes clear, as computer technology continues to evolve, writing center professionals will continue—in the interest of their student writers—to experiment with and wrestle with the practical and theoretical implications of this technology. I hope scholars find the bibliography useful in their pursuits. In any case, I must mention that it attempts to cover works from 1995 on, with only a sampling of works prior to 1995. For a complete bibliography of articles involving writing centers and computers, please see the Educational Technology section (and other sections) of *Writing Centers: An Annotated Bibliography*, (Greenwood, 1996), compiled by Christina Murphy, Joe Law, and me. Finally, I must thank Dr. Robert Royar for sending me a copy of the winter 1995-1996 issue of *ACE Newsletter*, which is dedicated entirely to articles exploring the writing center-computer connection.

ADMINISTRATIVE ISSUES

Crump, Eric. "Online Community: Writing Centers Join the Network World." *Writing Lab Newsletter* 17.2 (1992): 1-5.
Reviews the sense of isolation felt by writing center directors in distant parts of the nation and how WCenter, an email distribution list for writing center specialists has brought the profession together. Contends that WCenter gives writing center specialists to express concerns, discuss practical and theoretical issues, and enjoy a sense of community that conventions and print publications cannot, by themselves, provide.

Hobson, Eric. "Coming in Out of the Silence." *Writing Lab Newsletter* 17.6 (1993): 7-8.
Endorses WCenter, the email distribution list, as an invaluable source of information, advice, community, and easy communication for writing center specialists. Also discusses WCenter's potential as a research tool.

Holmes, Leigh Howard. "Expanding Turf: Rationales for Computers in Writing Labs." *Writing Lab Newsletter* 9.10 (1985): 13-14.
Suggests that the addition of computers to a writing lab can help disabuse professors and administrators of the notion that the lab serves only remedial writers, in part because

tutors can focus their efforts on assisting students of all abilities who are in the process of composing papers. Argues that computers help make the writing lab the hub of word processing and other activities related to composition."

Kinkead, Joyce. "The Electronic Writing Tutor." *Writing Lab Newsletter* 13.4 (1988): 4-5.

Discusses the advantages of using an Electronic Tutor" to meet the needs of nontraditional students whose jobs, distance from campus, and family responsibilities prevent them from using the writing center during regular hours. Presents email tutoring as a useful additional service writing centers can offer students with special needs, not as a replacement for face-to-face tutoring.

McKenzie, Lee. "The Union of a Writing Center with a Computer Center: What to Put in the Marriage Contract." *Writing Lab Newsletter* 14.3 (1989): 1-2, 8.

Examines the problems posed by the arranged marriage" of a writing center with a computer center administered by a social sciences department. Problems include dividing the responsibility for supervising the center, sharing access to computers, and training students to use the computers.

ETHICS OF ONLINE TUTORING

Baker, Jeffrey S. "An Ethical Question About Online Tutoring in the Writing Lab." *Writing Lab Newsletter* 18.5 (1994): 6-7.

Examines the ethics of online tutoring, citing problems that can occur because of the lack of face-to-face contact. Suggests that online tutoring can lead to students' misunderstanding of complex concepts raised by tutors and to students' incorporating a tutor's written response into their papers. Expresses concern about the inability of online dialogue to replicate the conceptual indeterminacy" and potential creativity of verbal conversations.

Crump, Eric. "A Dialogue on OWLing in the Writing Lab: Some Thoughts on Michael Spooner's Thoughts." *Writing Lab Newsletter* 18.6 (1994): 6-8.

Contends that the changing nature of writing—from print to electronic media—will inevitably change the nature of tutoring. Argues that writing centers must continue to provide face-to-face tutoring while exploring the new computer technologies and the possibilities they offer for online tutor-student interactions.

Spooner, Michael. "A Dialogue on OWLing in the Writing Lab: Some Thoughts About Online Writing Labs." *Writing Lab Newsletter* 18.6 (1994): 6-8.

Sees computers as primarily positive in writing instruction, but argues against a too-eager adoption of online tutoring because of the value of face-to-face contact between tutor and student. Considers facial expressions, tone of voice, gestures, and pauses for thought as essential aspects of the writing conference that online tutorials lack. Also raises ethical issues about the potential for online tutorials to become merely editing sessions.

HARDWARE AND SOFTWARE

Kock, Christian, and Lotte Rienecker. "A Writing Lab in Copenhagen, Denmark." *Writing Lab Newsletter* 20.9 (1996): 4-6, 8.

Among other topics, discusses the development of two computer-assisted composition programs—*Scribo* (written by Rienecker) and *The ToolBox* (written by Kock)—being used in this university writing lab.

HISTORICAL PERSPECTIVES

Mason, Richard G. "Computer Assistance in the Writing Lab." *Writing Lab Newsletter* 6.9 (1982): 1-5.
Defines computer-assisted instruction (CAI) and discusses its uses in the writing center. Though the word processing and text-analysis programs mentioned are obsolete, writing center specialists will find Mason's discussion of the challenges CAI may pose for writing centers in the future of historical interest.

Mullin, Joan. "Interview with Muriel Harris." *Composition Studies/Freshman English News* 23.1 (1995): 37-53.
Among other topics, this online interview touches on the creation of Purdue's online writing center. Harris states that the OWL is, in reality, only a small part of her writing lab's operation and doesn't seem to be meeting a student need as a way to engage in tutorials." Harris adds she is rethinking the OWL concept in hopes of improving student-tutor interactions.

PROGRAM DESCRIPTIONS

Campbell, John, and Greg Larkin. NAUWriter: "A Total, Automated Writing Environment." *EDU Magazine* 48 (1988): 11-13.
Describes NAUWriter, a computerized writing instruction program developed by an English professor and a computer specialist at the Northern Arizona University. Used in an English department writing lab and other campus facilities, NAUWriter includes an electronic editor that helps student writers focus on such issues as audience, purpose, and stance.

Douglas, Michael A. "A Successful Individualized Writing Lab Module." *Journal of Developmental Education* 16.3 (1993): 24-26.
Reports results of a year-long study of a computer-assisted learning programs designed by teachers to help underprepared students prepare for a state-mandated writing exam. Study shows an improvement in the percentage of students who passed the exam.

Feeman, Jeffrey. "The High School Writing Center: A Place Where Writing Is Fun!" *Thrust for Educational Leadership* 16.5 (1987): 21-22.
Describes the set-up of a high school writing center equipped with a Macintosh computer lab. Discusses the center's purpose, goals, software, staffing, and computer training sessions for students and teachers.

Kinkead, Joyce A., and Jeanette G. Harris. *Writing Centers in Context: Twelve Case Studies.* Urbana: NCTE, 1993.
Eight of the twelve profiles of individual writing centers include sections detailing the hardware and software that each center makes available to student writers. In an overview chapter, Kinkead also discusses the increasing use of computers in writing centers.

Lasarenko, Jane. PR(OWL)ING AROUND: An OWL by Any Other Name." *Kairos: A Journal for Teachers of Writing in Webbed Environments.* 1.1 (1996) <http://english.ttu.edu/kairos/1.1/ owls/ lasarenko/prowl.html> (10 June 1997).
Offers a taxonomy of OWLs, placing online writing labs into three categories: those that merely advertise a center's existence, those that provide handouts, information, and links to other OWLs, and those that provide a full range of tutoring services online. Reviews 14 online writing labs.

Reiss, Donna. "From WAC to CCCAC: Writing Across the Curriculum Becomes Communication, Collaboration, and Critical Thinking (and Computers) Across the Curriculum at Tidewater Community College." *National Writing Center Association Page.* 2 July 1996. <http://www2. colgate.edu/diw/NWCA/ WCResources.html>. (4 Aug. 1997).
This brief article describes the creation of a campus-wide literacy program involving computer-assisted instruction at Tidewater Community College. Also available at <http://www1.infi.net/tcc/tcresourc/faculty/dreiss/wachis. html>.

RESEARCH

Bush, Jonathan. "The OWL Resource Page." *Purdue Online Writing Lab.* <http://owl.english. purdue.edu/owl-bib.html> (10 June 1997).
Explains the concept of the online writing lab and offers a five-page annotated bibliography of scholarly research on online writing labs. Divides entries into three categories: issues and implications, narratives, and pedagogy.

Litton, Guy, et al. "Writing Centers in Transition." *National Writing Center Association Page.* <http: //www2.colgate.edu/diw/NWCA/WCResources.html> (5 August 1997).
Gives results of survey interviews with 27 writing center directors on such topics as funding, tutor training, number of students served, and computer services provided to student writers. Also available at <http://www.twu.edu/ as/engspfl/owl/owl4.html>.

Jordan-Henley, Jennifer. "A Snapshot: Community College Writing Centers in an Age of Transition." *Writing Lab Newsletter* 20.1 (1995): 1-4.
Gives results of a nationwide survey of community college writing center directors, including information on computer equipment and software. Indicates that as of 1995, 85% of community college writing centers made computers available to student writers.

STARTING A COMPUTERIZED WRITING CENTER, OWL MOO, OR MUD

Ericsson, Patricia, and Tim McGee. "The Virtual Writing Center: An Owl Flies at Dakota State University." *ACE Newsletter* 9.4 (1995-1996): 18-19.
Describes the creation of an online writing lab at Dakota State University and outlines the positive results of its first year of operation. Claims tutors have learned to avoid editing student papers, which are emailed to the OWL, and primarily address structure or logic of essays and answer specific questions about mechanics or citation styles.

Harris, Muriel. "Hatching an OWL (Online Writing Lab)." *ACE Newsletter* 9.4 (1995-1996): 12-14.
Recounts the creation of the Purdue Online Writing Center, including the coining of the term OWL, and candidly discusses the changes made and challenges faced as the OWL developed. Advises others who consider establishing an OWL to be flexible and to realize that electronic conferences cannot entirely replace face-to-face tutorials. Also mentions that future plans at Purdue may include offering hypertext tutorials and synchronous interactions between tutors and students.

Harris, Muriel, and Michael Pemberton. "Online Writing Labs (OWLs): A Taxonomy of Options and Issues." *Computers and Composition* 12 (1995): 145-59.
Explains the advantages and disadvantages of various technologies writing centers can use to take their services online. Discusses email, Gopher, the World Wide Web, newsgroups, synchronous chat systems, automated file retrieval systems and the factors to consider in choosing among them. Such factors include network security, computer illiteracy, institutional missions, writing center missions, computing center priorities, and programmers' attitudes.

Hoger, Elizabeth. "Identifying and Analyzing Audience Need for an Online Writing Lab." *ACE Newsletter* 9.4 (1995-1996): 5-6.
Examines the political and practical barriers to creating an online writing center and offers suggestions on how to overcome these barriers. Among other suggestions, urges directors to begin by determining the need for an OWL by seeking relevant information on courses and computer access from program directors, instructors, and students.

Kimball, Sara E. "The Undergraduate Writing Center at UT Austin Goes Online." *ACE Newsletter* 9.4 (1995-1996): 7-8.
Describes the establishment of an online writing lab at the University of Texas at Austin, which includes a Multi-User Domain (MUD) for synchronous discussions between tutors and student writers. Suggests the MUD allows for distance learning and encourages a sense of play in student writers.

Langston, Camille. "Resistance and Control: The Complex Process of Creating an OWL." *Kairos: A Journal for Teachers of Writing in Webbed Environments.* 1.1 (1996) <http://english.ttu.edu/ kairos/1.1/owls/Langston.html> (10 June 1997).
Recounts the efforts of a graduate student writing center director to establish an online writing center on her campus. Describes problems (ranging from apathy to active resistance to the OWL concept) with academic computer managers and others in the bureaucracy. Suggests that those seeking to start an OWL first muster support from those with the power and skill to help.

Nelson, Jane, and Cynthia A. Wambeam. Moving Computers into the Writing Center: The Path to Least Resistance." *Computers and Composition* 12 (1995): 135-43.
Urges writing center professionals to lead the way in integrating computer technologies into campus writing programs by collaborating with experts across the disciplines to develop appropriate electronic writing environments. Suggests that through such collaborative efforts as online writing labs (OWLs) and computer classrooms, writing centers can shape future directions of writing instruction.

Palmquist, Mike, and Jon Leydens. "The Campus Writing Center as the Focus for a Network Supported Writing Across the Curriculum Program." *ACE Newsletter* 9.4 (1995-1996): 15-17.
Explains how the creation of an online writing lab led the Colorado State University Writing Center to play a central role in the university's writing-across-the-curriculum program. Outlines the services the center provides, including multimedia instruction software and tutoring via electronic mail.

Palmquist, Mike, Dawn Rodrigues, Kate Kiefer, and Donald E. Zimmerman. "Network Support for Writing Across the Curriculum: Developing an Online Writing Center." *Computers and Composition* 12 (1995): 335-53.
Describes the formation of a writing-across-the-curriculum program housed in a writing center and supported by online tutoring sessions, instructional software, and network communication tools. Notes that offering these services transformed the writing center from an exclusively drop-in to an online facility. Outlines the steps taken in creating the online center.

Pitel, Vonna J. "Making the Writing Center Feel at Home in the Library." *Book Report* 10.2 (1991): 38-39.
Discusses the development of a computerized writing center in a high school library, through the collaborative efforts of the teacher and librarian. Describes how the library provided support for the writing center.

Rickly, Rebecca. "Locating the Writing Center in the Aviary." *ACE Newsletter* 9.4 (1995-1996): 22-24.
Describes the justification for an online writing lab and discusses the problems the director faced, including training cybertutors to respond effectively to submissions from student writers. Asserts that the OWL augments rather than replaces the face-to-face tutorials carried out in the writing center, allowing students to access help at their convenience. Also available online at <http://www-personal. umich.edu/~barthes/aceowl.html>.

Schipke, Rae. "Plugging the Writing Center into the Future." *ACE Newsletter* 9.4 (1995-1996): 1-2.
Argues that in order to make the most effective use of current computer technologies, a writing center director must first consider the resources, student needs, and tutoring philosophy specific to his or her institution. Also raises pedagogical and practical challenges directors may face as they introduce electronic learning environments to their campuses.

Selfe, Cynthia. *Creating a Computer-Supported Writing Facility: A Blueprint for Action.* Advances in Computers and Composition Studies. Houghton: Michigan Technological University, 1989.
Offers practical advice on establishing and maintaining a computer-supported writing center. Divides the process into three major sections: Planning for a Computer-Supported Writing Facility," Operating a Computer-Supported Writing Facility," and Improving a Computer-Supported Writing Facility."

Simons, Susan, Jim Bryant, and Jeanne Stroh. "Recreating the Writing Center: A Chance Collaboration." *Computers and Composition* 12 (1995): 161-70.
A writing center director, instructional designer, and computer coordinator discuss their cooperative effort to integrate computers into a community college writing center. Chronicles their search for a teaching/learning theory on which to base writing instruction via computer.

THEORY

Blythe, Stuart. "Networked Computers + Writing Centers = ? Thinking About Networked Computers in Writing Center Practice." *Writing Center Journal* 17.2 (1997): 89-110.

Examines the growing use of online services in writing centers and the varying perceptions writing center professionals have as to the value such services provide and the problems they pose. Contends that much of the scholarship about online and networked writing centers remains on the logistical rather than the theoretical level. Addresses three theories of technology—instrumental, substantive, and critical. Espouses critical theories of technology as democratic and empowering, therefore most closely reflecting the mission of the writing center.

Blythe, Stuart. "Why OWLs? Value, Risk, and Evolution." *Kairos: A Journal for Teachers of Writing in Webbed Environments.* 1.1 (1996) <http://english. ttu.edu/kairos/1.1/owls/blythe/ owl.html> (10 June 1997).
This hypertext presentation defines and explores the concept of the online writing lab. Discusses the arguments for and against the creation and use of OWLs, offers a theoretical overview, and provides links to other online resources.

Clark, Irene. "Information Literacy and the Writing Center." *Computers and Composition* 12 (1995): 203-09.
Argues that writing center personnel must become computer and information literate in order to help students make use of the ever-increasing wealth of available electronic information. Also suggests that anyone who wishes to have an important impact on students' literacy must play a part in creating the systems that deliver the information.

Collins, Paul. "The Concept of a Co-operative." *National Writing Center Association Page. National Writing Center Association Page.* 5 July 1997. <http://www2.colgate.edu/diw/NWCA/WC Resources.html> (4 August 1997).
Defines the idea of a writing cooperative—a group of writers who gather together to read and respond to one another's work—and compares it to the English coffeehouses of the eighteenth century. Argues that a cyberspace writing cooperative not only supplements a school's writing center but spreads its collaborative pedagogy throughout the campus. Sees the cyberspace writing cooperative, available to student writers at all hours, as the embodiment of Stephen North's original conception of a writing community.

Coogan, Dave. "The Idea of an Electronic Writing Center." *CCCC95 Online.* 20 Mar. 1995. <http:// www.missouri.edu/~cccc95/abstracts/coogan.html> (31 July 1997).
Examines the pros and cons of offering tutorial services over electronic mail. Discusses the methodological constraints of email tutoring and describes how such a program developed at the State University of New York, Albany.

Cooper, Marilyn M., and Cynthia L. Selfe. "Computer Conferences and Learning: Authority, Resistance, and Internally Persuasive Discourse." *College English* 52 (1990): 847-69.
Discusses the creation of a nontraditional discourse forum in which students discuss writing projects and issues via computer logs. Argues that this forum encourages students to resist traditional academic forms of language use because dialogues carried out on the computer are more egalitarian, shaped by students rather than teachers (who are cast in the role of peers rather than authority figures).

Denney, S. Erin, and Matthew J. Livesey. "Review of Internet Resources for Writing Centers." *Writing Center Journal* 16.2 (1996): 183-93.
Critiques three venues that offer online writing center services over the Internet: Gopher, the World Wide Web, and MOOs. Sees going online as a way to extend the impact of writing

center pedagogy beyond the walls of the center but cautions that the decision to provide online services calls for careful analysis of each center's goals, resources, and philosophy.

Farrell, Pamela B. "Writer, Peer Tutor, and the Computer: A Unique Relationship." *The Writing Center Journal* 8.1 (1987): 29-33.
Sees the computer as neutral ground," where a tutor and student writer can collaborate more or less as equals. Argues that composing on computers helps students relax about making revisions and encourages give-and-take dialogue between student writers and their tutors.

George, Diana. Wonder of it All: "Computers, Writing Centers, and the New World." *Computers and Composition* 12 (1995): 331-34.
Discusses the difficulties of fitting traditional educational models into the New World" of the information age. Argues that writing center practitioners and composition instructors need to construct theories about the nature of electronic discourse in ways that inform the teaching of writing.

Grimm, Nancy Maloney. "Computer Centers and Writing Centers: An Argument for Ballast." *Computers and Composition* 12 (1995): 323-29.
Argues that while writing centers and computer centers have different missions, and mergers between the two ought to proceed cautiously, both provide settings for extracurricular learning and institutional reform. Suggests that writing center professionals should work with computer professionals in order to accommodate students' differing educational needs.

Healy, Dave. From Place to Space: "Perceptual and Administrative Issues in the Online Writing Center." *Computers and Composition* 12 (1995): 183-93.
Discusses the effects on tutors and writing center directors of the move from a physical to a virtual writing center. Contends that moving online decenters the writing center and, among other effects, frees tutors from the constraints of time and place. Also explores practical and ethical problems involving scheduling, training, and supervision of tutors.

Johnson, J. Paul. Writing Spaces: "Technoprovocateurs and OWLs in the Late Age of Print." *Kairos: A Journal for Teachers of Writing in Webbed Environments.* 1.1 (1996) <http://english.ttu.edu/ kairos/1.1/owls/Johnson.html> (10 June 1997).
Points out that the term online writing lab" can stand for models ranging from a homepage that merely announces the existence of a center to a virtual space in which student writers and tutors carry on real-time conversations about writing. Describes several online writing labs, contending that they are changing the shape of literacy.

Kimball, Sara. Cybertext/Cyberspeech: "Writing Centers and Online Magic." *Writing Center Journal* 18.1 (1997): 30-49.
Discounts many of the conceptions writing center professionals have about the special nature of online tutoring, contending that some of the vaunted benefits of online tutoring are rooted in a magical" view of computer technology. For example, sees claims that virtual tutoring frees student writers from constraints of sex, race, age, and socioeconomic status as exaggerated. Embraces online tutoring, but cautions against a theoretically naïve approach to the evolving technology.

Mitchell, Margaret. "Initiated into the Fraternity of Powerful Knowers: How Collaborative Technology Has Ethically Legitimized Writing Centers." *Writing Lab Newsletter* 19.7 (1995): 11-13.
Contends that the recent movement toward computerized composition classrooms helps to validate the student-centered, collaborative-learning pedagogy of writing centers. Notes that email discussions by students in computerized classrooms means students are spending more time writing and responding to the writing of their peers. At the same time, teachers tend to exert less control over the email discussions than they do over oral class discussions—"exactly the things that writing centers had been promoting."

Selfe, Dickie. "Surfing the Tsunami: Electronic Environments in the Writing Center." *Computers and Composition* 12 (1995): 311-19.
Alerts writing center practitioners to the technological tsunami washing over higher education and reflects on the problems and opportunities computers present to writing centers. Argues that writing center practitioners must become conversant with MUDs, MOOs, the internet, and distance learning in order to avoid being overwhelmed by and to make intelligent use of such technological innovations.

Strickland, James. "The Politics of Writing Programs." *Evolving Perspectives on Computers and Composition Studies: Questions for the 1990s.* Ed. Gail E. Hawisher and Cynthia L. Selfe. Urbana: NCTC, 1991. 300-17.
Examines the political underpinnings that influence the teaching of writing via computer, including how computers have changed perceptions about teaching writing as a profession, the empowerment of student writers, and funding issues. Mentions writing centers as one site in which political issues and writing instruction intersect.

Veit, Richard C. "Are Machines the Answer?" *Writing Lab Newsletter* 4.4 (1979): 1-2.
Contends that newcomers to the writing center field tend to overestimate the effectiveness of machine-assisted instruction. Reviews the benefits face-to-face human contact between tutors and students and argues that humanistic labs" offer students acceptance, trust, and empathic understanding" that a machine cannot replace.

TRAINING TUTORS AND CYBERTUTORS

Chappell, Virginia A. "Theorizing in Practice: Tutor Training `Live, from the VAX Lab.'" *Computers and Composition* 12 (1995): 227-36.
Describes a tutor training program in which students participate in an email Party Line" to reflect on assigned readings in composition theory and apply theoretical concepts to their work as peer tutors in a writing center. Contends these discussions are more lively and far-reaching than individual journals in helping tutors to better understand and use collaborative pedagogy.

Childers, Pamela B. "Using Basic Technology as a Writing Center Tool to Train Tutors." *ACE Newsletter* 9.4 (1995-1996): 3-4.
Describes a tutor training program in which high school peer tutors carried on email discussions among themselves and with writing center specialists across North America. Contends that email discussions were valuable, in part, because the tutors had to express themselves in writing without making use of facial or verbal cues.

Clark, Irene L. *Writing in the Center: Teaching in a Writing Center Setting.* 2nd ed. Dubuque: Kendall/Hunt, 1992.
This tutor training manual includes a section on using computers in writing instruction.

Johanek, Cindy, and Rebecca Rickly. "Online Tutor Training: Synchronous Conferencing in a Professional Community." *Computers and Composition* 12 (1995): 237-46.
Describes a synchronous conferencing system (*Daedalus INTERCHANGE*) that Ball State University's writing center uses in training tutors. Claims that INTERCHANGE and other synchronous conferencing systems can support the goals of the training program by enhancing tutors' sense of community, encouraging them to participate in policy decisions, and allowing them to practice conversing in a virtual setting that combines elements of oral and written communication.

Kemp, Fred. Getting Smart with Computers: "Computer-Aided Heuristics for Student Writers." *The Writing Center Journal* 8.1 (1987): 3-10.
Takes issue with the notion that computers can or should replace the human tutor and argues that computers are merely tools, intended only to extend human understanding, much as telescopes extend human vision." Views computers as most useful to writers in word processing and in fulfilling a heuristic function. Describes several heuristic programs (*Topoi, SEEN, Writer's Helper, Idealog, LOGO*) that might augment human tutorials.

Meyer, Emily, and Louise Z. Smith. *The Practical Tutor.* New York: Oxford UP, 1987.
This textbook for tutor training provides detailed discussions of many aspects of tutoring, including working with computers in the writing center.

TUTORING IN ELECTRONIC ENVIRONMENTS

Andrews, Deborah C. OWL: "Online Writing Wisdom." *Business Communication Quarterly* 58.2 (1995): 9-10.
Profiles the operation of the Purdue University Online Writing Laboratory, in particular how universities and businesses around the world access the OWL's handouts on writing memos, resumes, and cover letters.

Coogan, David. "Email Tutoring, a New Way to Do New Work." *Computers and Composition* 12 (1995): 171-81.
Chronicles a tutor's experience with tutoring via email, demonstrating the benefits and uncertainties of commenting on student compositions without face-to-face contact. Reviews ways in which writing centers previously made use of computer technology—e.g., autotutorial programs and word processing—and argues that email tutorials closely reflect today's social constructivist views about the collaborative production of knowledge.

Cullen, Roxanne, and Sandra Balkema. "Generating a Professional Portfolio in the Writing Center: A Hypertext Tutor." *Computers and Composition* 12 (1995): 195-201.
Describes how a writing center uses a hypertext tutorial program to help students of various disciplines develop professional portfolios. Argues that, among other benefits, developing the hypertext tutorial has helped to maintain the writing center's primary role in the campus's writing-across-the-curriculum program.

Franz, Amelia F. Love and Enchiladas: "Students, Text, and Ownership in a High School Computer Writing Lab." *ACE Newsletter* 9.4 (1995-1996): 11-12.
Argues that the computer literacy encouraged in the writing lab builds students' self-esteem, gives them a greater sense of text ownership, and often leads to a better overall attitude toward writing.

Harris, Muriel. From the (Writing) Center to the Edge: "Moving Writers Along the Internet." *Clearing House* 69.1 (1995): 21-23.
Outlines the types of online services being offered by various writing centers. Suggests that email, MOOs, and internet resources are potent tools for learning in the writing center and will continue to enhance and change, in unpredictable ways, the character of tutor-writer interactions.

Jordan-Henley, Jennifer, and Barry Maid. "MOOving Along the Information Superhighway: Writing Centers in Cyberspace." *Writing Lab Newsletter* 19.5 (1995): 1-6.
Describes a Cyberspace writing center that links tutors at the University of Arkansas—Little Rock to students at Roane State Community College (TN). Argues that the resulting MOO (a multi-user, real-time, synchronous computer link) disrupts the traditional classroom hierarchy, gives students more responsibility for their own learning, and enhances narrative and computer programming skills.

Jordan-Henley, Jennifer, and Barry M. Maid. "Tutoring in Cyberspace: Student Impact and College/University Collaboration." *Computers and Composition* 12 (1995): 211-18.
Describes and evaluates the impact of an experimental program in which students at Roane State Community College (Tennessee) visit a cyberspace writing center and engage in synchronous conferences with graduate student tutors at the University of Arkansas—Little Rock. Contends that many of the skills tutors have developed in face-to-face tutorials apply to cyberspace tutorials. However, also notes key differences in style and affect of tutorials due to the lack of facial and verbal cues.

Kinkead, Joyce. Computer Conversations: "Email and Writing Instruction." *College Composition and Communication* 38.3 (1987): 337-41.
Explores the use of email as a teaching and tutoring tool. Describes a tutoring program in which a tutor responds, via email, to questions posed by nontraditional students who cannot make regular visits to the writing center. Reviews some of the advantages and disadvantages of this approach.

Klem, Elizabeth, and Charles Moran. "Computers and Instructional Strategies in the Teaching of Writing." *Evolving Perspectives on Computers and Composition Studies: Questions for the 1990s.* Ed. Gail E. Hawisher and Cynthia L. Selfe. Urbana: NCTE, 1991. 132-49.
Examines how the advent of computer technology has changed the character of composition and the teaching of composition. Offers strategies for addressing the needs of student writers composing on computers. Mentions computerized writing centers as one venue in which such teaching occurs.

Leff, Linda Ringer. "Computers and Writing Centers—a Marriage Made in Cyber-Heaven?" *ACE Newsletter* 9.4 (1995-1996): 19-21.
Describes how one writing center, dissatisfied with available software, designed its own set of user-friendly computer tutorials aimed at two different audiences: ESL students and first-year composition students. Contends that these programs, which are continually updated, have effectively combined computer technology and humane writing instruction.

Littleton, Bonnie. "Choose-Your-Own-Link' Fantasy Adventures." *ACE Newsletter* 9.4 (1995-1996): 10.
Describes a project in which an English teacher and writing lab supervisor had her students compose a fantasy story in hypertext markup language. The story allows readers to choose among various characters, settings, and plots. Argues that the assignment required students to draw on their story writing abilities while learning to use hypertext.

Luchte, Jeanne. "Computer Programs in the Writing Center: A Bibliographical Essay." *The Writing Center Journal* 8.1 (1987): 11-19.
Reviews contemporary scholarship linking writing centers and computers and explores how the new technology changes the way people teach, tutor, and write." Suggests ways that writing centers can use computers in helping students at all stages of the writing process—prewriting, organizing, drafting, revising, and proofreading. Also reviews relevant software programs.

Moody, Susan. "OWLs and ESL Students." *Kairos: A Journal for Teaching Writing in Webbed Environments* 1.1 (1996) <http://english.ttu/kairos/1.1/owls/moody.html> (10 June 1997).
Takes a brief look at eight online writing centers that offer help to English as a Second Language students. Points out that most of the available help involves grammar instruction and contends that more comprehensive online resources should be developed for ESL writers.

Morgan, M.C. Hands Off: "Ten Techniques for Tutoring on Word Processors." *National Writing Center Association Page.* 9 September 1995. <http://www2.colgate.edu/diw/NWCA/WC Resources.html> (4 August 1997).
Outlines a hands-off approach to tutoring on the word processor that fosters independence and self-discovery in student writers. Aims primarily to allow the student writer to retain full control of a developing text. Also available at <http://cal.bemidji.msus.edu/English/Morgan/Docs/TenTechniqueshtml>.

Scharton, Maurice. "The Third Person: The Role of the Computer in Writing Centers." *Computers and Composition* 7.1 (1989): 37-48.
Uses four case studies to examine the role of the computer in facilitating personalized writing instruction in tutorials. Suggests that computers act as mediators between tutor and student, enhancing one-to-one relationships, encouraging flexibility of thinking, and keeping the focus of the tutorial on issues of composition rather than grammar.

Simons, Susan. CAI: "Instruction and Change in the Writing Center." *Writing Lab Newsletter* 20.1 (1995): 11, 16.
Sees the increased use of computers in composition as empowering to student writers because composing on a word-processor helps students discover that text is fluid and writing

is a recursive process. Argues that insight into how computers are affecting the writing process allows tutors to intervene much more intelligently."

Swartz, Patti Capel. "Integrated Language, Integrated Writing: The Writing Center as Classroom." *ACE Newsletter* 9.4 (1995-1996): 8-9.
Describes a composition course which meets one class period per week in the writing center's computer cluster. Argues that this approach fosters collaboration and discussion of writing, encourages revision as the text develops, and leads to greater visibility for the writing center.

Wood, Gail F. "Making the Transition from ASL to English: Deaf Students, Computers, and the Writing Center." *Computers and Composition* 12 (1995): 219-26.
Describes five tutoring sessions with a deaf student (whose first language is American Sign Language). Tutor and student communicate in written English, via computer, in an attempt to decrease the student's dependence on ASL while expressing his thoughts. Notes an increase in fluency in written English and less reliance on signing before writing.

WORKS CITED

Adler, Paul and Terry Winograd. 1992. The Usability Challenge. *Usability: Turning Technologies into Tools*, Ed. Paul Adler and Terry Winograd. New York: Oxford UP.

AllWrite. 1997. New York: McGraw-Hill.

Almasy, Rudolph. 1976. Instructional Materials for the Writing Laboratory. *College Composition and Communication* 27: 400-03.

Amato, Joe. 8 September 1997. About tcomm/tcid. Email to David Coogan [online]. Available email: <coogan@charlie.cns.iit.edu>.

Anthony, Tobin. 1996. *Building and maintaining an intranet with the macintosh.* Indianapolis: Hayden.

Appel, F. S. 1936. A Writing Laboratory. *Journal of Higher Education* 7: 71-77.

Arden, Eugene. 21 July 1995. Ending the loneliness and isolation of adjunct professors. *Chronicle of Higher Education.* A44.

Arnold, H. J. 1930. Diagnostic and Remedial Techniques for College Freshman. *Association of American Colleges Bulletin* 16: 262-79.

Bailey, J. O. 1946. Remedial Composition for Advanced Students. *College English* 8: 145-48.

Baker, Jeffrey S. 1994. An Ethical Question About Online Tutoring in the Writing Lab. *Writing Lab Newsletter* 18.5: 6-7.

Baker, Tracey and Susan Wheallar.1982. The Comp-Lab Exercises: Use and Effectiveness with Basic Writers in the Writing Lab. *Proceedings: Writing Centers Association Fourth Annual Conference.* Columbus: Ohio Dominican College. 9-18.

Baldwin, Beth. 1996. *Conversations: Computer-mediated Dialogue, Multilogue, and Learning.* Dissertation. A RhetNet Project [online]. Available internet: <www.missouri.edu/HyperNews/get/rhetnet/conversations.html>.

Baldwin, Beth. 25 January 1996. Evolving past the essay-a-saurus: Introducing nimbler forms into writing classes. RhetNet [online]. Available internet: <www.missouri.edu/~rhetnet/baldwin_snap.html>.

Bazerman, Charles and David Russell Ed. *Landmark Essays on Writing Across the Curriculum.* Davis, CA: Hermagoras.

Beason, Larry. 18 August 1997. "The WAC Page." <http://ewu66649.ewu.edu/WAC.html>.

Beck, Charles E. and John A. Stibrany. 1985. User Perceptions of Improved Writing Quality through Extended Use of Word Processors. Le Van. 223-34.

Belanoff, Pat and Marcia Dickson. eds. 1991. *Portfolios: Process and Product.* Portsmouth, NH: Boynton/Cook.

Belenky, Mary, Blythe Clinchy, Nancy Goldberg, and Jill Tarule. 1986. Women's ways of knowing. New York: Basic Books.

Bell, Jim.1989. What Are We Talking About?: A Content Analysis of *The Writing Lab Newsletter*, April 1985 to October 1988. *The Writing Lab Newsletter* 13.7: 1-5.

Berlin, James. 1987. *Rhetoric and Reality: Writing Instruction in American College, 1900-1985.* Carbondale: Southern Illinois UP.

Berta, Renee. 1990. Computer Modifications for Disabled Students. *The Writing Lab Newsletter* 14.9: 6-7.

Blumenthal, Joseph C. 1993. *English 3200.* 4th ed. New York: Harcourt Brace.

Blythe, Stuart. 1997. Networked Computers + Writing Centers = ? Thinking About Networked Computers in Writing Center Practice. *The Writing Center Journal* 17: 89-110.

———. 1996. Why OWLs? Value, Risk, Evolution. *Kairos* 1 <http://english.ttu.edu/kairos/1.1/index.html>

———, et al. 1998. A Discussion on Collaborative Design Methods for Collaborative Online Spaces. Haviland, et. al.

Bødker, Susanne. 1991. *Through the Interface: A Human Activity Approach to User Interface Design.* Hillsdale, NJ: Lawrence Erlbaum.

Brannon, Lil and Jeanette Harris. 1978. Alternatives to Automated Learning. Paper presented at the Conference of the College Teachers of English of Texas. Dallas, ERIC ED153328.

Brereton, John C., ed. 1995. *The Origins of Composition Studies in the American College, 1875-1925.* Pittsburgh: U of Pittsburgh P.

Brown, Alan. 1990. Coping with Computers in the Writing Center. *The Writing Lab Newsletter* 15.4: 13-15.

Camp, Roberta, and Denise Levine. 1991. Portfolios Evolving: Background and Variations in Sixth-Through Twelfth-Grade Classrooms. Belanoff and Dickson.194-205.

Campbell, Elizabeth M. 1942. The Evolution of a Writing Laboratory. *College English* 3: 399-403.

Carino, Peter. 1996. Open Admissions and the Construction of Writing Center History: A Tale of Three Models. *The Writing Center Journal* 17.1: 30-48.

———. 1995. Early Writing Centers: Toward a History. *The Writing Center Journal* 15: 103-15.

———. 1995. Theorizing the Writing Center: An Uneasy Task. *Dialogue: A Journal for Writing Specialists* 2.1: 23-37.

Certeau, Michel de. 1984. *The practice of everyday life.* Translated by Steven Rendall. Berkley: U California P.

Chappell, Virginia A. 1995. Theorizing in Practice: Tutor Training 'Live, from the VAX Lab.' *Computers and Composition* 12: 227-36.

Clark, Irene. 1991. The Writing Center and the Research Paper: Computers and Collaboration. Wallace and Simpson. 205-15.

———. 1995. Information Literacy and the Writing Center. *Computers and Composition* 12: 203-09.

Colby, Elbridge. 1940. 'Laboratory Work' in English. *College English* 2: 67-69.

The Committee on Research of the National Council of Teachers of English. 1934. The Contributions of Research to Teaching and Curriculum-Making in English, January, 1933 through June, 1934. I. Composition, Grammar, and the Mechanics of English. *The English Journal* 23: 718-31.

Composition Clinic at Wayne. Sept. 15, 1950. *Higher Education* 7: 23.

Computers Called 'Fad' as Teaching Devices. 1968. *Automated Education Letter* 3: 5.

Conklin, F. R. 1931. Student Self-Help in Composition Drill. *The English Journal* (College Edition) 10: 50-53.

Coogan, David. 1995. Email Tutoring: A New Way to Do New Work. *Computers and Composition* 12: 171-181.

———. 1994. Towards a Rhetoric of Online Tutoring. *The Writing Lab Newsletter* 19.1: 3-5.

Cox, Bené Scanlon. 1984. Priorities and Guidelines for the Development of Writing Centers: A Delphi Study. Olson. 77-84.

Croft, Mary. 1983. Theresa Joins the Staff: A Microcomputer in the Writing Lab. Harris and Baker. 58-62.

Crump, Eric. 1994. A Dialogue on OWLing in the Writing Lab: Some Thoughts on Michael Spooner's Thoughts. *Writing Lab Newsletter* 18.6: 6-8.

Cuban, Larry. 1986. *Teachers and Machines: The Classroom Use of Technology Since 1920.* New York: Teachers College P.

Dorough, C. Dwight and Martin M. Shapiro. 1964. *Automated Instruction and Remedial English,* Vol. I. Washington, DC: University of Houston/US Department of Health, Education, and Welfare.

Dreyfus, Hubert L. 1992. *What Computers Still Can't Do: A Critique of Artificial Reason.* Cambridge, MS: MIT.

Duin, Ann Hill, and Craig J. Hansen. Ed. 1996. *Nonacademic Writing: Social Theory and Technology.* Mahwah, NJ: Lawrence Erlbaum.

———. 1996. Setting a Sociotechnological Agenda in Non-Academic Writing. Duin and Hansen.

Dykeman, John B. 1997. The complex new frontiers of electronic document management. *Managing Office Technology,* March, 20-22.

Ede, Lisa. 1989. Writing as a Social Process: A Theoretical Foundation for Writing Centers. *Writing Center Journal* 9.2: 3-13.

Ehn, Pelle. 1992. Scandinavian Design: On Participation and Skill. Adler and Winograd.

El-Khawas, Elaine and Deborah J. Carter. eds. 1988. *Community College Fact Book.* New York: Macmillan.

Epes, Mary and Carolyn Kirkpatrick. 1993. *Writing & Editing: The Comp-Lab Exercises Level 2,* 2nd ed. Englewood Cliffs: Prentice Hall.

———. 1983. Developing New Models of the Comp-Lab Basic Writing Course for Other Settings. Final Report. ERIC ED239258.

———. 1980. An Evaluation of the Comp-Lab Project: Final Report. ERIC ED194909.

———, and Michael G. Southwell. 1997. *Mastering Written English: The Comp-Lab Exercises,* 5th ed. Upper Saddle River: Prentice Hall.

———. 1979. The Autotutorial Lab at the CCCC. *The Writing Lab Newsletter* 3.8: 1.

———, Carolyn Kirkpatrick, and Michael G. Southwell. 1982. The Autotutorial Writing Lab: Discovering its Latent Power. Harris. 132-46.

———, Carolyn Kirkpatrick and Michael G. Southwell. 1979. The Comp-Lab Project: An Experimental Basic Writing Course. *Journal of Basic Writing* 2: 19-37.

———, and Others. 1979. The Comp-Lab Project: Assessing the Effectiveness of a Laboratory-Centered Basic Writing Course on the College Level. Final Report, September 1, 1977 through August 31, 1979. ERIC ED194908.

Farrell, Pamela B. ed. 1989. *The High School Writing Center: Establishing and Maintaining One.* Urbana: NCTE.

———. 1989. Computers Interact with Writers and Tutors. Farrell. 107-10.

———.1987. Writer, Peer Tutor, and Computer: A Unique Relationship. *The Writing Center Journal* 8.1: 29-34.

Feenberg, Andrew. 1989. The written world: On the theory and practice of computer conferencing. Mason and Kaye. 22-39.

Ferster, Teresa. 1937. An English Laboratory for Freshmen. *The English Journal* 26: 729-34.

Fountain, Alvin M. 1939. The Problem of the Poorly Prepared Student. *College English* 1: 309-22.

Frye, Edward B. 1964. Teaching Machines: The Coming Automation. *Educational Technology: Readings in Programmed Instruction.* Ed. John P. DeCecco. New York: Holt, Rinehart & Winston. 21-27.

Gardner, Clinton. 19 February 1998. MOO Discussions. *SLCC Online Writing Center.* May 1997. <http://www.slcc.edu/wc/papers/moocuss.htm>.

————. ed. 19 February 1998. No Frames version of *SLCC Online Writing Center.* SLCC Online Writing Center. July 1997. <http://www.slcc.edu/wc/noframes.htm>.

————. ed. 19 February 1998. Teachers Writing: A Clearinghouse of Pedagogy. *SLCC Online Writing Center.* July 1997. <http://www.slcc.edu/wc/teacher/papers.htm>.

————. 19 February 1998. Welcome to the SLCC Writing Center. *SLCC Online Writing Center.* 2 February 1998. <http://www.slcc.edu/wc/index.html>.

Gaskin, James E. 1997. *Corporate Politics and the Internet: Connection without Controversy.* Upper Saddle River: Prentice-Hall.

Genung, John Franklin. 1895. (Reprinted 1995). English at Amherst. Brereton. 172-77.

George, Diana. 1995. Wonder of it All: Computers, Writing Centers, and the New World. *Computers and Composition* 12: 331-34.

Giroux, Henry A. 1992. *Border crossings: Cultural workers and the politics of education.* New York: Routledge.

Goffman, Irving. 1950. *The Presentation of Self in Everyday Life.* Garden City: Doubleday.

Grandy, Adah G. 1936. A Writing Laboratory. *The English Journal* 25: 372-76.

Graphics, Visualization, & Usability (GVU) Center, Georgia Institute of Technology. 18 August 1997. Seventh WWW User Survey (April 1997). <http://www.cc.gatech.edu/gvu/user_surveys/>.

Graves, Gary, and Carl Haller. 1994. The Effect of Secondary School Structures and Traditions on Computer-Supported Literacy. Selfe and Hilligoss. 144-156.

Grimm, Nancy. 1996. Rearticulating the work of the writing center. *College Composition and Communication* 47.4: 523-548.

————. 1995. Computer Centers and Writing Centers: An Argument for Ballast. *Computers and Composition* 12: 171-81.

Grove, W. Alan. 1939. Freshman Composition: Its Great Middle Class. *College English* 1: 227-36.

Grubbs, Katherine. 1994. Some Questions About the Politics of Online Tutoring in Electronic Writing Centers. *Writing Lab Newsletter* 19.2: 7, 12.

Haas, Christina. 1996. *Writing Technology: Studies on the Materiality of Literacy.* Mahwah, NJ: Lawrence Erlbaum .

Hairston, Maxine.1982. The Winds of Change: Thomas Kuhn and the Revolution in the Teaching of Writing. *College Composition and Communication* 33.1: 76-88.

Hall, Christie. ed. 19 February 1998. *Cere: for the community.* July 1997. <http://www.slcc.edu/wc/cere/>.

Hall, R. M. R. and Beatrice L. Hall. 1967. Computer-Aided Instruction and Contrastive Analysis: A Look to the Future. *Journal of English as a Second Language* 2: 83-91.

Harris, Muriel.ed. 1983. *Tutoring Writing: A Sourcebook for Writing Labs.* Glenview, IL: Scott-Foresman.

———, and Tracey Baker. eds. 1983. *New Directions, New Connections: Proceedings of the Writing Centers Association Fifth Annual Conference.* West Lafayette, IN: Purdue University.

———. 1990. What's up and what's in: trends and traditions in writing centers. *The Writing Center Journal* 11.1: 15-26.

———. 1981. Process and Product: Dominant Models for Writing Centers. Hawkins and Brooks 1-8.

———, and Michael Pemberton. 1995. Online Writing Labs (OWLs): A Taxonomy of Options and Issues. *Computers and Composition* 12: 145-59.

Hart-Davidson, William F. 1997. Theorizing Professional Writing on the Network: An Action-Oriented Usability Study of Program and Staff Development. Diss. prospectus, Purdue U.

Hasek, Glenn. 1996. Data's new dimension. *Industry Week,* 16 December, 65+.

Haviland, Carol, et. al., eds. 1998. *Weaving Knowledge Together: Writing Centers and Collaboration.* Emmitsburg, MD: National Writing Centers Association.

Hawisher, Gail E., Paul Le Blanc, Charles Moran, and Cynthia L.Selfe. 1996. *Computers and the Teaching of Writing in American Higher Education,* 1979-1994. Norwood, NJ: Ablex.

——— and Anna O. Soter. eds. 1990. *On Literacy and Its Teaching: Issues in English Education.* Albany: SUNY.

Hawkins, Thom and Phyllis Brooks. eds. 1981. *New Directions for College Learning Assistance: Improving Writing Skills.* San Francisco: Jossey-Bass.

Haynes-Burton, Cynthia. Intellectual (Proper)ty in Writing Centers: Retro Texts and Positive Plagiarism. Stay, Murphy and Hobson. 84-93.

Healy, Dave. 1995. From Place to Space: Perceptual and Administrative Issues in the Online Writing Center. *Computers and Composition* 12: 183-93.

———.1995. In the Temple of the Familiar: The Writing Center as Church. Stay, Murphy and Hobson. 12-25.

Heath, Shirley Brice. 1990. The Fourth Vision: Literate Language at Work. Lunsford, Moglen and Slevin. 289-306.

Hickman, Larry A. 1990. *John Dewey's Pragmatic Technology.* Bloomington, IN: Indiana UP.

Hillocks, George, Jr. 1984. What Works in Teaching Composition: A Meta-analysis of Experimental Treatment Studies. *American Journal of Education* 43: 133-70.

Hobson, Eric. 1994. Writing Center Theory Often Counters Its Theory. So What? Mullin and Wallace. 1-10.

———. 1992. Maintaining Our Balance: Walking the Tightrope of Competing Epistemologies. *Writing Center Journal* 13.1: 65-75.

Holcomb, E. L. 1928. The English Laboratory. *The English Journal* 17: 50-52.

Holdstein, Deborah H. and Cynthia L. Selfe. eds. 1990. *Computers and writing: Theory, research, practice.* New York: MLA.

Hom, James. 3 February 1997. *The Usability Methods Toolbox.* 3 March 1996. <http://www.best.com/~jthom/ usability/>.

Homme, Lloyd E. and Robert Glaser. 1959. Relationship between the Programmed Textbook and Teaching Machines. *Automatic Teaching: The State of the Art.* Ed. Eugene Galender. New York: John Wiley & Sons. 103-07.

Horton, Sarah and Patrick Lynch. 18 August 1997. Yale C/AIM Web Style Guide. <http://info.med.yale.edu/caim/manual/interface/interface.html>.

Hunt, Russell. 5 September 1997. Audience: Imagined, virtual, and real. Alliance for Computers and Writing List [online]. Available email: ACW-L <listserv@ttacs6. ttu.edu>.

Huntley, John F. 1965. A Program for Programming English Composition. *The Journal of General Education* 17: 135-48.

―――. 1962. Programmed Teaching Involves Patience and Love. *College Composition and Communication* 13: 7-15.

Indiana University at Bloomington Campuswide Writing Program Home page. 18 August 1997. <http://www.indiana.edu/~wts/cwp/cwphome.html>.

Jacobson, Beatrice. 1983. The Apple in the Center. Harris and Baker. 105-107.

Johanek, Cindy and Rebecca Rickly. 1995. Online Tutor Training: Synchronous Conferencing in a Professional Community. *Computers and Composition* 12: 237-46.

Johnson, J. Paul. 1996. Writing Spaces: Technoprovocateurs and OWLs in the Late Age of Print. *Kairos* 1 <http://english.ttu.edu/kairos/1.1/index.html>

Johnson-Eilola, Johndan and Stuart A. Selber. 1996. After Automation: Hypertext and Corporate Structures. Sullivan and Dautermann. 115-141.

Jordan-Henley, Jennifer and Barry Maid. 1995. Tutoring in Cyberspace: Student Impact and College/University Collaboration. *Computers and Composition* 12: 211-218.

―――. 1995. MOOving Along the Information Superhighway: Writing Centers in Cyberspace. *The Writing Lab Newsletter* 19.5: 1-6.

Keller-Cohen, Deborah. ed. 1994. Literacy: interdisciplinary conversations. Cresskill, NJ: Hampton.

Kemp, Fred.1987. Getting Smart with Computers: Computer-Aided Heuristics for Student Writers. *The Writing Center Journal* 8.1: 3-10.

Key, Frances. 1983. Technology and the Writing Center: A Humane Approach. Harris and Baker. 133-37.

Kinkead, Joyce. 1996. The National Writing Centers Association as Mooring: A Personal History of the First Decade. *The Writing Center Journal* 16.2: 131-143.

―――. and Jeannette G. Harris. Ed. 1993. *Writing Centers in Context.* 216-26.

―――. 1988. The Electronic Writing Tutor. *The Writing Lab Newsletter* 12.4: 4-5.

Kinneavy, James. 1983 (reprinted 1994). Writing Across the Curriculum. Bazerman and Russell 65-78.

Kirkpatrick, Carolyn. 1981. The Case for Autotutorial Materials. Hawkins and Brooks 15-23.

Kroll, Keith. ed. 1990. *Maintaining Faculty Excellence.* Los Angeles: Educational Resources Information Center.

LeBlanc, Paul J. 1994. The Politics of Literacy and Technology in Secondary Schools. Selfe and Hilligoss. 22-36.

LeVan, Sally. ed. 1985. *Writing Centers Coping with Crisis: Proceedings of the Writing Centers Association: East Central, Seventh Annual Conference.* Erie, PA: Gannon University.

Lewis, Frances W. 1902. The Qualifications of the English Teacher. *Education* 23: 15-26.

Luchte, Jeanne. 1987. Computer Programs in the Writing Center: A Bibliographical Essay. *The Writing Center Journal* 8.1: 11-20.

Lumsdaine, A. A. 1960. Teaching Machines: An Introductory Overview. Lumsdaine and Glaser 5-22.

―――, and Robert Glaser, eds. 1960. *Teaching Machines and Programmed Learning: A Source Book.* Washington, DC: National Educational Association.

Lunsford, Andrea. 7 September 1997. Audience: Imagined, virtual, and real. Alliance for Computers and Writing List [online]. Available email: ACW-L <listserv@ttacs6.ttu.edu>.

———. 1991. Collaboration, Control, and the Idea of a Writing Center. *Writing Center Journal* 12.1, 3-10.

———, Helene Moglen, and James Slevin. eds. 1990. *The Right to Literacy.* New York: MLA.

Mallam, Duncan. January 9, 1943. A Writing Clinic at Iowa State College. *School and Society* 57: 51-53.

Marshall, Richard. 1985. Word Processing and More: the Joys and Chores of a Writing Lab Computer. LeVan. 166-8.

Mason, Robin and Anthony Kaye. eds. 1989. Mindweave. New York: Pergamon.

Medsker, Leland L. 1960. *The Junior College.* New York: McGraw-Hill.

Mills-Court, Karen and Minda Rae Amiran. 1991. Metacognition and the Use of Portfolios. Belanoff and Dickson.101-112.

Montague, Marjorie. 1990. *Computer, cognition, and writing instruction.* Albany: SUNY Press.

Moore, Dennis. 1983. What Should Computers Do in the Writing Center? Paper presented at the 1983 Midwest Writing Centers Conference, Iowa City. ERIC 208 553.

Moore, Robert H. 1950. The Writing Clinic and the Writing Laboratory. *College English* 11: 388-93.

Morton, F. Rand. 1960. The Teaching Machine and the Teaching of Languages: A Report on Tomorrow. *PMLA* 75: 1-6.

Mullin, Joan A. and Ray Wallace. eds. 1994. *Intersections: Theory-Practice in the Writing Center.* Urbana: NCTE.

Murphy, Christina, Joe Law, and Steve Sherwood. 1996. *Writing Centers: An Annotated Bibliography.* Westport: Greenwood.

———, and Joe Law. 1995. *Landmark Essays on Writing Centers.* Davis, CA: Hemagoras.

———. 1994. The Writing Center and Social Constructionist Theory. Mullin and Wallace. 25-38.

———. 1991. Writing Centers in Context: Responding to Current Educaitonal Theory. Wallace and Simpson. 276-288.

The National Center for Supercomputing Applications: University of Illinois at Urbana-Champaign. 19 February 1998. *A Beginner's Guide to HTML.* 12 January 1998. <http://www.ncsa.uiuc.edu/General/Internet/WWW/HTMLPrimer.html>.

Neuleib, Janice. 1984. Research in the Writing Center: What to Do and Where to Go to Become Research Oriented. *Writing Lab Newsletter* 9.4: 10-13.

———. 1983. Research in the Writing Center: What to Do and Where to Go to Become Research Oriented. Harris and Baker. 212-16.

———, and Maurice Scharton. 1990. Tutors and Computers, An Easy Alliance. *The Writing Center Journal* 11.1: 49-58.

Nielsen, Jakob. 1993. *Usability Engineering.* Boston, MA:Academic.

North, Stephen M. 1984. The Idea of a Writing Center. *College English* 46: 433-446.

———. 1984. Writing Center Research: Testing Our Assumptions. *Writing Centers: Theory and Administration.* Olson. 24-35.

Northern Illinois University Writing Across the Curriculum (WAC) Home Page. 18 August 1997. <http://www.niu.edu/acad/english/wac/wac.html>.

Norton, Don and Kristine Hanson. 1982. The Potential of Computer-Assisted Instruction. In *Tutoring Writing: A Sourcebook for Writing Labs.* Harris. 153-162.

Noyes, E. S. 1929. The Program of the Awkward Squad. *The English Journal* 18: 678-680.

Olson, Gary A. ed. 1984. *Writing Centers: Theory and Administration.* Urbana: NCTE.

Ong, Walter. 1982. *Orality and literacy: The technologizing of the word.* New York: Routledge.

Organization and Use of a Writing Laboratory: The Report of Workshop No. 9. 1951. *College Composition and Communication* 2: 17-18.

Otterbein, Leo E. 1973. A Writing Laboratory. *Improving College and University Teaching* 21: 296, 298.

Palmer, James C. 1992. The Scholarly Activities of Community College Faculty: Findings of a National Survey. Palmer and Vaughan.

———. Faculty Professionalism Reconsidered. *Maintaining Faculty Excellence.* Kroll. 29-38.

———. and George B. Vaughan. 1992. *Fostering a Climate for Faculty Scholarship at Community Colleges.* Washington, D.C.: The American Association of Community and Junior Colleges.

Partenheimer, David and Bill Emmett. 1987. Two Perspectives on Wandah/HBJ Writer. *The Writing Center Journal.* 8.1: 49-58.

Payne, Don. 1983. Integrating Computer Instruction into a Writing Center. Harris and Baker. 239-49.

Pegg, Bruce. 19 February 1998. Writing Centers Online. *National Writing Centers Association, an NCTE Assembly.* 21 October 1997. <http://departments.colgate.edu/diw/NWCAOWLS.html>.

Perrin, Porter G. 1947. Maximum Essentials in Composition. *College English* 8: 352-60.

Petit, Angela. 1997. The Writing Center as 'Purified Space': Competing Discourses and the Dangers of Definition. *The Writing Center Journal* 17.2: 111-22.

The Place of Individual Instruction in Composition. 1925. *The English Journal* 14: 329-30.

Postman, Neil. 1992. *Technopoly: The Surrender of Culture to Technology.* New York: Knopf.

Purdue University Writing Lab. 2 February 1998. *Online Writing Lab.* 1998. <http://owl.english.purdue.edu/>.

Report of the Workshop on Administering the Freshman Course: College. 1965. *College Composition and Communication* 16: 202-03.

Report of the Workshop on New Approaches in Teaching Composition. 1965. *College Composition and Communication* 16: 207-08.

Report of the Workshop on Students Needing Remedial Help. 1966. *College Composition and Communication* 15: 185-86.

Resnick, Lauren B. 1963. Programmed Instruction and the Teaching of Complex Intellectual Skills: Problems and Prospects. *Harvard Educational Review* 33: 439-71.

Riley, Terrance. 1994. The Unpromising Future of Writing Centers. *The Writing Center Journal* 15.4: 20-34.

Rodrigues, Dawn and Kathleen Kiefer. 1993. Moving Toward an Electronic Writing Center at Colorado State University. Kinkead and Harris. 216-26.

Rose, Mike. 1985. The Language of Exclusion: Writing Instruction at the University. *College English* 47: 341-59.

Rothwell, Kenneth S. 1962. Programmed Learning: A Back Door to Empiricism in English Studies. *College English* 23: 245-50.

Rowland, Devra. 1964. A Decade in the Life of a Programer. *College Composition and Communication* 15: 90-96.

Royar, Robert. 1986. Developing Word Processing Software for Composition. *Words Reaching Out to Worlds: Proceedings of the Writing Centers Association: East Central, Eighth Annual Conference.* Highland Heights, KY: Northern Kentucky University. 85-96.

Sacks, Peter. 1996. *Generation X Goes to College.* Chicago: Open Court.

Scharton, Maurice.1995. The Third Person: The Role of the Computer in Writing Centers. *Computers and Composition* 7.1: 37-48.

Schön, Donald A. 1987. *Educating the Reflective Practitioner: Toward a New Design for Teaching and Learning in the Professions.* San Francisco: Jossey-Bass.

———. 1983. *The Reflective Practitioner: How Professionals Think in Action.* New York: Basic Books.

Schramm, Wilbur. 1964. Programmed Instruction: Today and Tomorrow. *Four Case Studies of Programmed Instruction.* New York: Fund for the Advancement of Education. 98-115.

Scott, Fred Newton. 1895. English at Michigan. Brereton 177-81.

Selfe, Cynthia. 1995. Three Voices on Literacy, Technology, and Humanistic Perspective. *Computers and Composition* 12: 309-10.

———. 1992. Preparing English Teachers for the Virtual Age: The Case for Technology Critics. *Re-Imagining Computers and Composition: Teaching and Research in the Virtual Age.* Ed. Gail Hawisher and Paul LeBlanc. Portsmouth, NH: Boynton/Cook.

———. 1990. Computers in English departments: The rhetoric of techno/power. Holdstein and Selfe. New York: MLA. 95-103.

———. 1990. English Teachers and the Humanization of Computers: Networking Communities of Writers. Hawisher and Soter. 190-205.

——— and Susan Hilligoss. eds. 1994. *Literacy and Computers.* New York: MLA.

——— and Richard Selfe, Jr. 1994. The Politics of the Interface: Power and its Exercise in Electronic Contact Zones. *College Composition and Communication* 45: 480-504.

Selfe, Dickie. 1995. Surfing the Tsunami: Electronic Environments in the Writing Center. *Computers and Composition* 12: 311-22.

Severino, Carol. 1994. The Writing Center as Site for Cross-Language Research. *Writing Center Journal* 15.1: 51-61.

Shall 'Laboratory Work' in Composition Be Given Up? 1912. *The English Journal* 1: 48.

Simon, Charles. 1962. A Trial in Programmed Composition Teaching. *College Composition and Communication* 13: 16-19.

Simons, Susan. 1995. CAI: Instruction and Change in the Writing Center. *The Writing Lab Newsletter* 20.1: 11, 16.

SkillsBank Corporation. 13 August 1997. "SkillsBank Writing Education Solutions." <http://www.skillsbank.com/Pages/ writing.html>

Skinner, B. F. 1960. The Science of Learning and the Art of Teaching. Lumsdaine and Glaser. 99-113.

—-. 1960. Teaching Machines. Lumsdaine and Glaser 137-58.

Smith, Ray.18 August 1997. A Quick Guide to Minimal Marking. <http://www.indiana.edu/~wts/cwp/quickguide.html>

Southwell, Michael G. 1984. The Comp-Lab Writing Modules: Computer-Assisted Grammar Instruction. Wresch. 91-104.

Spear, Martin B., Evan Seymour, and Dennis McGrath. 1990. "The New Problem of Staff Development. Kroll. 21-28.

Spencer, Richard E. and Paul D. Holtzman. 1965. It's Composition...But Is It Reliable? *College Composition and Communication* 16: 117-21.

Spooner, Michael. 1994. A Dialogue on OWLing in the Writing Lab: Some Thoughts About Online Writing Labs. *Writing Lab Newsletter* 18.6: 6-8.

———. 1994. More Owlish Thoughts. *The Writing Lab Newsletter* 18.6: 8.

———, and Kathleen Yancey. 1996. Postings on a genre of email. *College Composition and Communication* 47.2: 252-278.

Stark, Meritt W., Jr. 1986. Word Processing: A Vital Skill to Enhance the Writing Center. *Issues in College Learning Centers* 4: 4-9.

Stay, Byron, Christina Murphy and Eric Hobson. eds. 1995. *Writing Center Perspectives.* Emmittsburg, MD: NWCA.

Suchman, Lucille. 1987. *Plans and Situated Actions: The Problem of Human-Machine Communication.* Cambridge: Cambridge UP.

Sullivan, Patricia. 1989. Beyond a Narrow Conception of Usability Testing. *IEEE Transactions on Professional Communication* 32: 256-264.

———. and Jennie Dautermann. eds. 1996. *Electronic Literacies in the Workplace.* Urbana: NCTE.

The Status of Freshman Composition. 1968. *College Composition and Communication* 19: 81-85.

Taber, Julian I., Robert Glaser and Helmuth H. Schaefer. 1965. *Learning and Programmed Instruction.* Reading, MA: Addison-Wesley.

Taylor, Michael. 1997. Intranets—A new technology changes all the rules. *Telecommunications,* January, 39-40.

Teaching the Disadvantaged: Methods of Motivation. 1966. *College Composition and Communication* 17: 37-40.

Teaching Machines and Programmed Instruction: Report of Workshop No. 15. 1961. *College Composition and Communication* 12: 181-83.

Teaching Machines and Programmed Instruction: Report of Workshop No. 19. 1966. *College Composition and Communication* 17: 192-93.

Thompson, John B. 19 February 1998. Writing Center Survey. Gardner. <http://www.slcc.edu/wc/papers/survpage.htm>.

Tomlinson, Barbara. 1975. A Study of the Effectiveness of Individualized Writing Lab Instruction for Students in Remedial Freshman Composition. Paper presented at the Annual Meeting of the Western College Reading Association. Anaheim, CA. ERIC ED108241.

Trowbridge, Dave. 1996. Developing intranets: Practical issues for implementation and design. *Telecommunications,* June, 51+.

Tuman, Myron C. ed. 1992. *Literacy online: The promise (and peril) of reading and writing with computers.* Pittsburgh: U Pittsburgh P.

University of Kansas Writing Consulting Faculty Resources Home Page. 18 August 1997. <http://falcon.cc.ukans.edu/~writingc/>

University of Michigan's Online Writing and Learning. 19 February 1998. 9 October 1996. <http://www.lsa.umich.edu/ecb/OWL/owl.html>.

University of Texas at Austin Team Web. 18 August 1997. Goals of Redesign of University Home Page of 20 December 96. <http://www.utexas.edu/teamweb/history/redesign2.html>.

Vasile, Kathy and Nick Ghizzone.1992. Computer-Integrated Tutoring. *The Writing Lab Newsletter* 16.9-10: 17-19.

Vaughan, George B. 1995. *The Community College Story: A Tale of American Innovation.* Washington, D.C.: The American Association of Community Colleges.

Wagner, Daniel A. 1994. Life-span and life-space literacy: National and international perspectives. Keller-Cohen.

Waldo, Mark L. 1987. More Than 'First Aid': A Report on the Effectiveness of Writing Center Intervention in the Writing Process. *Issues in College Learning Centers* 5: 13-22.

Wallace, Bob. 1996. Road to intranet paved with congestion issues. *Computerworld*, 18 November, 4.

Wallace, Ray. 1991. Sharing the Benefits and the Expense of Expansion: Developing a Cross-Curricular Cash Flow for a Cross-Curricular Writing Center. Wallace and Simpson. 82-101.

———— and Jeanne Simpson. eds. 1991. *Writing Centers: New Directions.* New York: Garland.

Weizenbaum, Joseph. 1976. *Computer Power and Human Reason: From Judgement to Calculation.* San Francisco: W.H. Freeman.

Willey, Malcom Macdonald. 1937. *Depression, Recovery and Higher Education. A Report by Committee Y of The American Association of University Professors.* New York: McGraw-Hill.

Winograd, Terry. 1995. Heidegger and the Design of Computer Systems. *Technology and the Politics of Knowledge.* Ed. Andrew Feenberg and Alastair Hannay. Bloomington, IN: Indiana UP.

———— and Fernando Flores. 1986. *Understanding Computers and Cognition: A New Foundation for Design.* Norwood, NJ: Ablex.

Wise, J. Hooper. 1939. A Comprehensive Freshman English Course in Operation. *The English Journal* 28: 450-60.

Wresch, William .ed. 1984. *The Computer in Composition Instruction: A Writer's Tool.* Urbana: NCTE.

Yancey, Kathleen Blake. ed. 1992. *Portfolios in the Writing Classroom: An Introduction.* Urbana: NCTE.

————. 1992. Portfolios in the Writing Classroom: A Final Reflection. Yancey.

Zeni, Jane. 1994. Literacy, Technology, and Teacher Education. Selfe and Hilligoss. 79.

CONTRIBUTORS

STUART BLYTHE, assistant professor of English at Western Kentucky University, is a former /chp coordinator of Purdue University's Online Writing Lab (OWL), one of the first OWLs in the country. He has presented at numerous conferences on the uses and effects of technology in writing instruction and his publications include "Networked Computers + Writing Centers = ?," which appeared in the spring 1997 issue of *The Writing Center Journal.* stuart.blythe@wku.edu

PETER CARINO is Professor of English at Indiana State University. A long-standing member and officer of the East Central Writing Centers Association and the National Writing Centers Association, he has lead the community as its historical critic, exploring early writing center design and theory in light of educational changes. His work has been recognized by the NWCA, which has awarded Peter its "Article of the Year" award on more than one occasion. ejcarino@root.indstate.edu http://isu.indstate.edu/writing

PAMELA B. CHILDERS, Caldwell Chair of Composition at The McCallie School, directs the writing center and the writing across the curriculum program. She previously taught English and created a WAC-based writing center in Red Bank Regional High School (NJ). Past president of NWCA and current treasurer of the Assembly on Computers in English, she serves on NCTE's Committee on Alternatives to Grading Student Writing. An international workshop presenter on writing centers, teaching writing in a visual culture, computers in writing, and writing across the curriculum, she has published numerous professional articles, chapters and poetry as well as *ARTiculating: Teaching Writing in a Visual Culture* (with Hobson and Mullin, Boynton/Cook,1998), *Programs and Practices: Writing Across the Secondary Curriculum* (with Gere and Young, Boynton/Cook,1994), and the award-winning *The High School Writing Center: Establishing and Maintaining One* (NCTE, 1989). pchilder@truth.mccallie.chattanooga.tn.us http://blue.mccallie.org/wrt_ctr

DAVID COOGAN teaches writing and poetry at the Illinois Institute of Technology, where he is also Associate Director of the Department of Humanities Writing Center and Interim Director of the Writing Program. His dissertation, *Electronic Writing Centers*, captured the 1996 Hugh Burns award for best dissertation in computers and composition. He is currently working on a book-length version of that work. coogan@charlie.acc.iit.edu

CLINTON GARDNER teaches writing, directs the Salt Lake Community College Writing Center, and developed and maintains the center's Online Writing Center. He served as a member of the local planning committee for the 3rd National Writing Centers Conference. cgardner@englab.slcc.edu http://www.slcc.edu/wc

ERIC HOBSON, Associate Professor of Humanities at the Albany College of Pharmacy, directs the school's faculty development efforts. The 1998 president of the National Writing Centers Association, Eric is a national leader in developing writing centers and WAC programs in health care education. His books include *ARTiculating: Teaching Writing in a Visual World* with Pamela Childers and Joan Mullin (Boynton/Cook 1998), *Writing Center Perspectives* with Christina Murphy and Byron Stay (NWCA 1995), and *Reading and Writing in High Schools* with R. Baird Shuman (NEA, 1990). hobson@panther.acp.edu

JEANETTE JORDAN teaches English and directs the writing center at Glenbrook North High School near Chicago. She represents high schools on the NWCA board of directors and is active in the Northshore Writing Center Consortium, a resource and support group for high school writing center directors in the Chicago area. JenJordan@aol.com

KURT KEARCHER manages the Writing Center and coordinates the Writing Across the Curriculum program at Owens Community College, located in Toledo, Ohio. His involvement in writing and technology instruction includes secondary and post-secondary levels, and industry. He has presented papers on composition and writing center issues, contributed to *Keywords in Composition* (Boynton 1996), and developed World Wide Web sites for the University of Toledo's writing center and Governor's Institute program. He is currently developing a computer-based writing center videoconferencing link to provide writing center support to another Owens campus. kkearcher@owens.cc.oh.us

SARA KIMBALL, Associate Professor with a joint appointment in the Division of Rhetoric and Composition and the Department of English at the University of Texas at Austin, directs the Undergraduate Writing Center, which she started in the fall of 1993. She is a linguist whose research interests include Indo-European and historical linguistics, Hittite, ancient Greek, literacy, and online discourse, and is the author of, *Handbook of Hittite Historical Phonology*. Currently, she is working on a dictionary of terms used in online communication and a study of literacy in the Hittite Empire. skimball@uts.cc.utexas.edu

NEAL LERNER is Writing Program Coordinator at the Massachusetts College of Pharmacy & Allied Health Sciences in Boston, MA. A member of the NWCA board of directors, his research interests include applying qualitative methodologies to composition research and understanding the historical precedents of the teaching of writing. He is a contributor to two forthcoming texts on writing centers and one forthcoming collection on qualitative research in composition. nlerner@mcp.edu http://www.mcp.edu/as/wc/wc.html

ELLEN MOHR has coordinated the Writing Center at Johnson County Community College in Overland Park, Kansas, since 1983. The JCCC Writing Center and its peer tutor program have been nationally and locally recognized through the state's Excellence in Education Award and numerous publications, including *Writing Centers in Context* (Kinkaid & Harris, 1993). Active in the Midwest Writing Center Association, hosting several of their conferences and serving as vice chair and chair, Ellen is a frequent presenter at MWCA and NWCA conferences. She is also engaged in staff development, serving as the JJCC WAC consultant, administrative intern, and the faculty director of the Center for Teaching and Learning. JCCC recently named Ellen as a recipient of the Distinguished Service Award for the third time. emohr@jcccnet.johnco.cc.ks.us

BARBARA MONROE is a member of the University of Michigan's Composition Board and has been instrumental in developing and maintaining the writing center's OWL. Her research into electronic writing centers includes studies about user habits and preferences, as well as a cybermentoring project linking local high schools and the university over the Web via the OWL. bjmonroe@umich.edu

BRUCE PEGG has a B.A. in English from Loughborough University and an M.A. in English from SUNY College at Brockport. In 1992, he became the first director of the writing center at Colgate University, where he also teaches in the Department of Interdisciplinary Writing. Since 1996, he has maintained the web site for the National Writing Centers Association. He is currently at work on a biography of rock musician Chuck Berry. bpegg@center.colgate.edu http://departments.colgate.edu/diw/NWCA.html http://departments.colgate.edu/diw/center.html

REBECCA J. RICKLY is a Visiting Assistant Professor at Texas Tech University. Formerly, she coordinated the Online Writing and Learning (OWL) program for the University of Michigan's English Composition Board. http://www.lsa.umich.edu/ecb/OWL/owl.html

STEVE SHERWOOD is the Coordinator of Peer Tutor Training at the William L. Adams Writing Center at Texas Christian University, where he has worked as a professional tutor and English instructor since 1988. A past President of the South Central Writing Centers Association, his work has appeared in *Writing Lab Newsletter, The Writing Center Journal, Writing Center Perspectives, Dialogue,* and other journals. With Christina Murphy, he co-edited *The St. Martin's Sourcebook for Writing Tutors* (1995), and with Chistina Murphy and Joe Law, he compiled *Writing Centers: An Annotated Bibliography* (Greenwood 1996). s.sherwood@tcu.edu

JIM UPTON teaches English at Burlington Community High School in Burlington, Iowa. He is a frequent author of articles about high school writing centers and serves on the NWCA board of directors. jupton@bchs.burlington.k12.ia.us

RAY WALLACE, a former President of the National Writing Centers Association, is Professor of English at Northwestern State University in Natchitoches, Louisiana. He has written or edited three books and numerous articles on writing center development and is a featured speaker at national and international conferences on the issue of technological implementations in education. He is the co-author of the only fully-funded five-year Title III grant written in the 1990s. wallace@ct-tel.net

INDEX

Academy for Community College Leadership and Advancement, Innovation, and Modeling (ACCLAIM), 75
action research, 112
Adler, Paul, 105, 111–112, 114
Air Force Institute of Technology, 179
Albany College of Pharmacy, 243
Alliance for Computers and Writing (ACW), 29
Almasy, Rudolph, 131
Amato, Joe, 25, 30–31
American Sign Language, 230
Amherst College, 120–121
Amiran, Minda Rae, 48
Andrews, Deborah, 227
Anthony, Tobin, 94, 97
Apple, F.S., 121
Arden, Eugene, 76
Arnold, H.J., 122
artificial intelligence, 180, 182
Assembly for Computers in English (ACE), 173–174, 218, 221–223, 226, 228–230, 242
audience, xvii–xviii, 51, 94, 113

Bailey, J.O., 124
Baker, Jeffrey, xviii, 217, 219
Baker, Tracey, 178
Baldwin, Beth, 29–30, 34–37, 42
Balkema, Sandra, 227
Ball State University, 177
Beason, Larry, 62
Beck, Charles, 179
Beginner's Guide to HTML, A, 83
behaviorism/behavioral psychology, 124–127, 131
Belenky, Mary, 37
Bell, Jim, 179
Bemidji State University, 199–200
Berlin, James, xvii,
Berta, Renee, 180
Bloom's Taxonomy, 160
Blumenthal, Joseph, 127, 129

Blythe, Stuart, v, xxi–xxii, 23–24, 103, 179, 190, 192, 218, 223–224, 242
Bødker, Susanne, 111
Bonwell, Chuck, vii
Book Report, 223
Brannon, Lil, 131
Brigham Young University, 173
   Hawaii Campus, 197
Brown, Alan, 180
browsers (see, Computer, search engines/web browsers)
Bruffee, Kenneth, 179
Bryant, Jim, 223
Burlington (IA) Community High School, 142–145, 245
Burns, Hugh, 173, 176
Bush, Jonathan, 221
Business Communication Quarterly, 227

CAI (see, Computer, assisted instruction)
California State University of Los Angeles, 201–202
California University of Pennsylvania, 201
Camp, Roberta, 44
Campbell, Elizabeth, 124
Campbell, John, 220
Carino, Peter, vi, xii, xvi–xvii, xix, xxvi, 120–122, 171, 242
Carter, Deborah, 76
Certeau, Michel de, 89–90
Chappell, Virginia, xiv, 187–188, 226
Chase, Geoffrey, 190
Childers, Pamela, vi, xiv, xviii, 137–138, 149–150, 182, 225–226, 242–243
Chronicle of Higher Education, 71
Clark, Irene, 183, 192, 224, 226
classroom
   instruction, xiii
      automated, 128
      drill-and-practice, 119, 121–124, 126, 128, 130, 134–135, 158, 173, 176

lecture and recitation, 120, 125, 127, 129–131, 133
    self, 135
    paperless, 93
Clearing House, The, 228
Colby, Elbridge, 121
Colgate University, 244
collaboration, xiii–xiv, xvii, xxiii, 27, 47, 59, 76–77, 82, 88, 91–93, 95, 97, 101, 147, 154, 179, 182–183, 216–217, 225
College Composition and Communication (CCC), 127, 130, 178, 217
College English (CE), 124, 128, 224
College Reading and Learning Association, 158
College Teachers of English of Texas, 131
Collins, Paul, 224
Colorado State Univeristy, 189, 202–203, 222
community college, x–xi, 75–84, 151–162, 188–189, 221, 223
Community College of Baltimore, 130
Comp-Lab project, 129–134, 171, 178–179
composition
    computer assisted, xv, 171, 173
    computerized classroom, xvi
Composition Studies/Freshman English News, 217, 220
Computer
    assisted instruction (CAI), 93, 124, 174, 176, 178, 181, 183–184, 220
    environments
        asynchronous, 119, 187
        MUD-Object Oriented (MOO), xiii, xxvi, 81, 95, 103–104, 135, 171, 173, 185, 188, 193, 217
        multi-user domains (MUDs), xiii, xxvi, 95, 103, 135, 171, 173, 217
        synchronous, 119
    file
        audio, 96, 100, 110
        email, 96
        multi-media, 119, 158, 174
        sharing, 88
        text, 96
        video, 96, 99–101, 110, 158
    hardware
        cable
            10BaseT, 98
            100BaseT, 99
            T1, 99, 147, 169

    T3, 99
    modem, 96, 98–99, 161, 169
    Pentium chip, 173
languages
    hypertext, 71, 119, 173–174, 180, 183, 190–191, 227
    HTML, xviii, xxii, 83, 197
        frames, 78, 84
mediated communication (CMC), 33, 174, 185
    chat rooms, 93–94, 169
    email, vii, xiii, 4, 29, 36, 43, 53, 57, 77–78, 92–96, 99, 101, 103, 106, 108, 147–150, 153, 158, 161, 165, 167, 169, 173, 187, 217
    lists, 93–94
    listserv, 108, 149, 158, 161, 183, 186, 190
    newsgroups/newslists, 77, 83
electronic bulletin boards, 77–78, 81, 86, 93, 100
networks, xiv, 29–30, 77, 87, 95–96, 103–106, 108, 140, 144, 158, 165, 169–170, 184
    administrator, 96–99
    gateway, 99
    local area (LANs), xviii, 77, 92, 98–99, 173–174, 180, 185, 187
    security, 99
    server, 85, 97–98
    wide area (WANs), 173–174
    personal, xiii, xviii,
platforms
    IBM/PC, ix, 98, 138, 163
    Macintosh/Apple, ix, 98, 138–139, 143–145, 147–150, 163–164, 177
    Sun, 98
    Unix, ix, 69
random access memory (RAM), 100, 216
search engines/web browser, 64, 79, 84–85, 88, 101
    Alta Vista, 62
    Lynx, 69
software
    Access, 146
    AllWrite!, 135
    Blue Pencil, 156, 158
    Citation, 158
    Compris, 158
    Correct Grammar, 158

Daedalus, 47–50, 54–57, 59
Editor, 158
Elements of Style, 158
Ellis, 157–158
Enhanced CuSee-Me, 109–110, 114
Eudora, 147–148
Excel, 146, 158
File Transfer Protocol (FTP), 78, 95,
    100
Gopher, xviii, 77
Grammatik, 158
Guides, 157–158
HBJ Writer, 181
Homer, 178, 180
HyperStudio, 144
HyperText, 144
Internet Explorer, 147, 163
Internet Protocol (IP), 98–99
Internet Relay Chat (IRC), 96, 100
Leading Edge Writer, 163
Learning Plus, 158
MicroLab, 155, 158
Microsoft Exchange, 158
Microsoft Scheduler, 158
Netscape/Netscape Gold, 146, 158,
    163
Netscape Communicator, 107
Office 97, 147
Perfect Copy, 158
Pine, 158
PLATO, 173, 176
PowerPoint, 144, 157–158
Que Intellectual, 158
Scribo, 219
SkillsBank, 135
SLIP, 99
Telnet, 78
TICCIT, 173, 176
The Toolbox, 219
Toefl, 158
Topoi, 173, 176
Transmission Control Protocol
    (TCP), 98–99
Tutor Tapes, 158
WANDAH, 171, 176, 180–181
Webchat, 74
Web Wizard, 158
Windows/Win95/Win97, 146,
    157–158, 162

Word, 146, 163
Word 97, 147
WordPerfect, 154, 157–158, 163
Wordstar, 163
Wordsworth, 171, 180
*Computer in Composition: A Writer's Tool,
    The*, 174, 179
Computers and Composition, vii, x–xi, 174,
    186, 217, 222, 224–226, 228–230
*Computers and the Teaching of Writing in
    American Higher Education, 1979-1994:
    A History*, 173
Computers and Writing Conference, 174
*Computers in the English Classroom: A
    Primer for Teachers*, 174
Conference on College Composition and
    Communication (CCCC), xv, 124, 127,
    130, 173–174
Conklin, F.R., 123
Coogan, David, v, xiv, xxiii, 25, 103, 187,
    217, 224, 227, 242
Cooper, Marilyn, 224
cost analysis, xxiv,
critical thinking, xvii–xviii, 53, 56, 160
critical reading, 49
critical reflection, 103–104, 112
Croft, Mary, 176
Crump, Eric, xiv, 185, 211, 218–219
Cuban, Larry, 120
Cullen, Roxanne, 227
cultural studies, 174–175, 182
Current Traditional Rhetoric, xvii, 173,
    175–179

Daiute, Collette, 93, 178
Dakota State University, 221
Denny, Erin, 224
Designated Technology Facilitators (DFTs),
    146
disabilities, xviii, 67, 160
discourse analysis, xxiii,
discourse communities, xvii–xviii,
distance education/learning, xviii, xxi, 159,
    183, 192
Dorough, C. Dwight, 129
Douglas, Michael, 220
Dreyfus, Hubert, 179–180, 182
Duin, Ann Hill, 103, 113
Dykeman, John, 95

East Central Writing Centers Association, 242

Eastern Illinois University, vii

Eastern Washington University, 62

Ede, Lisa, xvii, xix, 36

educational technology, (see, technology, educational/instructional)

EDU Magazine, 220

efficiency movement, 123

Ehn, Pelle, 106, 111–113

email, (see, computer, mediated communication)

Eliot, T.S., 191

El-Khawas, Elaine, 76

Emerson, Ralph Waldo, 191

Emmett, Bill, 181

emoticon, 14

English, Joel, 189

Epes, Mary, 132–134, 178

Epiphany Project, 212

English as a Second Language (ESL), 18, 67, 127, 135, 156–157

English Journal, 120, 122

Ericsson, Patricia, 221

expressivist rhetoric, xvii, 191

E-zines, 81

faculty/professional development, xii, 65, 71, 143, 146

Feenberg, Andrew, 33

feminist studies, 174, 182

Ferster, Teresa, 121

flaming, 54

Flores, Fernando, 112

Fountain, Alvin, 136

Franz, Amelia, 228

Freeman, Jeffrey, 220

Gardner, Clinton, v, xiv, xviii, xx, 75, 78, 81, 84, 151, 161, 243

Garrison, Roger, 175

Gaskin, James, 74

General Electric, 26–27

Generation X Goes to College, 151

Genung, John Franklin, 120–121

George, Diana, ix, 217, 225

George Washington University, 121, 212

Georgia Institute of Technology, 74

Gerrard, Lisa, 173, 176

Gere, Ann, 242

Ghizzone, Nick, 186

Giroux, Henry, 101–102

Glaser, Robert, 126

Glenbrook North High School, Northbrook, IL, 138, 243
    The Write Place, 138–142

Grandy, Adah, 121

Grant, Tripp, 148

Grove, W. Alan, 122

Goffman, Irving, 33, 72

Graves, Gary, 138

Grimm, Nancy, xx, 27, 225

Grubbs, Catherine, xviii

Hairston, Maxine, 178

Hall, Beatrice, 127

Hall, Christie, 81

Hall, R.M.R., 127

Haller, Carl, 138

Handbook of Usability Testing, 112

handbooks online, xix

Hansen, Craig, 103, 113

Hansen, Kristine, 176

hardware, (see, Computer, hardware)

Harris, Jeanette, 131, 220, 244

Harris, Muriel, 36, 104, 131, 134, 175–176, 186–188, 217, 220–222, 228

Harvard University, 189

Haseck, Glenn, 90

Hass, Christina, 103

Hawisher, Gail, 173, 175–176, 178–179,, 181–182, 185, 226

Hawthorne, Nathaniel, 191

Haynes-Burton, Cynthia, 190–192

Healy, David, x, 171, 189–190, 225

Heath, Shirley Bryce, 137

Heidegger, Martin, 112

Hickman, Larry, 105

Hilligoss, Susan, xxv

Hillocks, George, 136

hit counters, xxii, 84

Hobson, Eric, iii, v, viii–ix, xvii, xix, 218, 242–243

Hoger, Elizabeth, 222

Holcumb, E.L., 121

Holmes, Leigh, 218

Holtzman, Paul, 127

Hom, James, 112

homepage, x, 45, 85, 97, 168, 186
Homme, Lloyd, 126
Hunt, Russell, 29–30
Huntley, John, 127–128
hypertext, (see, Computer, languages)

Illinois Institute of Technology, 25, 242
Indiana State University, 242
Indiana University Bloomington, 70, 74
    Campuswide Writing Program, 70, 74
individualized instruction, xvii, 93,
    123–124, 126
Infobahn, 190, 192
internet, vii, 77, 79, 83, 90, 93, 98, 99, 144,
    149, 153, 162, 167, 174, 189
    access to, xi–xii, 68, 78, 84, 93, 140, 159
intranet, 63, 66, 74, 97, 85–102
Iowa State College/University, 124, 177
Ironwood Junior College, 121

Japan, 182
Johanek, Cindy, xiv, 187–188, 227
Johnson, Beatrice, 177
Johnson County Community College
    (JCCC), 151–162, 244
Johnson, Paul, 23, 225
Johnson-Eiola, Johndan, 71
Jordan, Jeanette, vi, xviii, 137–138,
    146–149, 243
Jordan-Henley, Jennifer, xiv, 103, 188–189,
    207, 221, 228
Journal of Developmental Education, 220
Joyce, James, 191

Kairos, xi, 222, 224–225, 229
Kaplan, Jonas, 45
Kearcher, Kurt, v, xx, 85, 243
Kemp, Fred, 181, 216, 227
Key, Francis, 177
Keifer, Kathleen, 189
Kiefer, Kate, 223
Kinkead, Joyce, xiv, xviii, 103, 171, 183,
    187, 219–220, 228, 244
Kinneavy, James, 65
Kimball, Sarah, v, 62, 222, 225, 243
Kirkpatrick, Carolyn, 132, 178
Klem, Elizabeth, 228
Kock, Christian, 219
Kuhn, Thomas, 178

laboratory approach/writing lab approach,
    119–124, 130
Landmark Essays, 171
Landow, George, 93–94
Langston, Camille, 222
Lanham, Richard, 178
Larkin, Greg, 220
Lasarenko, Jane, 220
Law, Joe, vii, x, 218, 245
learning community, 90
LeBlanc, Paul, 138, 173, 175–176, 178–179,
    81–182, 185
Leff, Linda, 229
Lerner, Neal, vi, 119, 244
Levine, Denise, 44
Lewis, Frances, 120
Leydens, Jon, 222
lists/listserv, (see, Computer, mediated
    communication)
literacy, xii–xiii, xvi, xxv, 36, 69, 94, 97, 101,
    103, 137, 148, 174, 183, 191–192
Littleton, Bonnie, 229
Litton, Guy, 221
Liu, Min-zhan, 193
Luchte, Jeanne, 181, 216, 229
L'Universite D'Ottawa, 211
Lunsford, Andrea, xvii, xix, 28, 187

Maid, Barry, xiv, 103, 188–189, 228
mailto/mailform, 4, 8, 11, 67, 71
Mallam, Duncan, 124
Marshall, Richard, 179
Mason, Richard, 220
Massachusetts College of Pharmacy and
    Allied Health Sciences, 244
McCallie School, The, 145–149, 242
McDonough, Carla, vii, xxvi
McGee, Tim, 221
McGrath, Dennis, 76
McGraw-Hill, 135
McKenzie, Lee, 219
McLuhan, Marshall, 188
Medsker, Leland, 76
Megabyte University, 186
mentoring, 27
Meyer, Emily, 227
Meyer, Paul, 186
Miami Dade Community College, 154
Miami Univeristy of Ohio, 122

Michigan State University, 197, 204
Michigan Technological University, xx,
Midwest Writing Centers Association, 176, 178
Mills-Court, Karen, 48
Mitchell, Margaret, 226
Mohr, Ellen, vi, xix–xx, 151, 244
MONDO 2,000 Users Guide to the New Edge, 191
Monroe, Barbara, v, xx, xxiii, 3, 46, 244
Montague, Marjorie, 93
MOO/MUD, (see, Computer, environments)
Moody, Susan, 229
Moore, Dennis, 178
Moore, Robert, 124
Moran, Charles, 173, 175–176, 178–179, 181–182, 185, 228
Morgan, M.C., 229
Morrison, Toni, 191
Morton, F. Rand, 128–129
Mullin, Joan, 86, 217, 220, 242–243
Murphy, Christina, vii, x, xvii, xix, 111, 218, 243, 245
Murray, Donald, 175

National Association of Independent Schools, 145
National Center for Supercomputing Applications, 83
National Council of Teachers of English (NCTE), xv, 122, 143, 174, 179, 242
National Directory of Writing Centers, 185
National Writing Centers Association (NWCA), xv, 59, 153, 159, 197, 215, 242–243
natural language processing, 181, 185
Nelson, Jane, 222
networks, (see, Computer, networks)
Neuleib, Janice, xxii, 177
Nielsen, Jakob, 106, 110, 113
North, Stephen, xxii, 51, 111, 179, 224
Northern Arizona University, 220
Northern Illinois University, 62, 69–70
North Shore Writing Center Consortium, 138, 243
Northwestern State University of Louisiana, vii, 245
Northwest Ohio Writing Education Consortium, 86

Norton, Don, 176
Noyes, E.S., 126

Olson, Gary, 132
online tutoring, (see, tutoring)
Online Writery, 211
Otterbein, Leo, 130
Owens Community College, 243

Palmer, James, 76
Palmquist, Mike, 222–223
paralinguistic cues, xxiii, 114, 188
Park College, 124
Partenheimer, David, 181
participatory design movement, 111
Payne, Don, 177–178
peer feedback, xvii, 76, 91
peer relationship, 8
peer tutoring, (see, tutoring)
Pegg, Bruce, vi, xi, xvii, 83, 244
Pemberton, Michael, vii, 186–188, 222
Perrin, Porter, 122
Petit, Angela, 193
Pitel, Vonna, 223
plagiarism, 190
Polytechnic University of New York, 134
portfolios, 44, 64
Postman, Neil, xii, 171, 178–179
primary school, 91
Proceedings of the Writing Center Fifth Annual Conference, 176
programmed instruction/learning, 124–132, 134–136
Project Synergy, 154
Purdue University, 78, 104, 190, 205, 217, 227, 242

real-time chat, 77, 173
Red Bank Regional High School (NJ), 145, 242
reflective practitioners, 44–61, 105
Reiss, Donna, 221
Reno, Steve, 146
research methods, xxii–xxiii, 104–110
Resnick, Lauren, 126
Rickly, Rebecca, v, xiv, xx, 44, 187–188, 223, 227, 244
Rienecker, Lotte, 219
Riley, Terrance, 171

Roane State Community College, 206
Rodrigues, Dawn, 189, 223
Rose, Mike, 123, 126
Rothwell, Kenneth, 128
Rowland, Devra, 128
Royer, Robert, 179, 218
Rubin, Jeffrey, 112

Sacks, Peter, 151
Salt Lake Community College (SLCC),
    75–84, 152–153, 204, 242
Scharton, Maurice, 182–185, 229
Schipke, Rae, 223
Schön, Donald, 44, 105
Schramm, Wilbur, 125
Schwartz, Helen, 94
Scott, Fred Newton, 120
Seamour, Evan, 76
search engines, (see, Computer, search
    engines/web browsers)
secondary school/high school, x–xi, xviii,
    xxiv, 44, 63, 68, 76, 85, 88, 90–91, 99,
    101, 120–121, 123, 133, 137–150, 152,
    182, 223, 228
Selber, Stuart, 71
Selfe, Cynthia, xiii–xiv, xxv, 95, 103, 105,
    137, 173, 175–176, 178–179, 181–182,
    185–186, 223–224, 226
Selfe, Richard, xi–xii, 105, 226
Severino, Carol, xxii
Shapiro, Martin, 129
Sherwood, Steve, vi–vii, x, 216, 245
Shuman, R. Baird, 243
Simon, Charles, 129
Simons, Susan, 186, 223, 229
Simpson, Jeanne, 180
SkillsBank Corp., 135
Skinner, B.F., 124–128, 136
Smith, Gordon, 24
Smith, Louis, 227
Smith, Ray, 70
Snow, Stu, 138
social construction/social pedagogy, xiv,
    xix, 47, 112–113, 174, 181–184, 191, 217
software, (see, Computer, software)
South Central Writing Centers Association,
    245
Southern Association of Colleges and
    Schools, 145

Southwell, Michael, 132, 178–179
Spear, Martin, 76
Spencer, Richard, 127
Spooner, Michael, xviii, 25, 28, 35, 193, 219
Stark, Meritt, 135
Stay, Byron, 243
Stibrany, John, 179
Strickland, James, 226
Stroh, Jeanne, 223
Suchman, Lucille, 105, 113
Swartz, Patti Chapel, 230

Taber, Julian, 126
Taylor, Michael, 90
teaching machines, 119, 124–125, 128, 130
technology, 26, 62
    access to, xv, 159
    audio, 95, 132
    educational/instructional, x, 119–120,
        163, 169
    film/filmstrips, 120, 132
    large bandwidth, 96
    lure of, 120, 135, 164
    video, 95, 167
Texas Christian University, 245
Texas Tech University, 244
Thompson, John, 83–84
Tidewater Community College, 221
Tomlinson, Barbara, 131
Trowbridge, Dave, 91
Tuman, Myron, 94
tutor training, xvii, 3, 44–61, 159, 171, 188
tutoring, 27
    autotutorial, 128, 130–132, 135, 177,
        179, 216
    face-to-face (f2f)/one-to-one, xvi, xxiii,
        3, 10–11, 16, 20, 24, 47, 96, 103, 108,
        114, 141, 148–149, 160, 169–172,
        180, 183, 188, 217, 219, 221
    online/virtual, xv–xvi, xviii, xxi, xxiii,
        3–24, 25–61, 84, 183, 188–189, 219,
        225
    analysis of, xxiii, 3–24
    asynchronous, xxiv, 48
    cybertutors, 60, 188–189, 223
    genre, 3, 7
    peer, 53, 59, 189, 191
    procedure for, 4
    structure of , 7, 11–23

successful, xxiii
synchronous, xxiv, 48, 103
*Tutoring Writing: A Sourcebook for Writing
    Labs*, 175–176

university/college, x, xxiv, 44, 46, 99,
    123–124
    mission, 164
University of
    Arkansas–Little Rock, 207
    Florida, 121
    Georgia, 207–208
    Houston, 128–129
    Illinois, 173
    Kansas, 62, 70
    Maine, 197
    Michigan, xix, 45–61, 84, 120, 244–245
    Minnesota, 121, 207
    Missouri, 211
    North Carolina, 124
    Richmond, 197, 212
    Tennessee–Chattanooga, 146
    Texas–Austin, 62–74, 209, 222, 243
    Wisconsin–Madison, 213
Upton, James, vi, xviii, 137–138, 146,
    149–150, 245
usability research, xxi, 103–116
Utah State University, 217

Vasile, Kathy, 186
Vaughn, George, 75–76, 83
Veit, Richard, 216, 226
video conferencing, xxi

Wagner, Daniel, 101
Walhstrom, Billie, 173
Waldo, Mark, 135
Wallace, Bob, 95–96
Wallace, Ray, vi–vii, xvi–xvii, xxvi, 163,
    180, 245
Wambeam, Cynthia, 222
Washington State University, 213
Way, Robert, 24
Wayne University, 124
Wcenter, x, 59, 134, 185, 218
webmaster, (see, network systems adminis-
    trator)
website/webpage, xv–xviii, xxii, 65, 71,
    78–79, 81, 83, 95–96, 108, 170

Weizenbaum, Joseph, 179–181, 193
Western Governors University, 192
Western Kentucky University, 242
West Virginia University Writing
    Laboratory, 131
What Computers Can't Do, 180
What Computers Still Can't Do, 180
Whealler, Susan, 178
WhitePine, 110, 114
Wilderman, Marion, 24
Wilkes University, 214
Willey, Malcolm, 121
Williams, Paula, 138
Winograd, Terry, 105, 111–112, 114
Wise, J. Hooper, 121
Wood, Gail, 230
word processing, 92–93, 156, 165, 176–177,
    216, 219
World War II, 124
World Wide Web (WWW or Web), ix, xiii,
    xxiv, 45, 57, 62, 70, 72, 74, 84, 88, 92, 95,
    100, 103, 109, 165, 183, 185, 192, 217
Wresch, William, 173, 178–179
Wright State University, vii
writing
    wirters block, 93
    co-writing, 27
    collaborative, 30, 149–150
    community, 90–92, 94–95, 101, 224
    computer mediated/assisted, xiv,
        85–102, 154, 167
    online, xiv, 47, 75
    paperless classroom, 92
    process/process pedagogy, xiii, xvii, 64,
        86–88, 90–93, 103, 130, 144, 153,
        170, 173, 176–179, 181, 183, 216
    recursiveness, 181
    social activity, 126
    to-learn, 146
    writing intensive courses, 62, 65, 67, 71
writing across the curriculum (WAC), 53,
    56, 62–74, 137–139, 149, 158, 164, 189,
    223, 227
writing center
    future of, xiii, xvi, xxv
    grammar hotline, 146, 153, 159, 166
    mission, xiv–xv, xxiv, 143, 153, 164, 216,
        218, 222, 225
    obsolescence, xvi, xxv, 189

online (OWL), x–xii, xiv–xix, xxii,
xxv–xxvi, 3–24, 44–61, 75–84,
141–142, 149, 168, 171, 173, 180,
185, 193, 217
outreach, 62–74, 78
tutorless, 120
"wired", x–xi, xiii, xiv, xix, xxi, xxv, 163
Writing Center Journal, The, x–xi, 180,
182–185, 193, 216, 223–225, 227, 229
Writing Center: New Directions, The, 180
Writing Centers: An Annotated Bibliography,
vii, x, 218
Writing Centers Association (now
ECWCA), 176
Writing Centers in Context, 189, 220

*Writing Centers: Theory and
Administration*, 132
Writing Lab Directory, 176
Writing Lab Newsletter, x–xi, 176, 179–180,
183, 185, 216–220, 226, 228–229

Yale C/AIM Web Style Guide, 66, 74
Yancey, Kathleen Blake, 25, 28, 35
York College of City University of New
York (CUNY), 132–133
Young, Art, 242

Zeni, Jane, 104, 112
Zimmerman, Donald, 223
ZooMoo, 211